The
FENIAN
ANTHOLOGY

The
FENIAN
ANTHOLOGY

JOE AMBROSE

MERCIER PRESS
WHAT YOU NEED TO READ

Mercier Press
Cork
www. mercierpress. ie

Trade enquiries to:

Columba Mercier Distribution,
55a Spruce Avenue
Stillorgan Industrial Park
Blackrock
County Dublin

ISBN: 978 1 85635 607 7

10 9 8 7 6 5 4 3 2 1

Mercier Press receives financial assistance from
the Arts Council/An Chomhairle Ealaíon

Printed and bound in the EU.

CONTENTS

FOREWORD

In our own time it sometimes seems that even our radical political revolutionaries have to be photogenic or reasonably media friendly. Che Guevara established the tradition and Osama Bin Laden, living or dead, keeps it alive. History is, on occasion, made by the soundbite.

It was not always thus. The nineteenth-century revolutionary image was that of a complex, multifaceted, bearded, biblical, besuited male. Fierce moustachioed men fulminated in smoky coffee houses, lived in damp dark accommodations down Parisian back streets or in the less salubrious parts of London or Dublin. It was the great era of the conspirator; the anarchist, the Zionist, the Marxist – a world of bomb factories, pamphlets, short-lived newspapers, long and often awful, vindictively imposed, terms of imprisonment. Very little success achieved in pursuit of, depending on one's point of view, high ideals or low intentions.

The Fenian Brotherhood, like the anarchists, caught the popular Victorian imagination. Like the Islamic resistance in our own time, Fenians were allegedly everywhere and up to all sorts. They tried to invade Canada. They let off bombs in England. They were a part of the political and judicial establishment in America. They were escaping from British imprisonment in Australia. They wrote hundreds of books and published more newspapers than Rupert Murdoch. They were formidable, ineffectual, terrible or magnificent.

Fenianism began in the 1850s, but the founding father of violent Irish separatism was Wolfe Tone whose 1798 United Irishmen rebellion was undertaken in collusion with the revolutionaries who'd overthrown the French monarchy. Nothing much happened, after that, until 1848 when the Young Irelanders, stylish cosmopolitan writers and theorists, made their Francophile plans in the parlours, talking shops and coffee houses of Dublin but struck out for their principles in and around Tipperary's rainy streets and hills. The socialist leader James Connolly, who helped found the Irish Republic in 1916, said that the Young Irelanders had been handed 'revolutionary material' but that they were 'unfit to use' that material. But an ideal took shape within Irish rebel hearts which would never lie down or back down, no matter how hopeless the odds. Their romantic but unsuccessful agitations soon gave rise, seamlessly, to the Fenian Brotherhood, a covert revolutionary belief system. From the ashes of Fenianism arose the twentieth-century Irish Republican Brotherhood (IRB). In 1919 members of the IRB, styling themselves the Irish Republican Army (IRA) started and subsequently won the Irish War of Independence. Another IRA rose from the ashes of a civil war to agitate, organise and fight in 1930s Spain. Yet another IRA emerged in the late 1960s and fought a war which went on for decades. Who knows what the future holds?

The Fenian Brotherhood's leaders were an unusual, dark and gifted bunch. James Stephens was a long-winded, arrogant schemer, ruthless and ultimately incompetent. John O'Leary, in effect a trust fund kid, was a bibliophile and a curiously modern man of refreshingly urbane opinions. According to Ireland's first president Douglas Hyde, however, O'Leary was a staunch conservative who did not believe that the masses had the right to elect their own rulers. O'Leary loathed the popular Fenian ballad 'God Save Ireland' and was affronted when, returning in triumph to Ireland after years in jail and exile, his welcoming brass band played that tune. He once undertook an undercover Fenian fundraising trip to New York in discreet disguise. When he landed on the other side of the Atlantic a brass band awaited him on the Battery pier and he was marched up Broadway, where a speech was demanded of him.

Michael Doheny was a troubled, idealistic, rough diamond on a doomed trajectory. Charles J. Kickham, blind and half deaf, took his place at every Irish hearth via the sentimental maudlin ballads which he wrote and via his novel, *Knocknagow or the Homes of Tipperary* (1879). None was odder than the scholarly, passionate, perpetually cash-strapped John O'Mahony.

By the early 1860s, Doheny was dead and John O'Mahony was temporarily the undisputed leader of the Fenian Brotherhood in New York. The Brotherhood, despite having Irish-born leaders, came to perceive Irish separatism through the prisms of American ideology, American capital and American requirements. Subsequent Fenian leaders such as John Savage persistently stressed the American nature of their organisation and its essential loyalty to American values.

The Fenian movement was re-organised in the 1870s with a new constitution. Thereafter it was mainly known as the Irish Republican (or Revolutionary) Brotherhood. Kickham then headed the secret council that controlled it.

In recent decades the scholarship surrounding the rise, fall, and rise again of the separatist ideology clustered around Fenianism has grown from a whisper into a scream. A strident desire to discredit generic 'Fenian' thinking has gone hand in hand, in the popular discourse, with a mellowing of attitudes towards the individuals involved. The creation of an Irish state which had its starting point in the Fenian/IRB-rooted 1916 Rising always ensured a solid bulwark of pro-Fenian establishment literature, scholarship, statuary, balladry, and sanitised propaganda which gave to 'the cause' a certain solidity and respectability. In the Ireland in which I grew up basic Fenian achievements, such as the Gaelic Athletic Association, the Irish language revival movement, and the incomplete resolution of the land question prevailed so complacently that they were taken for granted. It was difficult to perceive the somewhat rickety origins of the movement, the sheer hopelessness of many of its gestures, or the impossible complexity of some of its thinking.

The word 'Fenian' was so successfully launched onto the world by its founding fathers that the expression still has substantial resonance all over the world. In its simplest and purest form, it refers to an ideology which seeks to remove the British presence from Irish affairs by force of arms. In a slightly expanded form, it refers to a huge cultural empire which involves the Irish language, an interpretation of Irish history, the pursuit of Irish music and, most successfully, the propagation and playing of Irish games. Ironically, given the mutual antipathy which existed between the Fenians and the Catholic hierarchy, 'Fenian' became a sectarian term of abuse for Catholics. In its broadest and vaguest interpretation, the term might apply to a rebel of any kind, a nonconformist, a radical, or one who deviated from the norm. A troublesome child or a troublesome presence in society might be referred to, in certain circles, as 'a bit of a Fenian'. When the anarchist writer John McGuffin, the product of impeccable Ulster Protestant stock, died, he was buried wearing a t-shirt emblazoned with the words 'Unrepentant Fenian Bastard'.

A fundamental premise behind Fenian actions was the notion that Ireland could never realise its full potential until it was entirely independent. Michael Collins warmly embraced this idea in the notes posthumously published as *The Path to Freedom*. The prosperity enjoyed by the Irish Republic in recent years seems to give retrospective credence to that belief. The fact that the totally independent stance of de Valera-era Ireland went hand in hand with abject poverty, exploitation, and enforced emigration might contradict this belief. Contemporary Ireland's much-vaunted sophistication and self-confidence owes a great deal more to the country becoming a hugely Americanised construct with a fundamentally compromised foreign policy than it does to the island being a dynamic young democracy overflowing with miraculously successful entrepreneurs and entertainers.

The Fenians, their predecessors and their successors, were often impressive writers and polemicists. There is much with which to anthologise. Their stories are habitually told, in this book, by individuals who knew how to wield the pen as skilfully as they knew how to wield the sword. John Savage, Fenian historian, was also one of the most prominent and contentious Fenians in New York. Thomas Moore and Wolfe Tone were innate writers. Kickham was a professional author. Underground revolutionaries cannot always expect to get their own way in the real world and, all too often, the memoir and the polemic is the final refuge of the thwarted radical.

Vincent Comerford and other researchers have suggested that the Fenian attitude was more of a lifestyle option than a properly revolutionary belief system. For sure, the dithering behaviour of the famous chief organiser James Stephens marked him down as a very queer fish indeed. The exasperation and mystification which he inspired in his comrades is palpable in John O'Leary's remembrance of him. In his prime, Stephens always seemed to be demanding further funding while delivering, to put it mildly, disappointing results. It was said of O'Leary that he came to see his own life as a work of art, always a dangerous delusion, and there can be no doubt that his major contribution to Irish life was the cultural education which he bestowed upon W. B. Yeats. The baton which O'Leary passed on to Yeats is comparable to the baton which Woody Guthrie passed to Bob Dylan.

But there was, conversely, nothing imaginary about the suffering endured by the Fenian prisoners. This was no lifestyle option. There was nothing ineffectual about the work of the Land League whose leader, Michael Davitt, was very much a Fenian. The part the Fenians played in the rise and fall of Parnell was not a figment of their imagination. The GAA, to this day one of the most dynamic participants in the ongoing Irish adventure, is no talking shop. And the Republic of Ireland was the invention of men and women who signed up, at various times, to the pure Fenian position. They were all people who could, as de Valera told one left wing intellectual, hold their hand in the flame.

The Irish freedom which the Fenians saw in their mind's eye was a very specific model. It was hugely conservative, militaristic, and masculine. Fenians, in old age, tended to become American judges, members of the British Parliament, newspaper editors, significant engineers and entrepreneurs of various sorts. They did not tend to disappear without trace or to die in the gutter. Perhaps an Ireland crawling with American capital, American values and American visitors was exactly what they had in mind. It is certainly the case that Fenianism was an essentially American occurrence, and the substantial battles which Fenians and Young Irelanders fought during their first flowering were on behalf of radically different visions of what the United States should be in the American Civil War.

Despite Karl Marx's enthusiasm for their cause, the Fenian social agenda was disappointingly conventional. It was not until the powerful polemicist James Connolly threw in his lot with the IRB men in time for the 1916 Rising that Irish nationalism took on board a truly radical analysis. This Connolly strand, ably represented here by the likes of Seamus Costello, Peadar O'Donnell, Frank Ryan and the brave hearts who took their struggle to Spain during that country's civil war, gave to the separatist cause an intellectual and sentimental integrity which it previously lacked.

Joe Ambrose
www.joeambrose.net

Timeline

1798

United Irishmen rebellion: Lord Edward Fitzgerald, tries to arrange a rebellion involving a rural secret society network, but his efforts are undermined by informers. Brutal repression accompanies mass arrests. In Wexford Protestant yeomen go on the rampage, bringing about a response from the Catholic population led by Father John Murphy. After a surprise success at Oulart Hill, the Catholic rebels camp on Vinegar Hill. They begin killing Protestant prisoners and a barn containing Protestants is torched at Scullabogue, with survivors being harshly dealt with. Protestant United Irishman Bagnell Harvey takes command of the Catholics. He seeks to give some shape and purpose to the rebellion and unsuccessfully counsels restraint. The rebels liberate Wexford before being ferociously dealt with on Vinegar Hill. 50,000 are said to have died in the Wexford disturbances which effectively drove the entire Irish Protestant population into the pro-British camp.

1800

2 July: The Act of Union is passed, and puts an end to the Irish Parliament. In 1801 Ireland and England are united 'forever'. At first Irish Protestants oppose union on patriotic grounds whereas some Catholics imagine that the English will protect them.

1803

23 July: Second United Irishmen rebellion led by Robert Emmet whose plan was to seize Dublin Castle in the hope of encouraging the country to rise up. Emmet is remembered for his speech from the dock in which he said his epitaph should not be written until Ireland was a free nation. He is executed on 20 September.

1815

Agricultural prices collapse: The Catholic population expands, causing rural anxiety to fester amid secret society violence led by organisations such as the Ribbonmen. Landlords, often based in England, complain about the native population whom they deem incompetent and uncivilised.

1823

The Catholic Association, formed by Daniel O'Connell, organises mass political protest and demands economic, political and civil rights for Catholics.

1829

24 March: Catholic Emancipation is introduced, permitting Catholics to sit in the British Parliament.

1831

3 May, Tithe War: Members of the Irish Constabulary, under protest, seized cattle belonging to a priest in lieu of his tithe payment to the Church of Ireland.

1836

The Tithe Commutation Act lessens the tithe demanded from non-Anglicans and liberalises the enforcement of the system. This ends the Tithe War.

1830s

The Young Ireland movement, led by Protestant radicals, liberals and nationalists, founds a hugely influential paper, *The Nation.* The harp is adopted as a symbol of Irish nationalism.

1843

15 Aug.: Daniel O'Connell's 'Monster Meeting' takes place on the Hill of Tara, attracting a reported 750,000 people. O'Connell says that the size of the crowd should inspire pride and fear, and that they were approaching Repeal with the strides of a giant.

The Orange Order is reconstituted in response to O'Connell's seemingly rampant Repeal movement.

1845

The Irish Famine starts and rages for several years. A potato disease destroys two-thirds of Ireland's potato harvest, upon which the peasantry relies for food and nutriment.

The initial danger arises in Mayo, where 90% of the population survived on potatoes. Prime Minister Robert Peel says that the Irish tend to exaggerate.

1846

Every county is affected by the blight with 75% of the potato crop wiped out. Typhus is found all over the country. Peel orders American maize to be shipped to Ireland and organises a relief commission in Dublin which would organise committees of the wealthier people to supply cheap food and employment through public works. As a result of British intervention the price of bread falls, but many still can't afford it. Malthusian economics prevail and it is felt that the market should not be interfered with. The Irish could not be given free food because that would destabilise market prices.

British opinion is more concerned with the threat to property than with hunger. Curfews are introduced to control public disorder. Peel grumbles that violence and murder is being inflicted on supporters of the queen. An ample supply of food is on hand in Ireland, but it is not given to the famished (1.5 million are still starving). The government feels Irish landlords should be responsible for their people. Some landlords are active, cancelling rents and distributing food. Others evict tenants. *The Times* said the Irish were indolent. An estimated 5,000 people attacked a Listowel workhouse demanding 'bread or blood'. There are now insufficient coffins in Ireland to bury the dead and some of them have to be buried in mass pits.

1847

Daniel O'Connell dies.

Typhus and fever rage across Ireland, with even 'the better sort of people' infected. Liberal British opinion – encouraged by groups such as the Quakers – is finally mobilised and free food given out by soup kitchens. Help also comes from America. It is thought that in 1847 a quarter of a million people left Ireland, with 100,000 going to Liverpool. Over the next four years similar numbers left the country, the majority going to the United States. It was this human drain which was the basis of the powerful Irish Diaspora and which helped to bring about the decline of the Irish language (most widely spoken in those parts of the country worst affected by famine). The Diaspora eventually came back to haunt Britain via the Fenians and their successors. The revival of the language becomes a passionately held ambition for future generations of Irish separatists.

By the summer, three million are receiving assistance. There is a good, but small potato crop. Outdoor relief is introduced, but anyone with more than a quarter of an acre of land is ineligible so many have to give up their land. Some landlords are bankrupted and many farmers ruined.

1848

Young Ireland rebellion at Ballingarry, County Tipperary: Led by William Smith O'Brien, originally a member of O'Connell's Repeal movement who was radicalised by the famine. The Young Irelanders believe in an Irishness which brought Catholics and Protestants together. John Mitchel, son of a Presbyterian minister, founded the *United Irishman* which advocating rebellion. After Mitchel's arrest, Smith O'Brien becomes the leader of the movement. He goes to Tipperary where he encourages the famine-ravaged population to rise up. This doesn't happen, but there is a near-farcical skirmish at Ballingarry which became known as 'the battle of Widow MacCormack's cabbage garden'.

1849

The worst famine year. The Irish came to blame the British government for their plight and eventually concluded that they were better off looking after their own affairs. This belief became the central thrust of all Irish political activity until the end of the twentieth century. The population of Ireland shrinks from 8,175,124 in 1841 to 6,552,385 in 1851. As a result of famine 1.5 million people emigrate and 800,000 die.

1850s

Fenianism emerges under the guidance of men who had been footsoldiers in the failed Young Ireland movement.

1856

James Stephens undertakes a 3,000 mile covert tour of Ireland on foot weighing up revolutionary prospects. He finds that alienation was rife but that the people had no idea what to do about it.

1858

James Stephens helps found the Fenians or Irish Republican Brotherhood. They take an oath of loyalty to an independent democratic Irish Republic. In New York Michael Doheny, John O'Mahony and others found a parallel organisation, the Fenian Brotherhood.

Stephens organises the funeral of Fenian Terence Bellew MacManus and founds a Fenian paper, *The Irish People*, which is largely put together by John O'Leary with assistance from novelist Charles Kickham and others.

1865

The team behind the *Irish People* are arrested, but Stephens escapes. Despite claims that Stephens had 85,000 men ready for a fight, a decision is made to postpone the rebellion.

1866

Stephens states that this was the year for the Fenian rising but, once again, it is postponed. He is toppled by American Fenians.

2 June: American Fenians skirmish with Canadian forces.

1867

11 Feb.: An ill-conceived Fenian rising commences with an attack on Chester Castle which is undermined by an informer and called off.

5 March: A second attack at Chester is betrayed by the same informer. In Ireland Fenians capture a police barracks and a coastguard station.

September: Colonel Thomas Kelly and Captain Timothy Deasy are arrested. Some thirty Fenians surround their Manchester prison van, killing a policeman but rescuing Kelly and Deasy. The

'Manchester Martyrs' are found guilty of killing the policeman and are hung. Popular sentiment is greatly exercised and their declaration from the scaffold, 'God save Ireland' becomes one of the catchphrases of the era, immortalised in the eponymous popular ballad.

Fenian organiser Richard Burke, locked up in Clerkenwell, is the subject of a daring rescue attempt involving the blowing up of a prison wall. Several adjacent houses are demolished by the blast and twelve people are killed. The incident – regarded as a massacre – brings Ireland's state of affairs to the attention of British opinion and liberal politicians. Gladstone, in and out of office, begins to consider the Irish land question and also starts toying with the idea of giving the country Home Rule. Charles Stewart Parnell, a Protestant landlord, is active in the Home Rule movement. Ex-Fenian Michael Davitt calls him 'an Englishman of the strongest sort moulded for an Irish purpose'. There are substantial Home Rule initiatives in 1886, 1893 and 1912. Attracted by Parnell's charismatic leadership and competence, many able Fenians turn to constitutionalism.

1879

Davitt campaigns for an end to evictions and a shift in the ownership of Irish land from landlords to their tenants via the Land League. With Parnell as president, the organisation ranks are filled with Fenians, dissidents and tenant's associations.

Their movement involves violence against, and intimidation of, landlords and their agents. The most famous mode of intimidation, favoured by the non-violent Parnell, is the boycott, taking its name from the campaign of isolation waged against west of Ireland landlord Captain Boycott.

1881

Parnell says that he wants the crown to be the only link between Britain and Ireland.

1881–2

A series of Land Acts strengthens security of tenure.

1882

The chief secretary for Ireland is killed in the Phoenix Park. His killers are former IRB members called the Invincibles.

1884

The Gaelic Athletic Association is formed, with Fenian support and Parnell's blessing, to propagate Irish games.

1885

Parnell's Home Rule/Parliamentary Party wins 80% of the Irish seats in the British general election. He holds the balance of power between Liberals and Conservatives in Parliament. Gladstone supports Home Rule.

1886

The First Home Rule Bill fails.

1886–9

The Plan of Campaign and Land League disturbances dominate political debate in Ireland.

1887

Parnell is accused of instigating the Phoenix Park murders.

1889

Parnell's disgrace and fall commences when his affair with a married woman, Kitty O'Shea, becomes pubic knowledge. Gladstone calls for Parnell's resignation.

1890

A turbulent meeting of the Parliamentary Party votes to get rid of Parnell who subsequently adopts a more radical stance, turning to the Fenians – the 'men of the hills' – for support. A broken man, he dies from a heart attack at the age of 45.

The Home Rule Party continues in a diminished form and dominates Irish political and social discourse until the rise of Sinn Féin in 1918.

1892

Liberals succeed in getting a Home Rule Bill passed in the Commons.

1893

The Second Home Rule Bill is rejected by the House of Lords.

1900

Queen Victoria successfully visits Ireland.

One-time Parnellite John Redmond heals the split in the Parliamentary Party.

1903

King Edward makes a trip to Ireland.

1904

Sinn Féin is founded by the journalist and agitator Arthur Griffith. Griffith's moderate solution to the 'Irish problem' is eventually superseded by a more strident desire for a wholly independent republic.

Patrick Pearse, a poet and teacher, founds St Enda's, a school which preaches the idea of an Ireland Gaelic and free.

1913

The Irish Transport Union instigates a bitter and ultimately unsuccessful six-month strike. Dublin's slums are believed to be the worst in Europe.

1914

The First World War commences. Home Rule, now on the statute books, is postponed. John Redmond, signing the Parliamentary Party's death warrant, encourages Irish Volunteers to join the British army and fight in the war. The Volunteers split. A small minority, mainly made up of IRB men and women, hold on to the name Irish Volunteers. These subsequently become the nucleus of the IRA.

Tom Clarke, a one time Fenian bomber, is heavily involved in Dublin IRB affairs. The IRB has been revived by the likes of Bulmer Hobson and enjoys more support that at any previous time.

1915

The death and stage-managed funeral of Fenian O'Donovan Rossa. Pearse gives an important graveside oration.

1916

17 March: The Irish Volunteers and James Connolly's Irish Citizen Army undertake St Patrick's Day marches in Dublin.

24 April: The Easter Rising, under the command of Connolly and Pearse, commences. It declares for an Irish Republic.

Within a week the rebels are defeated and, in quick succession, the signatories of the Proclamation of the Irish Republic are executed, causing a wellspring of sympathy for the revolutionaries which, over the next two years, spreads like wildfire throughout the nationalist population.

1917

Griffith effectively loses control over Sinn Féin and figures such as Éamon de Valera and Michael Collins come to the fore. Sinn Féin nominates Count Plunkett, the father of 1916 Rising leader Joseph Plunkett, in a by-election, and he is triumphantly elected.

De Valera becomes the leader of Sinn Féin while Michael Collins takes over the IRB.

1918

Sinn Féin enjoy what is regarded as being a landslide victory in the British general election.

1919

January: Tipperary IRB men, under the leadership of Seán Treacy and Dan Breen, kill two RIC men. The incident, though it is not the first outbreak of hostilities, is generally regarded as being the opening volley of the Irish War of Independence because of the political stance of open rebellion subsequently adopted by the Tipperary men.

De Valera goes to New York where he is feted as the president of the Irish Republic. He encounters some resistance from old school Fenians.

In Ireland the war, known sometimes as the Tan War (because of the involvement of the ruthless British Black and Tan force), rages with the British seemingly unable to stop it.

1921

July: De Valera meets with the British and a truce is signed.

December: The Anglo-Irish Treaty is agreed to by a delegation led by Collins and Griffith. Ireland is divided into the 26 county Free State with the other six counties being turned into the Unionist-dominated Northern Ireland. Both states exist under the British crown.

De Valera is against the Treaty, but it is ratified by Dáil Éireann, the Sinn Féin parliament

1922–24

The Irish Civil War begins because of disagreement over the Treaty. During this bloody interlude some of Ireland's most interesting and talented leaders – like Collins, radical Liam Mellows, and novelist Erskine Childers – are killed. The pro-Treaty Free Staters win the war but, in the long run, it is De Valera and his new constitutional party, Fianna Fáil, who eventually win the peace. He and his followers come to dominate Irish political life for the rest of the twentieth century. The rest is history.

THE UNITED IRISHMEN

The Condition of Ireland — 1798[*]

The country was steadily improving, and no serious danger was felt till the French Revolution burst upon Europe. In every country it stimulated the smouldering elements of disorder. In few countries was its influence more fatal than in Ireland. I have very lately described at length the terrible years of growing conspiracy, anarchy, and crime; of fluctuating policy, and savage repression, and revived religious animosity, and maddening panic, deliberately and malignantly fomented, that preceded and prepared the rebellion. It is sufficient here to say that in the beginning of 1798 three provinces were organised to assist a French invasion. But at the last moment the leaders were betrayed and arrested; the French did not arrive; the rebellion was almost confined to a few Leinster counties, and it broke out without leaders and without a plan.

In most places the rebels proved to be wretched bands of marauders intent only on plunder, and, although they committed many murders, they were utterly incapable of meeting the loyalists in the field. But in Wexford, priests put themselves at the head of the movement and turned it into a religious war, deriving its main force from religious fanaticism, and waged with desperate courage and ferocity. The massacre of Protestants on Vinegar Hill, in Scullabogue Barn, and on Wexford Bridge, and the general character the rebellion in Leinster assumed, at once and forever checked all that tendency to rebellion which had so long existed among the Protestants of Ulster.

---

[*] *A History of England during the Eighteenth Century* (1892), William Lecky.

Wolfe Tone – Rebel without a Pause[*]

During his student days Tone was something of a drinker or party animal. While still at Dublin's Trinity College he eloped with a mid-teens girl, called Elizabeth, changed her name to Matilda (presumably because he didn't want his wife to bear the name of a prominent English monarch) and had two sons and a daughter with her. She outlived her rebel husband by fifty years. She reared their children, and died, in America. The fact that the Tone family, after the revolutionary leader's death, passed their time in the United States played some part in obscuring Wolfe Tone's virulently anti-American views.

It was Wolfe Tone, a big and honourable icon, who gave to Irish separatism some of its most basic tenets and most fervently cherished ideals. He said that:

> To subvert the tyranny of our execrable government, to break the connection with England, the never failing source of all our political evils, and to assert the independence of my country – these were my objects. To unite the whole people of Ireland, to abolish the memory of all past dissentions, and to substitute the common name of Irishman, in the place of the denominations of Protestant, Catholic, and Dissenter – these were my means.

Tone and his co-conspirators in the United Irishmen were as radical as a revolutionary organisation could be before the evolution of socialist and anarchist theory. Tone, mischievous and confrontational, said that, 'If the men of property will not support us, they must fall. Our strength shall come from that great and respectable class, the men of no property.'

English radical Thomas Paine's *Rights of Man* had a huge influence upon smart radical thinkers in Ireland and the book, printed in Dublin, was constantly reprinted and circulated, its

[*] Joe Ambrose.

anti-monarchy and anti-privilege messages striking a progressive chord amongst radical Presbyterians and Catholics.

In 1791, Tone penned a pamphlet, *A Northern Whig*, said to have sold over 10,000 copies. In it, he sought to apply the principles of the French Revolution concerning equality and liberty to a contemporary Irish political situation where the majority of the Catholic population were ruled by a London-connected Protestant parliament located in central Dublin. Known as Grattan's Parliament, in honour of liberal Henry Grattan who provided the assembly with a moral compass, this sporadically tolerant assembly oversaw an unfair tithe system which required the Catholic majority (and Jews and Presbyterians) to pay a substantial levy to the establishment Anglican church.

It was also in 1791 that Tone, with Napper Tandy and a number of Northern Presbyterian radicals, first established the United Irishmen. Their political idea was to create an organisation to bring progressive Catholics and Protestants with shared (French) republican ideals together inside one pressure group which would seek, by parliamentary means, to reform Ireland's social and sectarian injustices.

As in all pseudo-democratic systems where a compromised mandate determines the nature of government, pressure groups and lobbyists exerted considerable influence in Grattan's Dublin. At first, the United Irishmen seemed to be one such pressure group whose existence could be tolerated by the ruling classes. Most of the organisation's supporters were socially well connected.

As with any united front, there were left/right clashes within the United Irishmen. Tone, a fan of both Paine and of French revolutionary Danton, confidently led the organisation's left flank. A free-thinking character, almost eccentric in his liberalism, he came to believe that only revolutionary means would persuade a well-established and well-padded rulers to give up a lifestyle and system which obviated the interests of the Irish majority population.

By 1794, the United Irishmen were looking longingly towards revolutionary France for a solution to the problems they perceived in their own country. The French Revolution was one of the most important European developments since the emergence of Christianity as the dominant religion on the continent. It seemed to provide a quick fix solution to all of the world's ills and seemed, like the 1917 Russian Communist revolution, the 1950s spread of television, or the 1990s Internet avalanche, to be a fundamentally life-changing phenomenon.

The English state, which declared war on France and its revolution in 1793, loathed and dreaded the spread of revolutionary ideas. They regarded the emergent Irish Jacobins with classic right-wing fear and loathing.

In 1794, an English cleric and French Revolutionary called William Jackson visited Ireland on behalf of the French Committee of Public Safety, then the dominant political force in Paris where the guillotine was wet with aristocratic blood. Jackson met with the United Irishmen and Tone led him to believe that Ireland was ready for revolution. In 1794, Jackson was arrested and charged with treason against England. United Irishmen were rounded up, their papers seized, and many of their leaders fled to France. Tone, rather peculiarly for an unremitting revolutionary, used his connections in high places to cut a deal. Jackson festered in prison before committing suicide in 1795. Tone was allowed to go free and to emigrate so long as he furnished the authorities with information concerning his dealings with Jackson and eschewed all future revolutionary activities. He emigrated with his family to America, arriving in May 1795. Before this departure, at Belfast's Cave Hill, Tone made a secret pact with other United Irishmen that they would never stop their political efforts, 'until we subvert the authority of England over our country and asserted our independence'.

He did not like America or the Wasp establishment he encountered there. He found the people of Philadelphia to be a 'churlish, unsocial race, totally absorbed in making money'. George Washington did not make a great impression on him either: 'I do believe from my very soul that Washington is a very honest man but he is a high-flying aristocrat.' He felt that Washington and his cohorts pursued political policies that sought to 'bring in more dollars to the chests of the Mercantile Peerage of America.'

'I bless God I am no American', he wrote to an old Irish friend. Offered the opportunity to become a farmer involved in taming the 'Wild West' he commented laconically, 'as I have no great talent for the tomahawk, I have therefore given up going into the woods.' Tone's pro-French political sympathies and anti-American prejudices ensured that, for the next fifty years, Irish separatists inevitably looked towards Paris, rather than towards America, for salvation.

Fifty years later, in 1848, Paris was still be the first port of call for fleeing rebels, but the Young Ireland conspirators eventually moved their centre of operations to New York where they founded the Fenians, an organisation inextricably linked into American structures and thought-processes. From the time of the Fenians up until the Good Friday Agreement, America remained the dominant external force putting pressure on London to do something about Ireland. Though the Provisional IRA, during the 1970s, enjoyed considerable support from French intellectuals and radicals, post-1848 Irish separatists no longer expected much from the French state.

One of the first things that Wolfe Tone did when he arrived in America was to contact the French representative there, presenting him with a document concerning the state of Ireland. Over the next few months, spurning invitations to go west, Tone received letters from revolutionary friends at home lamenting the condition of Ireland and encouraging him to go to Paris. He did not need much encouragement and, in February 1796, the vivacious, fun-loving Tone washed up in the equally vivacious and fun-loving, but dangerous and shark-infested, Paris. He soon had access to senior figures in the revolutionary establishment – men interested in exporting their revolution were reported as being impressed by his energy, sincerity, and ability. He was given a commission in the French army and assured that a meaningful French military expedition would be put at his disposal so the British could be driven out of Ireland.

In December 1796, a French expedition containing some 14,000 men set sail from France accompanied by Tone. They tarried a while near Bantry Bay but, due to bad weather, were unable to reach land. In June 1797, Tone played his part in a scheme for a Dutch invasion of Ireland, with French support. The Dutch fleet was detained for weeks by bad weather. By the time that it could put to sea in October, Tone was back in Paris, busily scheming.

The diaries which Tone kept during his time in Paris represent some of the finest writing there is by an Irish political rebel. Full of the quickness and clarity which defines all good writing, they allow this unrepentant troublemaker's exuberant spirit to reach out across the dusty centuries and to touch us. Short of money, hoping for the best, drunk again, Wolfe Tone speaks to us in a shockingly modern way.

PARIS DIARY[*]

July 5, 1796
'Twas a sad rainy night, but the morning is fine. I think it rains as much at Paris as in Ireland and that kills me. I am devoured this day with the spleen, and I have not settled with Clarke & yet, and everything torments me.[†] Time! Time! I never felt the *taedium*

---

[*] *Life of Theobald Wolfe Tone* by himself, continued by his son, with his political writings (1826), edited by W. T. Wolfe Tone.
[†] *Clarke*: a senior French general.

vitae‡ in my life, till the last two or three months, but at present I do suffer dreadfully, that is the truth of it. Only think, there is not at this moment, man, woman, nor child in Paris, that cares one farthing if I were hanged, at least for my sake. I may say the Executive Directory are my nearest connection ... I respect them all, and wish them sincerely well on every account, but I would rather spend an hour talking nonsense with PP than a week with any one of them, saving at all times my business here. I do not speak of the loss of the society of my dearest love, and our little family, for that is not to be replaced. Well, if ever I find myself at Paris, Ambassador from Ireland, I will make myself amends for my former privations; 'I will, by the God of war!' And I will have PP here too, and I will give him choice Burgundy to drink, *ad libitum* and he and I will go to the opera together, and we will be as happy as the day is long.§ 'Visions of glory, spare my aching sight'. This is choice castle building, but what better can I do just now to amuse myself? Trifling as these memorandums are, they are a great resource to me, for when I am writing them, I always fancy I am chatting with PP and my dearest love. I wish I had my commission though; I long to see myself in regimentals.¶ (Sings) 'Zounds, I'll soon be a brigadier!' That is choice.

Evening, 5 o'clock. It was not for nothing that I have been in the horrors all the forenoon. On the 26th May I wrote to my wife respecting the immediate removal of my family to France and today I see in an English paper given me that the vessel which carried my letter, an American, the *Argus*, was carried into Plymouth on the 25th June last, and is detained. That is pleasant! This event throws my private affairs into unspeakable confusion, and I am too angry just now to see how to rectify them. I was this very morning counting that my dearest love would have my letter in about a fortnight. Was there ever anything so

---

‡ *Taedium vitae:* boredom.
§ *Ad libitum:* as he wishes.
¶ *My commission*: papers making him an officer in the French army.

distressing? ... I am infinitely embarrassed by this event; one thing consoles me. In all my letters, I have hardly mentioned one word of politics, or of my business here, and the little I have said is calculated to mislead; for at the time I wrote, appearances were as gloomy as possible. Well, this is the second time in my life I am indebted for a serious evil to master John Bull. He hunted me out of my own country first, and now he is preventing me from bringing my family to France; and does he think I will forget all that? No! That I won't, no more than his attempt to press me for a sailor on my passage out to America.* Well, it does not signify cursing or swearing; I am in too great a fury to write any longer. God knows now when my family will get my letters, or whether they will ever get them.

July 6, 1796

Saw Clarke this morning; he is almost recovered; and tells me my business is delayed solely by the absence of General Hoche, who is coming up with all privacy to Paris to confer with the Directory; that on his arrival everything will be settled; that I must be introduced to him, and communicate with him, and most probably return with him to the army where my presence would be necessary.† All this is very good. I shall be glad to be introduced to Hoche; it looks like serious business. Clarke also told me he wanted to have my commission expedited instantly by the Minister of War, but that Carnot had decided to wait for Hoche.‡ I told him it was the same to me, and also begged to know when he expected Hoche. He replied, 'Every day.' I then took occasion to mention the state of my finances, that in two or three days I should be run out, and relied upon him to

* *Passage out to America:* an attempt was made to press-gang Tone into the British army when the British boarded the vessel taking him into exile off the American coast.
† *Hoche:* one of the outstanding military leaders of Revolutionary France, Napoleon's major rival during their early days.
‡ *Carnot:* the 'Organiser of Victory' during the Revolutionary Wars.

prevent my falling into difficulties. He asked me could I carry on the war some little time longer. I answered, I could not, for I did not know a soul in Paris but the Government. He seemed a little taken aback at this, by which I see that money is not their forte at present. Damn it for me! I am sure I wish there was not a guinea in the world. So here I am, with exactly two louis in my exchequer, negotiating with the French Government, and planning revolutions. I must say it is truly original. 'Crescit amor nummi, quantum ipsa pecunnia crescit.'§ That is not true as to me, for my passion increases as my funds diminish. I reckon I am the poorest Ambassador today in Paris, but that gives me no great concern. Huzza! *Vive la Republique!* 'When Christmas comes about again, Oh then I shall have money.' To be sure I am writing most egregious nonsense, *mais c'est égal*.¶ I told Clarke of the miscarriage of my letters, by way of precaution against certain unknown apprehensions which I felt.

How lucky it was that I hardly mentioned a word of my business to anyone. Well, Lazarus Hoche, I wish you were come with all my soul. Here I am 'in perplexity and doubtful dilemma,' waiting your arrival. Sad! Sad! I am gnawing my very soul with anxiety and expectation. And then I have a vision of poverty in the background, which is truly alarming …

After leaving Clarke, I sat down in an outside room, and wrote him a note, desiring him to apply to Carnot for such assistance in the premises as he might think fit; adding that any money advanced to me was to be considered as advanced on public account, and that I would call on him the day after tomorrow. In the meantime I will devour my discontents, 'and in this harsh world draw my breath with pain'. Maybe my friend Lazarus, 'who is not dead, but sleepth,' may make his appearance by that time. It is, to be sure, most excessively ridiculous … that I should be run out of money.

---

§ *The love of money increases as wealth increases* is a quote from Juvenal's *Satires*.
¶ *Mais c'est égal:* but all the same.

July 7, 1796

In order to divert myself, and get rid of a little of my superfluous cash, I went last night to the opera, where, by-the-by, I go most frequently. I am more and more pleased with that spectacle. Nothing can be more perfect in its kind, than the representation of *Oedipe à Colonne.** It is a complete Greek tragedy ... I have seen it now I believe a dozen times, and am every time more pleased with it, which is a rare thing to be able to say of an opera.

July 11, 1796

Called on Clarke, who took down my name and the day and place of my birth, in order to have my commission filled up, which he expects to have done tomorrow. He was very civil, and mentioned that if it rested with him, the business would have been done long since. He then asked me did I know one Duckett? I answered, I understood ... that he was a blackguard. He seemed a little taken aback at this, and said, 'Ay, but he is clever.' I answered I knew nothing more about him, that it was disagreeable to me to speak ill of anybody, especially of a person whom I knew merely by report, but in a business of such consequence as ours, I felt it my duty to speak without the least reserve. Clarke said, 'undoubtedly', and so the matter rested.

I am to call the day after to-morrow, at which time I hope my eternal commission will be ready. Bought the *Reglement pour le service de la Cavalerie* and sat down to study it. I must get a sensible sous officer to drill me a little before I join the regiment.† I am tired now of tactics, so I think I will go walk a little to refresh me.

---

* *Oedipe à Colonne*: an opera featuring a libretto based on Sophocles' *Oedipus at Colonus*.
† *Sous officer:* non-commissioned officer.

Wolfe Tone's Character[‡]

He rises far above the dreary level of commonplace which Irish conspiracy in general presents. The tawdry and exaggerated rhetoric; the petty vanity and jealousies; the weak sentimentalism; the utter incapacity for proportioning means to ends, and for grasping the stern realities of things, which so commonly disfigure the lives and conduct even of the more honest members of his class, were wholly alien to his nature. His judgement of men and things was keen, lucid and masculine, and he was alike prompt in decision and brave in action.

Tone's Speech from the Dock[§]

No name is more intimately associated with the national movement of 1798 than that of Theobald Wolfe Tone. He was its mainspring, its leading spirit. Many men connected with it possessed, as he did, brilliant talents, unfailing courage and determination; but the order of his genius raised him above them all, and marked him out from the first as the head and front of the patriot party. He was one of the original founders of the Society of United Irishmen, which was formed in Belfast in the year 1791. In its early days this society was simply a sort of reform association having for its chief object the removal of the frightful oppressions by which the Catholic people of Ireland were tortured and disgraced. But in the troubled and portentous condition of home and foreign politics, the society could not long retain this character.

---

‡ *A History of England during the Eighteenth Century* (1892), William Lecky.
§ *Speeches from the Dock, or protests of Irish Patriots: Speeches Delivered After Conviction* (1868), A. M. Sullivan.

The futility of seeking a redress of the national grievances by parliamentary means was becoming apparent to every understanding. The system of outrage and injustice towards the Catholics continued to exasperate the actual sufferers and to offend all men of humane feelings and enlightened principles; and, at the same time, the electric influence of the American War of Independence and the French Revolution was operating powerfully in every heart, evoking there the aspiration for Irish freedom. In the midst of such exciting circumstances the society could not continue to stand on its original basis. In the year 1794, after a debate among the members, followed by the withdrawal of the more moderate or timid among them from its ranks, it assumed the form and character of a secret revolutionary organisation; and Tone, Thomas Addis Emmet, James Napper Tandy, with a number of other patriotic gentlemen in Belfast, Dublin, and other parts of the country, found themselves in the full swing of an insurrectionary movement, plotting and planning for the complete overthrow of British power in Ireland.

Such was the state of affairs when, in the early part of 1794, an emissary from the French government arrived in Ireland, to ascertain to what extent the Irish people were likely to co-operate with France in a war against England. This individual was the Rev. William Jackson, an Irish Protestant clergyman, who had for some years been resident in France, and had become thoroughly imbued with Democratic and Republican principles. Unfortunately, he was not one of the most prudent of envoys. He revealed his mission to an acquaintance of his, an English attorney, named Cockayne, who repaid his confidence by betraying his secrets to the government. Cockayne was immediately employed as a spy upon Jackson's further proceedings, in which capacity he accompanied his unsuspecting victim to Ireland, and acquired cognisance of most of his negotiations.

On the 28th of April 1794, Jackson was arrested on a charge of high treason. He was brought to speedy trial, was found guilty, but was not sentenced, for, on the day on which the law's award was to have been announced to him, he contrived to swallow a dose of poison, from the effects of which he expired in the dock. Tone, with whom Jackson was known to have been in confidential communication, was placed by those events in a very critical position. Owing, however, to some influence which had been made with the government on his behalf, he was permitted to exile himself to America.

He left Dublin for Philadelphia on the 20th of May, 1795. One of his first acts, after arriving, was to present to the French Minister there resident a memorial on the state of Ireland. During the remaining months of the year letters from his old friends came pouring in on him, describing the brightening prospects of the cause at home, and urging him to proceed to the French capital and impress upon the Directory the policy of despatching at once an expedition to ensure the success of the Irish revolutionary movement.

Tone was not the man to disregard such representations. He had at the time a fair prospect of securing a comfortable independence in America, but with the full concurrence of his heroic wife, who had accompanied him across the Atlantic, he sacrificed those chances and resumed the perilous duties of an Irish patriot. On the 1st of January, 1796, he left New York for Paris to try what he could do as a diplomatist for the cause of Ireland. Arrived at the French capital, he had his business communicated to the Directory through the medium of an Irish gentleman and also by memorial, representing always that the landing of a force of 20,000 men in Ireland, with a supply of arms for the peasantry, would ensure the separation of Ireland from England.*

Not satisfied with the slow progress he was achieving, he went on the 24th of February direct to the Luxemburg Palace, and sought and obtained an interview with the War Minister, the celebrated Carnot, the 'organiser of victory'. The Minister

---

* *By memorial:* by presenting a document, a memo.

received him well, listened attentively to his statements, discussed his project with him, and appeared much impressed with the prospects it presented.

The result was that on the 16th of December a splendid expedition sailed from Brest for Ireland. It consisted of seventeen sail of the line, thirteen frigates and fifteen transports, with some smaller craft, and had on board 15,000 troops, with a large supply of arms for the Irish patriots.

Tone himself, who had received the rank of Adjutant-General in the French service, was on board one of the vessels. Had this force been disembarked on the shores of Ireland, it is hardly possible to doubt that the separation of this country from England would have been effected. But the expedition was unfortunate from the outset. It was scattered on the voyage during a gale of wind, and the Admiral's vessel, with Hoche, the Commander, on board, was separated from the others.

A portion of the expedition entered the magnificent Bay of Bantry and waited there several days in expectation of being rejoined by the vessel containing the Admiral and Commander; but they waited in vain. Tone vehemently urged that a landing should be effected with the forces then at hand – some 6,500 men – but the officers procrastinated, time was lost, the wind which had been blowing from the east (that is out the harbour) rose to a perfect hurricane, and on the 27th and 28th of the month the vessels cut their cables and made the best of their way for France.

This was a terrible blow to the hopes of the Irish organiser. Rage and sadness filled his heart by turns as the fierce storm blew his vessel out of the bay and across the sea to the land which he had left under such favourable auspices. But yet he did not resign himself to despair. As the patient spider renews her web again and again after it has been torn asunder, so did this indefatigable patriot set to work to repair the misfortune that had occurred. His perseverance was not unproductive of results.

The Dutch Republic, then in alliance with France, took up the project that had failed in the Bay of Bantry. In the month of July 1797, they assembled an expedition for the invasion of Ireland, nearly, if not quite, as formidable in men and ships as that which had left Brest in the previous year. Tone was on board the flagship, even more joyous and hopeful than he had been on the preceding occasion. But again, as if by some extraordinary fatality, the weather interposed an obstacle to the realisation of the design. The vessels were ready for sea, the troops were on board. Nothing was wanted but a slant of wind to enable the fleet to get out. But for five weeks it continued to blow steadily in the adverse direction.

The supplies ran low; the patience of the officers, and of the government, became exhausted – the troops were disembarked and the project abandoned! The second failure was a heavy blow to the heart of Tone. Elaborate and costly efforts like those which had ended so poorly, he felt, could not often be repeated. The drift of the war was cutting out other work for the fleets and armies of France and the unwelcome conviction began to settle darkly on his mind that never again would he see such a vision of hope for Ireland as that which had shone before him on those two occasions, and vanished in doubt and gloom.

Yet there was no need to despair. Assurances reached Tone every day that the defeat and humiliation of England was a settled resolve of the French Government, one which they would never abandon. And for a time everything seemed to favour the notion that a direct stroke at the heart of England was intended.

In the latter part of 1797 the Directory ordered the formation of 'The Army of England', the command of which was given to General Bonaparte. Tone's heart again beat high with hope, for now matters looked more promising than ever. He was in constant communication with some of the chief officers of the expedition, and in the month of December he had several interviews with Bonaparte himself, which however he could hardly consider of a satisfactory nature.

On the 20th of May, 1798, General Bonaparte embarked on board the fleet at Toulon and sailed off – not for Ireland or England, but for Egypt.

On the Irish leaders at home these repeated disappointments fell with terrible effect. The condition of the country was daily growing more critical. The government, now thoroughly roused and alarmed, and persuaded that the time for 'vigorous measures' had arrived, was grappling with the conspiracy in all directions. Still those men would, if they could, have got the people to possess their souls in patience and wait for aid from abroad before unfurling the banner of insurrection; for they were constant in their belief that without the presence of a disciplined army on Irish soil to consolidate their strength and direct it, a revolutionary effort of the Irish people could end only in disaster.

On the 23rd of May, three days after Bonaparte had sailed from Toulon for Alexandria, the Irish insurrection broke out. The news of the occurrence created the most intense excitement among the Irish refugees then in Paris.

Tone rushed to and fro to the Directory and to the generals, pleading for the despatch of some assistance to his struggling countrymen. Various plans were suggested and taken into consideration, but while time was being wasted in this way, the military forces of the British Government were rapidly suppressing the insurrection of the unarmed and undisciplined Irish peasantry. In this condition of affairs a gallant but rash and indiscreet French officer, General Humbert, resolved that he would commit the Directory to action, by starting at once with a small force for the coast of Ireland. Towards the middle of August, calling together the merchants and magistrates of Rochelle, he forced them to advance a small sum of money, and all that he wanted, on military requisition; and embarking on board a few frigates and transports with 1,000 men, 1,000 spare muskets, 1,000 guineas, and a few pieces of artillery.

He compelled the captains to set sail for the most desperate attempt which is, perhaps, recorded in history. Three Irishmen were on board the fleet – Matthew Tone, brother to Theobald, Bartholomew Teeling, and Sullivan, an officer in the French service, who was enthusiastically devoted to the Irish cause. Humbert landed at Killala, routed with his little handful of men a large force of royal troops, and held his ground until General Lake, with 20,000 men marched against him.

After a resistance sufficient to maintain the honour of the French arms, Humbert's little force surrendered as prisoners of war. The Irish who had joined his standard were shown no mercy. The peasantry were cruelly butchered. Of those who had accompanied him from France, Sullivan, who was able to pass as a Frenchman, escaped; Teeling and Matthew Tone were brought in irons to Dublin, tried, and executed. The news of Humbert's expedition and the temporary success that had attended it created much excitement in France, and stirred up the Directory to attempt something for Ireland more worthy of the fame and power of the French nation, and more in keeping with their repeated promises to the leaders of the Irish movement. But their fleet was at the time greatly reduced, and their resources were in a state of disorganisation.

They mustered for the expedition only one sail of the line and eight small frigates, commanded by Commodore Bompart, conveying 5,000 men under the leadership of General Hardy. On board the Admiral's vessel, which was named the Hoche, was the heroic Theobald Wolfe Tone. He knew this expedition had no chance of success, but he had all along declared, 'that if the government sent only a corporal's guard, he felt it his duty to go along with them.'

The vessels sailed on the 20th of September 1798; it was not till the 11th October that they arrived off Lough Swilly – simultaneously with an English squadron that had been on the lookout for them. The English ships were about equal in number to the French, but were of a larger class, and carried a much heavier armament. The French Admiral directed some of his smaller craft to endeavour to escape by means of their light draught of water, and he counselled Tone to transfer himself to that one of them which had the best chance of getting away. The Frenchmen, he observed, would be made prisoners of war, but for the Irish rebel a worse fate was reserved if he should fall into the hand of his enemies.

To this suggestion Tone declined to accede. 'Shall it be said,' he replied, 'that I fled while the French were fighting the battles of my country'. In a little time the Hoche was surrounded by four sail of the line and one frigate, who poured their shot into her upon all sides. During six hours she maintained the unequal combat, fighting 'till her masts and rigging were cut away, her scuppers flowed with blood, her wounded filled the cockpit, her shattered ribs yawned at each new stroke, and let in five feet of water in the hold, her rudder was carried off, and she floated a dismantled wreck on the water. Her sails and cordage hung in shreds, nor could she reply with a single gun from her dismounted batteries to the unabating cannonade of the enemy.'

During the action Tone commanded one of the batteries, 'and fought with the utmost desperation, as if he was courting death.' But, as often has happened in similar cases, death seemed to shun him, and he was reserved for a more tragic fate.

The French officers who survived the action, and had been made prisoners of war, were, some days subsequently, invited to breakfast with the Earl of Cavan, who commanded in the district in which they had been landed. Tone, who up to that time had escaped recognition, was one of the party, and sat undistinguished among them until Sir George Hill, who had been a fellow-student of his in Trinity College, entered the room and accosted him by his name. This was done, not inadvertently, but with the intention of betraying him. In a moment he was in the hands of a party of military and police who were in waiting for him in the next room.

Seeing that they were about to put him in fetters, he complained indignantly of the offering of such an insult to the uniform which he wore, and the rank – that of Chef de Brigade – which he bore in the French army. He cast off his regimentals, protesting that they should not be so sullied and then, offering his limbs to the irons, exclaimed – 'For the cause which I have embraced, I feel prouder to wear these chains, than if I were decorated with the Star and Garter of England'.

He was hurried off to Dublin, and though the ordinary tribunals were sitting at the time, and the military tribunals could have no claim on him, as he had never belonged to the English army, he was put on his trial before a court-martial. This was absolutely an illegal proceeding, but his enemies were impatient for his blood, and would not brook the chances and the delays of the ordinary procedure of law.

On the 10th of November 1798 his trial, if such it might be called, took place in one of the Dublin barracks. He appeared before the Court 'dressed,' says the *Dublin Magazine* for November, 1798, 'in the French uniform: a large cocked hat, with broad gold lace and the tri-coloured cockade; a blue uniform coat, with gold-embroidered collar and two large gold epaulets; blue pantaloons, with gold-laced garters at the knees; and short boots, bound at the tops with gold lace.'

In his bearing there was no trace of excitement. 'The firmness and cool serenity of his whole deportment,' writes his son, 'gave to the awestruck assembly the measure of his soul'. The proceedings of the Court are detailed in the following report, which we copy from the *Life of Tone* by his son, published at Washington, U.S., in 1826: –

The members of the Court having been sworn, the Judge Advocate called on the prisoner to plead guilty or not guilty to the charge of having acted traitorously and hostilely against the King.

Tone replied – 'I mean not to give the court any useless trouble, and wish to spare them the idle task of examining witnesses. I admit all the facts alleged, and only request leave to read an address which I have prepared for this occasion.'

Colonel Daly – 'I must warn the prisoner that, in acknowledging those facts, he admits, to his prejudice, that he has acted traitorously against his Majesty. Is such his intention?'

Tone – 'Stripping this charge of the technicality of its terms, it means, I presume, by the word traitorously, that I have been found in arms against the soldiers of the King in my native country. I admit this accusation in its most extended sense, and request again to explain to the court the reasons and motives of my conduct.'

The court then observed they would hear his address, provided he kept himself within the bounds of moderation.

Tone rose, and began in these words – 'Mr President and Gentlemen of the Court-Martial, I mean not to give you the trouble of bringing judicial proof to convict me legally of having acted in hostility to the government of his Britannic Majesty in Ireland. I admit the fact.

'From my earliest youth I have regarded the connection between Great Britain and Ireland as the curse of the Irish nation, and felt convinced that, whilst it lasted, this country could never be free or happy. My mind has been confirmed in this opinion by the experience of every succeeding year, and the conclusions which I have drawn from every fact before my eyes.

'In consequence, I was determined to employ all the powers which my individual efforts could move, in order to separate the two countries. That Ireland was not able of herself to throw off the yoke, I knew; I therefore sought for aid wherever it was to be found. In honourable poverty I rejected offers which, to a man in my circumstances, might be considered highly advantageous. I remained faithful to what I thought the cause of my country, and sought in the French Republic an ally to rescue three millions of my countrymen from –'

The President here interrupted the prisoner, observing that this language was neither relevant to the charge, nor such as ought to be delivered in a public court. A Member said it seemed calculated only to inflame the minds of a certain description of people (the United Irishmen), many of whom might be present, and that the court could not suffer it. The Judge Advocate said – 'If Mr Tone meant this paper by way of extenuation, it must have quite a contrary effect, if the foregoing part was suffered to remain.'

The President wound up by calling on the prisoner to hesitate before proceeding further in the same strain.

Tone then continued – 'I believe there is nothing in what remains for me to say which can give any offence. I mean to express my feelings and gratitude towards the Catholic body, in whose cause I was engaged.'

President – 'That seems to have nothing to say to the charge against you, to which you are only to speak. If you have anything to offer in defence or extenuation of the charge, the court will hear you, but they beg you will confine yourself to that subject.'

Tone – 'I shall, then, confine myself to some points relative to my connection with the French army. Attached to no party in the French Republic – without interest, without money, without intrigue – the openness and integrity of my views raised me to a high and confidential rank in its armies. I obtained the confidence of the Executive Directory, the approbation of my generals, and I will venture to add, the esteem and affection of my brave comrades.

'I feel a secret and internal consolation which no reverse of fortune, no sentence in the power of this court to inflict, can deprive me of. Under the flag of the French Republic I originally engaged with a view to save and liberate my own country. For that purpose I have encountered the chances of war amongst strangers. For that purpose I repeatedly braved the terrors of the ocean, covered, as I knew it to be, with the triumphant fleets of that power which it was my glory and my duty to oppose.

'I have sacrificed all my views in life; I have courted poverty; I have left a beloved wife unprotected, and children whom I adored fatherless. After such a sacrifice, in a cause which I have always considered – conscientiously considered – as the cause of justice and freedom, it is no great effort, at this day, to add the sacrifice of my life. But I hear it said that this unfortunate country has been a prey to all sorts of horrors. I sincerely lament it. I beg, however, it may be remembered that I have been absent four years from Ireland. To me these sufferings can never be attributed.

'I designed by fair and open war to procure the separation of the two countries. For open war I was prepared, but instead of that a system of private assassination has taken place. Atrocities, it seems, have been committed on both sides. I do not less deplore them. I detest them from my heart; and to those who know my character and sentiments I may safely appeal for the truth of this assertion; with them I need no justification.

'In a case like this success is everything. Success, in the eyes of the vulgar, fixes its merits. After a combat nobly sustained – combat which would have excited the respect and sympathy of a generous enemy – my fate has been to become a prisoner.

'I was brought here in irons like a felon. I mention this for the sake of others; for me, I am indifferent to it. I am aware of the fate which awaits me, and scorn equally the tone of complaint and that of supplication. As to the connection between this country and Great Britain, I repeat it – all that has been imputed to me (words, writings, and actions), I here deliberately avow. I have spoken and acted with reflection and on principle, and am ready to meet the consequences. Whatever be the sentence of the court, I am prepared for it. Its members will surely discharge their duty – I shall take care not to be wanting in mine.'

The court having asked if he wished to make any further observation, Tone said – 'I wish to offer a few words relative to one single point – the mode of punishment. In France our émigrés, who stand nearly in the same situation in which I now stand before you, are condemned to be shot. I ask that the court shall adjudge me the death of a soldier, and let me be shot by a platoon of grenadiers. I request this indulgence rather in consideration of the uniform I wear – the uniform of a Chef de Brigade in the French army – than from any personal regard to myself. In order to evince my claim to this favour, I beg that the court may take the trouble to peruse my commission and letters of service in the French army. It will appear from these papers that I have not received them as a mask to cover me, but that I have been long and *bona fide* an officer in the French service.'

Judge Advocate – 'You must feel that the papers you allude to will serve as undeniable proof against you.'

Tone – 'Oh, I know they will. I have already admitted the facts, and I now admit the papers as full proof of conviction.'

The papers were then examined. They consisted of a brevet of Chef de Brigade from the Directory, signed by the Minister of War, of a letter of service granting to him the rank of Adjutant-General, and of a passport.*

General Loftus – 'In these papers you are designated as serving in the army of England.'

Tone – 'I did serve in that army but I have also served elsewhere.'

The Court requested if he had anything further to observe. He said that nothing more occurred to him, except that the sooner his Excellency's approbation of the sentence was obtained the better.

This is Tone's speech, as reported in the public prints at that time, but the recently-published 'Correspondence' of Lord Cornwallis – Lord Lieutenant in those days – supplies a portion of the address which was never before published, the Court having forbade the reading of it at the trial. The passage contains a noble outburst of gratitude towards the Catholics of Ireland. Tone himself, as every reader is aware, was a Protestant, and there can have been no reason for its suppression except the consideration that

* *Brevet:* a certificate or diplomatic licence.

45

it was calculated to still more endear the prisoner to the hearts of his countrymen. We now reprint it, and thus place it for the first time before the people for whom it was written: –

'I have laboured to create a people in Ireland by raising three millions of my countrymen to the rank of citizens. I have laboured to abolish the infernal spirit of religious persecution, by uniting the Catholics and Dissenters. To the former I owe more than ever can be repaid. The services I was so fortunate as to render them they rewarded munificently; but they did more: when the public cry was raised against me – when the friends of my youth swarmed off and left me alone – the Catholics did not desert me; they had the virtue even to sacrifice their own interests to a rigid principle of honour.

'They refused, though strongly urged, to disgrace a man who, whatever his conduct towards the government might have been, had faithfully and conscientiously discharged his duty towards them; and in so doing, though it was in my own case, I will say they showed an instance of public virtue of which I know not whether there exists another example.'

The sad sequel of those proceedings is soon told. The request of the prisoner to receive a military execution was refused and Tone was sentenced to die 'the death of a traitor' within forty-eight hours. But he – influenced, it must be confessed, by a totally mistaken feeling of pride, and yielding to a weakness which every Christian heart should be able to conquer – resolved that, rather than allow his enemies to have the satisfaction of dangling his body from a gibbet, he would become his own executioner.

On the night of the 11th of November he contrived, while lying unobserved in his cell, to open a vein in his neck with a penknife. For the space of seven days afterwards did the unfortunate gentleman endure the agonies of approaching death. On the 19th of November, 1798, he expired.

PEARSE ON TONE[*]

Wolfe Tone's Bodenstown grave has long been a totemistic place of pilgrimage for republicans, alleged republicans, and the vast array of fringe leftist organisations which accept, *à la* James Connolly, that the first job that socialists must bring to a close is the solving of the 'national question', which they regard as being unsolved.

Wolfe Tone was the patron saint of Fenianism, his devil-may-care rebel spirit mixing nicely with their own social, political and revolutionary predilections. Fenianism became better known as the IRB (Irish Republican or Revolutionary Brotherhood) and, in the early years of the twentieth century, was profoundly revived by a new generation of leaders such as Bulmer Hobson.

The Bodenstown speech delivered by the IRB's representative at the annual Wolfe Tone Commemoration was important. It announced to the world what way the organisation's thinking was going. Three years before the 1916 Rising, on 22 June 1913, Patrick Pearse was chosen to deliver the oration. This was a sign that Pearse had arrived, that he was seen as a man to be respected and followed. The IRB's endorsement was underlined two years later when Pearse got the job of speaking at the freshly dug grave of Fenian O'Donovan Rossa.

Pearse shared with the previous generation of IRB men a taste for dressing up, a literary facility, and a belief in nihilistic propaganda-by-deed. He was not a colourful life force, a charismatic rogue, or even a terribly likeable man. He was interested in language revival and was somewhat pious or holier-than-thou. He was, nevertheless, part of the spark which lit the flame that led to the War of Independence. His mother said that he was a disciple of the old Fenian Tom Clarke who, perhaps, saw in him

---

[*] Joe Ambrose.

that quality which took sixty years of Fenian rhetoric very seriously and meant to do something with that rhetoric.

THEOBALD WOLFE TONE[*]

We have come to the holiest place in Ireland; holier to us even than the place where Patrick sleeps in Down. Patrick brought us life, but this man died for us. And though many before him and some since have died in testimony of the truth of Ireland's claim to nationhood, Wolfe Tone was the greatest of all that have made that testimony, the greatest of all that have died for Ireland whether in old time or in new. He was the greatest of Irish Nationalists; I believe he was the greatest of Irish men. And if I am right in this I am right in saying that we stand in the holiest place in Ireland, for it must be that the holiest sod of a nation's soul is the sod where the greatest of her dead lies buried.

I feel it difficult to speak to you today; difficult to speak in this place. It is as if one had to speak by the graveside of some dear friend, a brother in blood or a well-tried comrade in arms, and to say aloud the things one would rather keep to oneself. But I am helped by the knowledge that you who listen to me partake in my emotion: we are none of us strangers, being all in a sense brothers to Tone, sharing in his love. I have then, only to find expression for the thoughts and emotions common to us all and you will understand even if the expression be a halting one.

We have come here not merely to salute this noble dust and to pay our homage to the noble spirit of Tone. We have come to renew our adhesion to the faith of Tone; to express once more our full acceptance of the gospel of Irish Nationalism which he was the first to formulate in worthy terms, giving clear

* Speech by Patrick Pearse at Bodenstown, 12 June 1913.

definition and plenary meaning to all that had been thought and taught before him by Irish-speaking and English-speaking men; uttered half articulately by Shane O'Neill in some defiance flung at the Englishry, expressed under some passionate metaphor by Geoffrey Keating, hinted at by Swift in some biting gibe, clearly and greatly stated by Wolfe Tone, and not needing now ever to be stated anew for any generation.[†]

He has spoken for all time, and his voice resounds throughout Ireland, calling to us from this grave, when we wander astray following other voices that ring less true.

This, then, is the first part of Wolfe Tone's achievement – he made articulate the dumb voices of the centuries. He gave Ireland a clear and precise and worthy concept of Nationality. But he did more than this: not only did he define Irish Nationalism, but he armed his generation in defence of it. Thinker and doer, dreamer of the immortal dream and doer of the immortal deed – we owe to this dead man more than we can ever repay him by making pilgrimages to his grave or by raising to him the stateliest monument in the streets of his city. To his teaching we owe it that there is such a thing as Irish Nationalism, and to the memory of the deed he nerved his generation to do, to the memory of '98, we owe it that there is any manhood left in Ireland.

I have called him the greatest of our dead. In mind he was great above all the men of his time or of the after time; and he was greater still in spirit. It was to that nobly-dowered mind of his that Kickham, himself the most nobly-dowered of a later generation, paid reverence when he said:

Oh, knowledge is a wondrous power;
'Tis stronger than the wind ...
And would to the kind heavens
That Wolfe Tone were here today.

[†] *Geoffrey Keating*: seventeenth-century priest, poet and historian. Wrote *Lament on the Sad State of Ireland* about the Flight of the Earls. His influential *History of Ireland* appeared around 1634.

Sean Bhean Bhocht translates into 'Poor Old Woman'. The un-fortunate lady in question is Ireland, and this poetic device, the representation of Ireland as a stricken but great lady, is a popular one in the rebel ballad tradition. This song relates specifically to the abortive effort made by Wolfe Tone and the French to land an invading force at Bantry Bay in 1796.

Both *Boolavogue* and *Father Murphy* celebrate 1798 events that took place near Enniscorthy, Co. Wexford. Father John Murphy from Boolavogue led his congregation into battle late in May 1798. For a while, Wexford smouldered ominously but, eventually, the British regained control of the situation in June at the battle of Vinegar Hill. Father Murphy was hanged amid bloody reprisals. Both sides carried out sectarian butchery.

Boolavogue was composed in 1898 by P. J. McCall to go with the surge of 1798 commemorative events which accompanied the United Irishmen centenary. McCall also wrote the stirring *Follow Me Down to Carlow* and the rousing *Kelly the Boy from Killane*. Seán Ó Riada used *Boolavogue* in his groundbreaking score for the 1959 Tan War documentary, *Mise Éire*.

The Rising of the Moon was first published in an 1866 col-lection, *A Wreath of Shamrocks*. Popularised in the 1960s by the Clancy Brothers, it was referred to by Bobby Sands in the diary which he kept during the 1981 hunger strike which ended with his death.

Roddy McCorley is about a youthful Antrim Presbyterian, a United Irishman whose family were evicted from their land before the 1798 rebellion, in which he participated. He managed to avoid the British authorities for a year after the rising failed, but was eventually captured and tried in Ballymena. He was

[*] Joe Ambrose.

executed on Good Friday 1799 in the town of Toomebridge, by the 'bridge of Toome'.

Ethna Carbery from Ballymena (1866–1902) wrote the popular ballad about him which was performed, with some gusto, by Shane McGowan on his 1995 album, *The Snake*. Carbery – her real name was Anna MacManus – was a typical writer of the nationalist persuasion. She co-founded two nationalist journals, *The Northern Patriot* and *The Shan Van Vocht*.

The Croppy Boy concerns a boy who wears his hair cropped in solidarity with the anti-wig anti-aristocratic faction during the French revolution. The British authorities suspected any young man who wore his hair thus of having pro-French sympathies. There are two important Croppy songs – the other one is the loyalist *Croppies Lie Down*. The British experimental Maoist composer Clarence Cardew drew inspiration for the croppies and Seamus Heaney's 1966 poem *Requiem for the Croppies* muses on the turbulence of 1798.

Kelly the Boy from Killane immortalises John Kelly of Killane who was badly injured during the fighting around New Ross. While recuperating in Wexford town he was arrested and hanged. The farmers of Shelmalier and Bargy used to shoot wildfowl on the nearby sloblands. For this purpose, they used the long-barrelled guns referred to in P. J. McCall's song which was recorded with respect and affection by Luke Kelly.

Sean Bhean Bhocht

'Oh the French are on the sea,' says the Sean Bhean Bhocht,
'The French are on the sea,' says the Sean Bhean Bhocht,
'Oh The French are in the Bay, they'll be here without delay,
And the Orange will decay,' says the Sean Bhean Bhocht.

'And their camp it will be where?' says the Sean Bhean Bhocht,
'Their camp it will be where?' says the Sean Bhean Bhocht.
'On the Curragh of Kildare and the boys will all be there
With their pikes in good repair,' says the Sean Bhean Bhocht

'And what will the yeomen do?' says the Sean Bhean Bhocht,
'What will the yeomen do?' says the Sean Bhean Bhocht,
'What will the yeomen do but throw off the red and blue,
And swear that they'll be true to the Sean Bhean Bhocht.'

'Then what colour will be seen?' says the Sean Bhean Bhocht,
'What colour will be seen?' says the Sean Bhean Bhocht,
'What colour should be seen where our fathers' homes have been
But our own immortal green?' says the Sean Bhean Bhocht,

'And will Ireland then be free?' says the Sean Bhean Bhocht,
'Will Ireland then be free?' says the Sean Bhean Bhocht,
'Yes old Ireland will be free from the centre to the sea,
And hurrah! for liberty,' says the Sean Bhean Bhocht.

The Wind that Shakes the Barley

I sat within a valley green,
Sat there with my true love.
My fond heart strove to choose between
The old love and the new love.

The old for her, the new that made
Me think on Ireland dearly,
While soft the wind blew down the glade
And shook the golden barley.

'Twas hard the mournful words to frame
To break the ties that bound us.
But harder still to bear the shame
Of foreign chains around us.
And so I said, 'The mountain glen
I'll seek at morning early,
And join the brave United Men.'
While soft winds shook the barley.

'Twas sad I kissed away her tears,
Her arms around me clinging.
When to my ears that fateful shot
Come out the wildwood ringing.
The bullet pierced my true love's breast
In life's young spring so early.
And there upon my breast she died
While soft winds shook the barley.

I bore her to some mountain stream
And many's the summer blossom
I placed with branches soft and green
About her gore-stained bosom.
I wept and kissed her clay-cold corpse
Then rushed o'er vale and valley,
My vengeance on the foe to wreak,
While soft winds shook the barley.

'Twas blood for blood without remorse

I took at Oulart Hollow.[*]
I placed my true love's clay-cold corpse
Where mine full soon may follow.
Around her grave I wander drear
Noon, night and morning early
With aching heart when e'er I hear
The wind that shakes the barley

Boolavogue

At Boolavogue as the sun was setting
O'er the bright May meadows of Shelmalier
A rebel hand set the heather blazing
And brought the neighbours from far and near.

Then Father Murphy from old Kilcormack
Spurred up the rocks with a warning cry:
'Arm! Arm!' he cried, 'For I've come to lead you
For Ireland's freedom we'll fight or die'!

He led us on against the coming soldiers
And the cowardly yeomen we put to flight.
'Twas at the Harrow the boys of Wexford
Showed Bookey's regiment how men could fight.[†]

Look out for hirelings, King George of England,
Search every kingdom where breathes a slave.
For Father Murphy of County Wexford
Sweeps o'er the land like a mighty wave.

---

* *Oulart Hollow:* the battle of Oulart Hill took place on 27 May 1798 when a United Irishmen force of 1,000 poorly armed and trained farmers and peasants wiped out a detachment of militia sent from Wexford town to destroy their encampment.
† *Bookey:* on 26 May 1798 Fr Murphy led an attack against marauding yeomen near Boolavogue. The insurgents killed Captain Bookey, thus instigating the United Irishmen rebellion in Wexford.

We took Camolin and Enniscorthy
And, Wexford storming, drove out our foes
'Twas at Slieve Coilte our pikes were reeking
With the crimson blood of the beaten Yeos.

At Tubberneering and Ballyellis
Full many a Hessian lay in his gore.‡
Ah, Father Murphy, had aid come over,
The Green Flag floated from shore to shore!

At Vinegar Hill, o'er the pleasant Slaney
Our heroes vainly stood back to back
And the Yeos at Tullow took Father Murphy
And burned his body upon a rack.

God grant you glory, brave Father Murphy,
And open Heaven to all your men.
The cause that called you may call tomorrow
In another fight for the Green again.

Father Murphy

Come all you warriors and renowned nobles,
Give ear unto my warlike theme.
While I relate how brave Father Murphy
He lately roused from his sleepy dream.
Sure Julius Caesar nor Alexander
Nor brave King Arthur ever equalled him
For armies formidable he did conquer
Though with two pikemen he did begin.

---

‡ *Hessian:* German mercenaries rushed to Ireland in 1798 to assist in the brutal suppression of the rebellion in Wexford. They played a major role in the battle of Vinegar Hill and in subsequent atrocities.

Camolin cavalry he did unhorse them.
Their first lieutenant he cut him down.
With shattered ranks and with broken columns,
They soon returned to Camolin town.
At the hill of Oulart he displayed his valour
Where a hundred Corkmen lay on the plain.
At Enniscorthy his sword he wielded
And I hope to see him once more again.

When Enniscorthy became subject unto him
'Twas then to Wexford, we marched our men,
And on the Three Rock took up our quarters,
Waiting for daylight the town to win.
The loyal townsmen gave their assistance
We will die or conquer, they all did say,
The yeomen cavalry made no resistance,
For on the pavement their corpses lay.

With drums a-beating the town did echo
And acclamations came from door to door.
On the Windmill Hill we pitched our tents then,
We drank like heroes but paid no score.
On Carraig Rua for some time we waited
And next to Gorey we did repair.
At Tubberneering we thought no harm,
But the bloody army was waiting there

The issue of it was a close engagement,
While on the soldiers we played warlike pranks.
Through the sheepwalks, hedgerows and shady thickets
There were mangled bodies and broken ranks.
The shuddering cavalry, I can't forget them,
We raised the brushes on their helmets straight.

They turned about and made straight for Dublin
As though they ran for a ten pound plate.

Now, some crossed Donnybrook and more through Blackrock
And some up Shankill without wound or flaw
And if Barry Lawless be not a liar
There was more went groaning up Luggela.
To the Windmill Hill of Enniscorthy,
The British Fencibles they fled like deers.
But our ranks were tattered and sorely scattered
By the loss of Kyan and his Shelmaliers.

The streets of England were left quite naked
Of all their army both foot and horse.
The Highlands of Scotland were left unguarded.
Likewise the Hessians the seas did cross.
But if the Frenchmen had reinforced us,
And landed transports at Baginbun,
Father John Murphy, he would be their seconder,
And sixteen thousand with him would come.

Success attend you sweet County Wexford
Throw off the yoke and to battle run
Let them not think we gave up our arms
For every man still has a pike and gun

The Rising of the Moon

'O come tell me Seán O'Farrell, tell me why you hurry so?'
'Hush a bhuachaill, hush and listen', and his cheeks were all
    aglow,
'I bear orders from the captain: get you ready quick and soon
For the pikes must be together at the rising of the moon.'
By the rising of the moon, by the rising of the moon,
For the pikes must be together at the rising of the moon.

'O then tell me Seán O'Farrell where's the gathering due to
    be?'
'In the old spot by the river, right well known to you and me.
One more word for signal token: whistle up a marching tune,
With your pike upon your shoulder, by the rising of the moon.'
By the rising of the moon, by the rising of the moon
With your pike upon your shoulder, by the rising of the moon.

Out from many a mud wall cabin eyes were watching through
    the night,
Many a manly heart was beating for the coming morning light.
Murmurs ran along the valleys to the banshee's lonely croon
And a thousand pikes were flashing at the rising of the moon.
At the rising of the moon, at the rising of the moon.
And a thousand pikes were flashing at the rising of the moon.

Roddy McCorley

Oh see the fleet-foot host of men, who march with faces drawn,
From farmstead and from fishers' cot, along the banks of Ban;
They come with vengeance in their eyes. Too late! Too late are
    they,
For young Roddy McCorley goes to die on the bridge of Toome
    today.

Oh Ireland, Mother Ireland, you love them still the best
The fearless brave who fighting fall upon your hapless breast,
But never a one of all your dead more bravely fell in fray,
Than he who marches to his fate on the bridge of Toome today.

Up the narrow street he stepped, so smiling, proud and young.
About the hemp-rope on his neck, the golden ringlets clung;
There's ne'er a tear in his blue eyes, fearless and brave are they,
As young Roddy McCorley goes to die on the bridge of Toome
    today.

When last this narrow street he trod, his shining pike in hand
Behind him marched, in grim array, an earnest stalwart band.
To Antrim town! To Antrim town, he led them to the fray,
But young Roddy McCorley goes to die on the bridge of Toome
    today.

The grey coat and its sash of green were brave and stainless then,
A banner flashed beneath the sun over the marching men;
The coat hath many a rent this noon, the sash is torn away,
And Roddy McCorley goes to die on the bridge of Toome to-
    day.

Oh, how his pike flashed in the sun! Then found a yeoman's heart,
Through furious fight, and heavy odds he bore a true man's part
And many a red-coat bit the dust before his keen pike-play,
But Roddy McCorley goes to die on the bridge of Toome to-
    day.

There's never a one of all your dead more bravely died in fray
Than he who marches to his fate in Toomebridge town today;
True to the last! True to the last, he treads the upwards way,
And young Roddy McCorley goes to die on the bridge of Toome
    today.

The Croppy Boy

'Good men and true in this house who dwell,
To a stranger buachaill I pray you tell,
Is the priest at home, or may he be seen?
I would speak a word with Father Green.'

'The priest's at home, boy, and may be seen;
'Tis easy speaking with Father Green;
But you must wait till I go and see
If the holy father alone may be.'

The youth has entered a silent hall –
What a lonely sound has his light footfall!
And the gloomy chamber's chill and bare,
With a vested priest in a lonely chair.

The youth has knelt to tell his sins.
'Nomine Dei,' the youth begins;
At 'Mea culpa' he beats his breast,
And in broken murmurs he speaks the rest.

'At the siege of Ross did my father fall,
And at Gorey my loving brothers all,
I alone am left of my name and race,
I will go to Wexford and take their place.

'I cursed three times last Easter Day –
At Mass-time once I went to play;
I passed the churchyard one day in haste
And forgot to pray for my mother's rest.

'I bear no hate against living thing,
But I love my country above the King.

Now, Father, bless me and let me go
To die if God has ordained it so.'

The priest said naught, but a rustling noise
Made the youth look up in wild surprise:
The robes were off, and in scarlet there
Sat a Yeoman captain with fiery glare.

With fiery glare and with fury hoarse,
Instead of a blessing he breathed a curse:
"'Twas a good thought, boy, to come here and shrive,*
For one short hour is your time to live'.

'Upon yon river three tenders float,
The priest's in one – if he isn't shot –
We hold this house for our lord the King,
And, Amen, say I, may all traitors swing!'

At Geneva Barracks that young man died,
And at Passage they had his body laid.
Good people, who live in peace and joy,
Breathe a prayer, shed a tear, for the Croppy Boy.

Kelly the Boy from Killane

What's the news? What's the news? O my bold Shelmalier,
With your long-barrelled gun of the sea?
Say what wind from the south blows his messenger here
With a hymn of the dawn for the free?
'Goodly news, goodly news, do I bring, Youth of Forth;
Goodly news shall you hear, Bargy man!
For the boys march at dawn from the South to the North,
Led by Kelly, the Boy from Killane!'

* *Shrive:* to obtain absolution by confession.

'Tell me who is that giant with the gold curling hair –
He who rides at the head of your band?
Seven feet is his height, with some inches to spare,
And he looks like a king in command!' –
'Ah, my lads, that's the pride of the bold Shelmaliers,
'Mong our greatest of heroes, a Man! –
Fling your beavers aloft and give three ringing cheers
For John Kelly, the Boy from Killane!'

Enniscorthy's in flames, and old Wexford is won,
And the Barrow tomorrow we cross,
On a hill o'er the town we have planted a gun
That will batter the gateways of Ross!
All the Forth men and Bargy men march o'er the heath,
With brave Harvey to lead on the van;*
But the foremost of all in the grim Gap of Death
Will be Kelly, the Boy from Killane!'

But the gold sun of Freedom grew darkened at Ross,
And it set by the Slaney's red waves;
And poor Wexford, stripped naked, hung high on a cross,
Her heart pierced by traitors and slaves!
Glory O! Glory O! to her brave sons who died
For the cause of the long downtrodden man!
Glory O! to Mount Leinster's own darling and pride –
Dauntless Kelly, the Boy from Killane!'

---

* *Bagnell Harvey:* temporarily President of the Wexford Republic during the 1798 rebellion.

Robert Emmet – A Man for whom Fame was dearer than Life[†]

One of the foundations of the militant tradition that has Fenianism at its core is the notion that dashed, hopeless, youthful idealism or folly is a fine thing. The 1803 farrago which was Robert Emmet's botched rising embodies this somewhat contradictory, erroneous, but sincerely held point of view.

In most situations, in the history of most countries, Emmet's rebellion and subsequent execution would amount to the merest of historical footnotes, just another young life lost in silly pursuit of an unattained ideal.

Because of a handful of colourful Victorian hagiographers and hacks, Emmet's speech from the dock became part of the basic canon of Irish separatism. His declaration that his epithet should not be written until Ireland had taken its place amongst the nations of the earth has become, ironically, one of the most significant epithets in Irish history.

The likes of Tone and Emmet have gradually faded from the popular discourse. Orators addressing Sinn Féin rallies and government soirees sometimes summon up their reputations, like spirits at séances. It was as heroic, almost cartoon-like, figures in once-popular books that they entered into mass consciousness, causing real excitement and giving real inspiration to the independence generation.

Emmet owes much of his fame to A. M. Sullivan (1829–1884) who edited and wrote the bestselling *Speeches from the Dock* (1868). Sullivan was an originator of the school of maudlin sentimental populist reportage and propaganda-as-news that dominates Irish journalism to this day. He was also the founding father of that school of Irish journalism which sees the hack

---

† Joe Ambrose.

writer as part celebrity, part moral arbiter, part entrepreneur, part man of action. The Victorian era was the great era of the complex, contradictory, thrusting middle-aged male and Sullivan was the archetypal Victorian man.

A. M. and his brother T. D. (author of the popular Manchester Martyrs ballad *God Save Ireland*), were great moulders of public opinion and sentiment through their control, between 1861 and 1884, of Thomas Davis' old paper, *The Nation*. A.M.'s phenomenally popular, sentimental, and influential books included, in addition to *Speeches from the Dock, The Story of Ireland* and *The Wearing of the Green.*

To some extent, in his low debased way, Sullivan fulfilled Thomas Davis' dream of building or manufacturing a body of literature which told the Irish their own story from a separatist anti-English point of view. Intellectual debate was, however, sacrificed in favour of cheap rabble rousing. Sullivan, this being the case, magnificently captured the spirit of his age.

Growing up in Bandon, the putative media mogul was just the right age to be influenced by Young Irelanders. Family tradition had it that, in July 1848, he set out for Tipperary, determined to make a stand alongside Smith O'Brien and the others. According to the same tradition, his family interceded and persuaded him to stay at home. In later years, a veritable high priest of conservative Dublin nationalism, some of the rough edges had been smoothed off. An admirer of Henry Grattan, he was largely responsible for a statue in honour of the Protestant parliamentarian being erected in Dublin.

Robert Emmet was born in Dublin in 1778. His father was a well-connected surgeon, part of the British establishment in Ireland. While studying at Trinity College Emmet joined the United Irishmen. He was considered by his contemporaries at college to be a very intelligent.

When London declared war on France in 1793, the United Irishmen were banned. To avoid arrest Robert's brother, Thomas

Addis Emmet, an important United Irishmen, escaped to France. After 1798, Robert Emmet went into voluntary exile in Paris.

In 1802, he, like Tone before him, was granted an audience by Bonaparte during which he sought the French leader's support for an Irish rebellion. According to A. M. Sullivan, 'the United Irishmen put themselves into communication with Bonaparte, then First Consul, and again they received flattering promises of assistance. Robert Emmet obtained an interview with that great man, and learned from him that it was his settled purpose, on the breaking out of hostilities, which could not long be deferred, to effect an invasion of England.'

Emmet was being naive, however, if he thought that he enjoyed Napoleon's real or active support. Events were soon to prove that Emmet was, whatever intellectual gifts he might have enjoyed, an impractical and perhaps vain man determined to follow an entirely self-destructive trajectory.

When European conflict was renewed in 1803, Emmet returned to Ireland where, together with co-conspirators, he instigated the manufacture of weapons and ammunition at a variety of covert Dublin locations. A premature explosion at an arms dump forced him to bring forward the date of his planned rising.

Not all of Emmet's comrades supported his ambition to lead a rebellion and some of the more competent and charismatic activists refused to throw in their lot with him. As a result he led an ill-conceived and poorly supported Dublin rising which took place on 23 July 1803. A scruffy force of revolutionaries, incompetents and drunken corner boys attacked a scarcely defended Dublin Castle, but failed to capture it. They then repaired to nearby Thomas Street where a riot of sorts ensued.

As chance would have it, the lord chief justice of Ireland, Lord Kilwarden, happened to pass that way and, once spotted, was dragged from his carriage and hacked to death by the mob. Emmet is said to have seen a dragoon being pulled from his horse and piked to death. The sight of this raw violence caused him to call off his rising in order to avoid further bloodshed. History does not record what contradictory spirit made Emmet lead a violent uprising against the crown which he then cancelled when he saw violence being used against a member of the crown forces.

He went into hiding near Harold's Cross, a Dublin suburb which he chose as a bolthole because it allowed him to be near his girlfriend, Sarah Curran. There he was captured. Tried for treason on 19 September, the crown presented a weak case to a corrupt court so Emmet was efficiently found guilty and sentenced to be hanged, drawn and quartered. The following day this sentence was carried out.

It fell to A.M. Sullivan, 65 years later in *Speeches from the Dock*, to tell the world that, 'in all Irish history there is no name which touches the Irish heart like that of Robert Emmet'. He wrote that in the character of Robert Emmet 'there was such a rare combination of admirable qualities, and in his history there are so many of the elements of romance, that the man stands before our mental vision as a peculiarly noble and loveable being, with claims upon our sympathies that are absolutely without a parallel.' The 'patriot chief,' is further credited with 'fervid eloquence' and 'admirable reasoning'. Small wonder that Emmet was hugely admired by the 1916 leaders and the IRA fighters who came after them. As is so often the case in Irish history, it was the strong myth, rather than the harsh reality, which was the most important thing.

Emmet's speech from the dock is based on contemporary reportage which was assembled by Sullivan. It is not based on notes or manuscript sources left behind by Emmet. It is much concerned with his reputation. There is also an understandably shrill tone, reasonable from a young man of privileged background about to face immediate unnecessary death. There is sabre rattling about what Emmet would have done had the French invaded Ireland and seized it as a colony, declarations that seem sad and pathetic in the context of the wretched little rebellion which he actually did lead.

As he envisaged, Robert Emmet owes his survival in the eyes of the world to this speech. It is easy to see why, with its potent sentiments and rich oratory, it became such an influential communication.

ROBERT EMMET'S SPEECH FROM THE DOCK[*]

The jury, without leaving their box, returned a verdict of guilty against him; after which, having been asked in due form why sentence of death should not be pronounced upon him, he delivered this memorable speech, every line of which is known and dear to the hearts of the Irish race: –

'My Lords – I am asked what have I to say why sentence of death should not be pronounced on me, according to law. I have nothing to say that can alter your predetermination, nor that it will become me to say, with any view to the mitigation of that sentence which you are to pronounce, and I must abide by. But I have that to say which interests me more than life, and which you have laboured to destroy.

'I have much to say why my reputation should be rescued from the load of false accusation and calumny which has been cast upon it, I do not imagine that, seated where you are, your minds can be so free from prejudice as to receive the least impression from what I am going to utter. I have no hopes that I can anchor my character in the breast of a court constituted and trammelled as this is. I only wish, and that is the utmost that I expect, that your lordships may suffer it to float down your memories untainted by the foul breath of prejudice, until it finds some more hospitable harbour to shelter it from the storms by which it is buffeted. Was

---

[*] *Speeches from the Dock, or Protests of Irish Patriotism: Speeches Delivered After Conviction* (1868), A.M. Sullivan.

I only to suffer death, after being adjudged guilty by your tribunal, I should bow in silence, and meet the fate that awaits me without a murmur; but the sentence of the law which delivers my body to the executioner will, through the ministry of the law, labour in its own vindication, to consign my character to obloquy. For there must be guilt somewhere, whether in the sentence of the court, or in the catastrophe, time must determine.

A man in my situation has not only to encounter the difficulties of fortune, and the force of power over minds which it has corrupted or subjugated, but the difficulties of established prejudice. The man dies, but his memory lives. That mine may not perish, that it may live in the respect of my countrymen, I seize upon this opportunity to vindicate myself from some of the charges alleged against me. When my spirit shall be wafted to a more friendly port – when my shade shall have joined the bands of those martyred heroes who have shed their blood on the scaffold and in the field in the defence of their country and of virtue, this is my hope – I wish that my memory and name may animate those who survive me, while I look down with complacency on the destruction of that perfidious government which upholds its domination by blasphemy of the Most High – which displays its power over man, as over the beasts of the forest – which sets man upon his brother, and lifts his hand, in the name of God, against the throat of his fellow who believes or doubts a little more or a little less than the government standard – a government which is steeled to barbarity by the cries of the orphans, and the tears of the widows it has made.'

[Here Lord Norbury interrupted Mr Emmet, saying – 'that the mean and wicked enthusiasts who felt as he did, were not equal to the accomplishment of their wild designs.']*

---

* Known as the hanging judge, Norbury was born in Tipperary in 1745. He was, at various times, lord chief justice, solicitor general and a member of Grattan's Parliament. He had a reputation for being a corrupt and feared judge. He had poor legal skills but used his booming vocal style to intimidate lawyers and defendants with his barbed jokes. His courts were said to be like a wild theatre. His most

'I appeal to the immaculate God – I swear by the Throne of Heaven, before which I must shortly appear – by the blood of the murdered patriots who have gone before me – that my conduct has been, through all this peril, and through all my purposes, governed only by the conviction which I have uttered, and by no other view than that of the emancipation of my country from the super-inhuman oppression under which she has so long and too patiently travailed; and I confidently hope that there is still union and strength in Ireland to accomplish this noblest of enterprises. Of this I speak with confidence.

'Think not, my lords, I say this for the petty gratification of giving you a transitory uneasiness. A man who never yet raised his voice to assert a lie, will not hazard his character with posterity, by asserting a falsehood on a subject so important to his country, and on an occasion like this. Yes, my lords, a man who does not wish to have his epitaph written until his country is liberated, will not leave a weapon in the power of envy, or a pretence to impeach the probity which he means to preserve, even in the grave, to which tyranny consigns him.'

[Here he was again interrupted by the court]

'Again I say that what I have spoken was not intended for your lordship, whose situation I commiserate rather than envy – my expressions were for my countrymen. If there is a true Irishman present, let my last words cheer him in the hour of his affliction.'

[Here he was again interrupted. Lord Norbury said he did not sit there to hear treason.]

'I have always understood it to be the duty of a judge, when a prisoner has been convicted, to pronounce the sentence of the law. I have also understood that judges sometimes think it their duty to hear with patience, and to speak with humanity; to ex-

---

famous trial was Robert Emmet's. Daniel O'Connell despised him and initiated an investigation into his conduct throughout a trial during which he fell asleep. He was eventually removed from the bench in 1827 due to absent-mindedness and his inclination to fall asleep.

hort the victim of the laws, and to offer, with tender benignity, their opinions of the motives by which he was actuated in the crime of which he was adjudged guilty. That a judge has thought it his duty so to have done, I have no doubt; but where is the boasted freedom of your institutions – where is the vaunted impartiality, clemency, and mildness of your courts of justice if an unfortunate prisoner, whom your policy, and not justice, is about to deliver into the hands of the executioner, is not suffered to explain his motives sincerely and truly, and to vindicate the principles by which he was actuated? My lords, it may be a part of the system of angry justice to bow a man's mind by humiliation to the proposed ignominy of the scaffold; but worse to me than the proposed shame, or the scaffold's terrors, would be the shame of such foul and unfounded imputations as have been laid against me in this court. You, my lord, are a judge; I am the supposed culprit. I am a man; you are a man also. By a revolution of power we might change places, though we never could change characters. If I stand at the bar of this court, and dare not vindicate my character, what a farce is your justice! If I stand at this bar and dare not vindicate my character, how dare you calumniate it? Does the sentence of death, which your unhallowed policy inflicts on my body, condemn my tongue to silence and my reputation to reproach?

'Your executioner may abridge the period of my existence; but while I exist I shall not forbear to vindicate my character and motives from your aspersions; and, as a man, to whom fame is dearer than life, I will make the last use of that life in doing justice to that reputation which is to live after me, and which is the only legacy I can leave to those I honour and love, and for whom I am proud to perish. As men, my lords, we must appear on the great day at one common tribunal; and it will then remain for the Searcher of all hearts to show a collective universe, who was engaged in the most virtuous actions or swayed by the purest motives – my country's oppressor, or …'

[Here he was interrupted and told to listen to the sentence of the law].

'My lords, will a dying man be denied the legal privilege of exculpating himself in the eyes of the community from an undeserved reproach, thrown upon him during his trial, by charging him with ambition, and attempting to cast away for a paltry consideration the liberties of his country? Why did your lordships insult me? Or rather, why insult justice, in demanding of me why sentence of death should not be pronounced against me? I know, my lords, that form prescribes that you should ask the question. The form also presents the right of answering. This, no doubt, may be dispensed with, and so might the whole ceremony of the trial, since sentence was already pronounced at the Castle before the jury were empanelled. Your lordships are but the priests of the oracle, and I insist on the whole of the forms.'

[Here Mr Emmet paused, and the court desired him to proceed.]

'I am charged with being an emissary of France. An emissary of France! And for what end? It is alleged that I wished to sell the independence of my country; and for what end? Was this the object of my ambition? And is this the mode by which a tribunal of justice reconciles contradiction? No; I am no emissary; and my ambition was to hold a place among the deliverers of my country, not in power nor in profit, but in the glory of the achievement. Sell my country's independence to France! And for what? Was it a change of masters? No, but for my ambition.

'Oh, my country, was it personal ambition that could influence me? Had it been the soul of my actions, could I not, by my education and fortune, by the rank and consideration of my family, have placed myself amongst the proudest of your oppressors. My Country was my Idol. To it I sacrificed every selfish, every endearing sentiment; and for it I now offer up myself, O God! No, my lords; I acted as an Irishman, determined on delivering my country from the yoke of a foreign and unrelenting tyranny, and the more galling yoke of a domestic faction, which is its joint partner and perpetrator in the patricide, from the ignominy existing with an exterior of splendour and a conscious depravity.

'It was the wish of my heart to extricate my country from this doubly riveted despotism – I wished to place her independence beyond the reach of any power on earth. I wished to exalt her to that proud station in the world. Connection with France was, indeed, intended, but only as far as mutual interest would require. Were the French to assume any authority inconsistent with the purest independence, it would be the signal for their destruction. We sought their aid – and we sought it as we had assurance we should obtain it – as auxiliaries in war, and allies in peace. Were the French to come as invaders or enemies, uninvited by the wishes of the people, I should oppose them to the utmost of my strength. Yes! my countrymen, I should advise you to meet them upon the beach with a sword in one hand, and a torch in the other. I would meet them with all the destructive fury of war. I would animate my countrymen to immolate them in their boats, before they had contaminated the soil of my country. If they succeeded in landing, and if forced to retire before superior discipline, I would dispute every inch of ground, burn every blade of grass, and the last entrenchment of liberty should be my grave. What I could not do myself, if I should fall, I should leave as a last charge to my countrymen to accomplish; because I should feel conscious that life, any more than death, is unprofitable when a foreign nation holds my country in subjection.

'But it was not as an enemy that the succours of France were to land. I looked, indeed, for the assistance of France; but I wished to prove to France and to the world that Irishmen deserved to be assisted – that they were indignant at slavery, and ready to assert the independence and liberty of their country. I wished to procure for my country the guarantee which

Washington procured for America – to procure an aid which, by its example, would be as important as its valour; disciplined, gallant, pregnant with science and experience; that of a people who would perceive the good, and polish the rough points of our character. They would come to us as strangers, and leave us as friends, after sharing in our perils and elevating our destiny. These were my objects; not to receive new taskmasters, but to expel old tyrants. It was for these ends I sought aid from France; because France, even as an enemy, could not be more implacable than the enemy already in the bosom of my country.'

[Here he was interrupted by the court.]

'I have been charged with that importance in the emancipation of my country, as to be considered the keystone of the combination of Irishmen; or, as your lordship expressed it, 'the life and blood of the conspiracy.' You do me honour over much; you have given to the subaltern all the credit of a superior. There are men engaged in this conspiracy who are not only superior to me, but even to your own conceptions of yourself, my lord – men before the splendour of whose genius and virtues I should bow with respectful deference, and who would think themselves disgraced by shaking your blood-stained hand.'

[Here he was interrupted.]

'What, my lord, shall you tell me, on the passage to the scaffold, which that tyranny (of which you are only the intermediary executioner) has erected for my murder, that I am accountable for all the blood that has and will be shed in this struggle of the oppressed against the oppressor – shall you tell me this, and must I be so very a slave as not to repel it? I do not fear to approach the Omnipotent Judge to answer for the conduct of my whole life; and am I to be appalled and falsified by a mere remnant of mortality here? By you, too, although if it were possible to collect all the innocent blood that you have shed in your unhallowed ministry in one great reservoir your lordship might swim in it.'

[Here the judge interfered.]

'Let no man dare, when I am dead, to charge me with dishonour. Let no man attaint my memory by believing that I could have engaged in any cause but that of my country's liberty and independence; or that I could have become the pliant minion of power, in the oppression and misery of my country. The proclamation of the Provisional Government speaks for our views; no inference can be tortured from it to countenance barbarity or debasement at home, or subjection, humiliation, or treachery from abroad. I would not have submitted to a foreign oppressor, for the same reason that I would resist the foreign and domestic oppressor. In the dignity of freedom, I would have fought upon the threshold of my country, and its enemy should enter only by passing over my lifeless corpse. And am I, who lived but for my country, and who have subjected myself to the dangers of the jealous and watchful oppressor, and the bondage of the grave, only to give my countrymen their rights, and my country her independence, am I to be loaded with calumny, and not suffered to resent it? No; God forbid!'

Here Lord Norbury told Mr Emmet that his sentiments and language disgraced his family and his education, but more particularly his father, Dr Emmet, who was a man, if alive, that would not countenance such opinions. To which Mr Emmet replied: –

'If the spirits of the illustrious dead participate in the concerns and cares of those who were dear to them in this transitory life, oh! ever dear and venerated shade of my departed father, look down with scrutiny upon the conduct of your suffering son, and see if I have, even for a moment, deviated from those principles of morality and patriotism which it was your care to instil into my youthful mind, and for which I am now about to offer up my life. My lords, you are impatient for the sacrifice. The blood which you seek is not congealed by the artificial terrors which surround your victim – it circulates warmly and unruffled through the channels which God created for noble purposes, but which you are now bent to destroy, for purposes so grievous that they cry to heaven. Be yet patient! I have but a few more words to say – I am going to my cold and silent grave – my lamp of life is nearly extinguished – my race is run – the grave opens to receive me, and I sink into its bosom. I have but one request to ask at my departure from this world, it is the charity of its silence. Let no man write my epitaph; for as no man who knows my motives dare now vindicate them, let not prejudice or ignorance asperse them. Let them and me rest in obscurity and peace; and my tomb remain uninscribed, and my memory in oblivion, until other times and other men can do justice to my character. When my country takes her place among the nations of the earth, then and not till then, let my epitaph be written. I have done.'

This affecting address was spoken – as we learn from the painstaking and generous biographer of the United Irishmen, Dr Madden – 'in so loud a voice as to be distinctly heard at the outer doors of the court-house; and yet, though he spoke in a loud tone, there was nothing boisterous in his manner; his accents and cadence of voice, on the contrary, were exquisitely modulated. His action was very remarkable, its greater or lesser vehemence corresponded with the rise and fall of his voice. He is described as moving about the dock, as he warmed in his address, with rapid, but not ungraceful motions – now in front of the railing before the bench, then retiring, as if his body, as well as his mind, were spelling beyond the measure of its chains. His action was not confined to his hands; he seemed to have acquired a swaying motion of the body when he spoke in public, which was peculiar to him, but there was no affectation in it.'

YOUNG IRELAND

Thomas Davis' Solemn Starlight[*]

Thomas Davis (1814–1845) was a youthful intellectual and poet who set the agenda for the Young Ireland movement. He found the entire concept of 'Ireland' to be in a poor state, its people ignorant of a bright heritage and colourful past, and he set about restoring – or inventing – Ireland's past national glories and dignity.

Davis played a vital role in the formulation of Irish cultural nationalism. Pearse, Sinn Féin founder Arthur Griffith and Fenian John O'Leary regarded themselves as followers of his. Griffith said he was 'the prophet I followed throughout my life, the man whose words and teachings I tried to translate into practice in politics'.

According to Davis, it was not blood lineage which made one Irish, but a simple willingness to jump on board and declare oneself a part of the Irish nation.

The son of a British army surgeon, who died before Thomas was born, and of an Irish Protestant mother, he went to Trinity College, Dublin in 1831 where he studied history, law, and politics. He told Trinity's Historical Society in 1840 that Trinity, heavily institutionally prejudiced against Catholics, was 'the laughing stock of the literary world' and 'an obstacle to the nation's march', that its library was 'the mausoleum of literature', and that its 'effete system of education rendered it ridiculous abroad'. He spoke of its bigoted rules and implied that it was hardly surprising that it was a hated institution in Ireland.

Griffith quoted him approvingly: 'A people without a language of its own is only half a nation. A nation should guard its language more than its territories – 'tis a surer barrier and more important frontier than fortress or river ... To lose your native tongue, and learn that of an alien, is the worst badge of conquest

[*] Joe Ambrose.

– it is the chain on the soul. To have lost entirely the national language is death; the fetter has worn through.'

In 1842, Davis, with his friends John Blake Dillon and Charles Gavan Duffy, took a stroll from Dublin's Four Courts to the nearby Phoenix Park. While walking, they decided that they would found a newspaper, *The Nation*, which would take on board, broadly speaking, the French egalitarian republican ideal. It would not be in hock to some faction or a mouthpiece for British opinion.

The first edition of *The Nation* was published in October 1842. Within weeks it reached a circulation of over 10,000, making it the best-selling paper in Ireland. Passed from hand to hand or read aloud to groups and gatherings, its success and influence was immediate. Davis wrote most of the editorials for the first three years, as well as a stream of engaged articles, book reviews, poems and ballads.

At a time when widespread famine in Ireland was challenging the Union, *The Nation*'s popularity and stance did damage to the connection between Britain and Ireland. John Mitchel recalled years later how 'many an eager boy, from the Giant's Causeway to Cape Clear, cut open the weekly sheet with a hand shaken by excitement.'

'Educate that you may be free', was Davis' invariable message. His Unionist pal, the scholar Samuel Ferguson, said that Davis sounded, 'the intellectual reveille of a whole people, and, if they had slept long, they awoke refreshed'.

Gavan Duffy wrote of Davis in his book *Young Ireland*: 'Davis was our true leader … his comrades had the same careless confidence in him men have in the operations of nature, where irregularity and aberration do not exist.' He died of scarlet fever aged 31.

John Mitchel, writing in *The Last Conquest of Ireland (Perhaps)* said, 'For a year before his death, Davis had been busy in furthering the preparation of a series of small volumes, called the "Library of Ireland", each of which was to narrate some important period of Irish history, or to present gems of Irish literature, or give a biography of some Irishman of whom we could all be proud.'

A Nation Once Again is proof positive of Davis' forcefully held belief that the concept of Irish nationhood could be nurtured through popular ballads. According to Professor Malcolm Brown: 'Davis was as avid for music as any other Irishman, and one of the few surviving glimpses into his early youth depicts him listening in tears to the old airs played on a fiddle by "a common country fellow".' The editor of *The Citizen,* the journal that had published several of his early essays, was Henry Hudson, one of the great line of Irish musicologists who opened for the public the treasure of Irish folk music, described by Sir Arnold Bax as 'the most varied and beautiful folk music to be found anywhere on earth'.

Davis felt that it was 'the duty of every patriot' to make the fullest use of Ireland's love of music since, as Professor Brown pointed out, 'a fine old tune could escort a good idea past barriers of indifference at any social level.' When Davis investigated the Irish popular ballad industry, he found that they were poorly written, pompous, politically confused, and poorly printed. 'A high class of ballads,' he concluded, 'would do immense good.'

A Nation Once Again is the higher class of ballad which Davis sought out. Dylanesque in its understated powerfulness, it has now survived almost three centuries. The superior recording, by Luke Kelly and the Dubliners, can be readily heard on YouTube.

A Nation Once Again

When boyhood's fire was in my blood
I read of ancient freemen,
For Greece and Rome who bravely stood,
Three hundred men and three men;*

* *Three hundred men and three men:* a reference to the Battle of Thermopylae, which took place in Greece in 480 BC. Any well educated man of Davis' generation would have been familiar with this epic conflict when 300 Spartan warriors were said to have

And then I prayed I yet might see
Our fetters rent in twain,
And Ireland, long a province, be
A Nation once again!

Chorus
A Nation once again,
A Nation once again,
And lreland, long a province, be
A Nation once again!

And from that time, through wildest woe,
That hope has shone a far light,
Nor could love's brightest summer glow
Outshine that solemn starlight;
It seemed to watch above my head
Through foreign field and fame,
Its angel voice sang round my bed,
A Nation once again!
(*Chorus*)

It whisper'd too, that freedom's ark
And service high and holy,
Would be profaned by feelings dark
And passions vain or lowly;
For, Freedom comes from God's right hand,
And needs a Godly train;
And righteous men must make our land
A Nation once again!

---

heroically held off a vastly numerically superior invading Persian army. Thermopylae
came to symbolise, in the popular imagination of the Romantic period, the correctness
of heroic, though often futile, action. The inclusion of the classical reference in *A
Nation Once Again* is entirely in keeping with Davis' desire to create an intellectually
sourced and reliable literature with which to stimulate the sense of nationality he felt
was dormant in the population. He was also seeking to put the Irish struggle on an
equal footing to the activities of the ancient Greeks and Romans.

So, as I grew from boy to man,
I bent me to my bidding
My spirit of each selfish plan
And cruel passion ridding;
For, thus I hoped some day to aid,
Nor can such hope be vain,
When my dear country shall be made
A Nation once again!

JAMES FINTAN LALOR[*]

After Davis, Mitchel, Duffy, and perhaps Father Kenyon, Lalor
ranks as the most vigorous intellect of the Young Ireland movement; but he was rather in the movement than of the movement.[†]
The restoration of the soil to the peasantry was a greater ideal to
him than the restoration of political liberty to the nation.

Repeal of the Union was to him sometimes a doubtful experiment, sometimes a question for the town populations, never
a matter of concern to contrast with the settlement of the question of the ownership and possession of the soil. His indifference or opposition to repeal did not spring from a desire for
complete separation of the two countries. While he condemned
Repeal and declared a dual monarchy impossible, he favoured

---

[*] By Arthur Griffith, from his Preface to *James Fintan Lalor, Patriot & Political
Essayist (1807–1849)*, (1919), L. Fogarty.

[†] *Fr Kenyon:* regarded as the moral compass underpinning Young Ireland, John
Kenyon once said that John Mitchel's pro-slavery views were such 'as the truest
lover of liberty and of the Catholic religion may lawfully adopt … We are all slaves'.
When Mitchel founded the *Southern Citizen* in Knoxville, however, Kenyon wrote
to him saying, 'Actively to promote the slavery system for its own sake would be
something monstrous.'

Federal Union. Ireland and England might bear the same relation to each other as 'New York and Pennsylvania'. But New York and Pennsylvania have a Washington above them.

Thus as a political thinker, Lalor failed: he knew little of history and less of political constitutions. As a writer, he was often fallacious and sometimes contradictory, but the vigour of his style and the swing of his rhetoric concealed from many the occasional weakness of his argument. To an extreme shrewdness he sometimes united a childish simplicity as when he naively wrote that but for certain Young Irelanders who did not accept his views of the immediate policy 'We could walk down the whole force of England in a month', Ireland being then divided, distracted, disarmed, and famished, and England being then the strongest power in the world.

His strength, his influence on his contemporaries, and his subsequent influence on Irish movements came from his intense Agrarianism. He flung the Agrarian question across the path of the national movement and foretold ruin for the latter if it did not link itself to the former. Beside the Land question 'Repeal dwarfed down into a petty parish question' and deliverance from the bondage of landlordism was more necessary than deliverance from the bondage of foreign Government.

He believed the people in 1848 would not fight for political liberty but would fight for the land. Events proved him wrong; the nation was too weak and ill to fight for anything, but he impressed Mitchel to a degree with the belief that Agrarianism could be used to promote the cause of political liberty. To Mitchel the question of the land was a question to help Ireland to political independence. To Lalor the political independence was a question to help the peasantry to regain the soil. Both Mitchel and Lalor failed in 1848, but thereafter Nationalism and Agrarianism become closely identified and the Land League was the ultimate fruit of Lalor's creed and Mitchel's action.

CLEARING THE DECKS[*]

It is never the mass of a people that forms its real and efficient might. It is the men by whom that mass is moved and managed. All the great acts of history have been done by a very few men. Take half a dozen names out of any revolution upon record, and what would have been the result?

Not Scotland but Wallace barred and baffled Edward. Not England but Cromwell struck a king from his seat. Not America but six or eight American men, put stripes and stars on the banner of a nation. To quote examples, however, is needless. They must strike at once on every mind.

If Ireland be conquered now or what would be worse still, if she fails to fight, it will certainly not be the fault of the people at large, of those who form the rank and file of the nation. The failure and fault will be that of those who have assumed to take the office of commanding and conducting the march of a people for liberty, without perhaps having any commission from nature to do so, or natural right.

The general population of this island are ready to find and furnish everything which can be demanded from the mass of a people – the numbers, the physical strength, the animal daring, the health, hardihood, and endurance. No population on earth of equal amount would furnish a more effective military conscription. We want only competent leaders, men of courage and capacity, men whom nature meant and made for leaders. Those leaders are yet to be found.

Can Ireland furnish them? It would be a sheer and absurd blasphemy against nature to doubt it. The first blow will bring them out. But very many of our present prominent leaders must first retire or be dismissed. These men must first be got rid of

* James Fintan Lalor. First published in *The Irish Felon*, 22 July 1846.

utterly. They must. There is nothing else for it. They are stopping our way, clinging round our arms, giving us up to our enemies. Many came into this business from the mere desire of gaining a little personal distinction on safe terms and at a cheap and easy rate of obtaining petty honours and offices, of making a small Dublin reputation, of creating a parish fame, or a tea-table fame. They will never suffer the national movement to swell beyond the petty dimensions which they are able themselves to manage and command; and are, therefore, a source not of strength but of weakness and the source of all our weakness. But for them we could walk down the whole force of England in one month.

In a movement of the nature of that which has been going on for years in this country, it was impossible to prevent the intrusion into offices of command of that class of men who mar success instead of making it. The movement naturally, and of necessity, belonged to them.

The class of men who make revolutions, and who doubtless exist here as well as elsewhere, have been altogether disgusted and driven away from the service of their country by the peculiar character of that sort of 'struggle for freedom', the system of 'moral agitation' which Ireland thought fit to adopt, and from which their pride of manhood and pride of country revolted. The leaders which that system created and has left behind it is composed of men utterly unfit and unwilling to take charge of a military struggle, and who ought at once to be superseded and replaced. For two generations may history forget to mention them. Those men have been working to do this, the best work that ever yet was done for tyranny to take from the people the terror of their name and make popular movement a mockery. And what now are they working to do?

To hold Ireland down hand and foot while her chains are being locked and double-locked, and her four noble prisoners sent fettered and handcuffed to a penal colony of England for saying that Ireland should suffer famine no more. Worse for us than the foreign tyrant is the native traitor and worse than the open traitor in the enemy's ranks is the vile trickster and the base craven in our own. Away with them! They must quit at once or be quashed.

But how are you to know them, these menials of England in the green livery of their country? By this shall ye know them. Any man who objects to every plan of armed resistance that is proposed, while he produces none or no better of his own. Or any man who tells you that any act of armed resistance even if made so soon as tomorrow, even if offered by ten men only, even if offered by ten men armed only with stones – any man who tells you that such an act of resistance would be premature, imprudent, or dangerous – any and every such man should at once be spurned and spat at. For, remark you this and recollect it, that somewhere, somehow, and by somebody, a beginning must be made; and that the first act of resistance is always, and must be ever premature, imprudent, and dangerous.

There are men who speak much to you of prudence and caution, and very little of any virtue beside. But every vice may call itself by the name of some virtue or other. Cowardice may call itself, and readily pass for, caution, and of those who preach prudence, it behoves to enquire what kind of prudence it is they speak of, and to what class of prudent persons they belong themselves. There is a prudence the virtue of the wisest and bravest, there is a prudence the virtue of beggars and slaves.

Which class do those belong to who are prating now for prudence, and against premature insurrection; while rejecting every proceeding and plan for preparation?

Against the advice of those men, and all men such as them, I declare my own. In the case of Ireland now there is but one fact to deal with, and one question to be considered. The fact is this – that there are at present in occupation of this country some 40,000 armed men, in the livery and service of England. The question is how best to kill and capture those 40,000 men.

If required to state my own individual opinion, and allowed to choose my own time, I certainly would take the time when the full harvest of Ireland shall be stacked in the haggards.* But not infrequently God selects and sends his own seasons and occasions; and oftentimes, too, an enemy is able to force the necessity of either fighting or failing. If opportunity offers, we must dash at that opportunity. If driven to the wall, we must wheel for resistance. Wherefore, let us fight in September if we may but sooner if we must.

Meanwhile, however, remember this: that somewhere, and somehow, and by somebody, a beginning must be made. Who strikes the first blow for Ireland? Who draws first blood for Ireland? Who wins a wreath that will be green for ever?

MICHAEL DOHENY, YOUNG IRELANDER
AND FENIAN FOUNDER†

Michael Doheny (1805–1862) was one of the originators of the Fenian ideal. He came to prominence when he, like most of the men who built Fenianism, participated in the 1848 Young Ireland rebellion. Born near Fethard, County Tipperary, he was in his early forties by the time he undertook the extraordinary adventures and feats of physical endurance chronicled in his widely read *The Felon's Track*.

While a law student in London, he'd grown sympathetic to the Chartists, a political and social reform movement. By January 1847, he, like the other Young Irelanders, had become wholly disillusioned with Daniel O'Connell's Repeal movement. He was more sympathetic than other Young Irelanders – many of whom held decidedly right-of-centre views on certain social issues – to

---

* *Haggards:* outhouses in a farmyard.
† Joe Ambrose.

James Fintan Lalor's leftist vision. Following the 1848 Paris uprising, Doheny addressed a Chartist rally at the Manchester Free Trade Hall. Soon afterwards, sharing a platform with Chartist leader Fergus O'Connor, he announced, 'I am an Irish Chartist'.

In May 1848, Doheny, along with Thomas Francis Meagher, addressed the gathered Young Ireland supporters on the slopes of Tipperary's Slievenamon mountain. He told the crowd: 'How proud I am at meeting so many of my school-fellows who are here today to shed their last drop of blood for their country.' It was his various bombastic public pronouncements which first brought him to the attention of the British authorities. Other future Fenian leaders involved in the disastrous 1848 rising included James Stephens, John O'Leary, John O'Mahony and Charles Kickham.

After a revolutionary debacle at Ballingarry, County Tipperary the entire Young Ireland experiment was thrown into utter disarray. Doheny and John O'Mahony retreated to Fethard where they were looked after and hidden by sympathetic locals. Then they walked to Carrick-on-Suir, eventually crossing the Suir and heading for Rathgormack County Waterford, where O'Mahony went his own way and James Stephens joined Doheny.

These two walked across Munster together, keeping one another company and lifting each other's flagging morale, until they could escape from Ireland. Initially they headed for the Cistercian monastery at Mount Melleray, crossing over the mountains into Dungarvan. Unable to get passage to England, they trudged on towards Dunmanway in West Cork. Then they travelled all over west Munster, washing up in various towns and ports before salvation reached them. During their time on the run, if captured, they would almost certainly have been sentenced to death. For two months Doheny, a well fed, comfortably off, middle-aged barrister, lived in the hills, leading the life of the outlaw raparee.

Stephens, later the chief organiser of the Fenians, wrote about their escapade many years later: 'I can never resist wondering at and admiring the heroic way he [Doheny] bore himself in the face of his difficulties and the hazardous stands we were forced to make and confront throughout that felon's track of ours. It was nothing for a young man like me, without wife or child, to have gone on my way singing; but that he, having a woman he loved, and an interesting family he adored, bore up as he did, as well, if not better than myself, raised him to a heroic level in my estimation.'

Stephens got away first, heading to Paris via England. Ultimately Doheny was sent by boat to Bristol. From there, he too headed for Paris, arriving on 4 October 1848. Stephens acted as Doheny's guide to the Parisian social whirl but, whereas Stephens took to Parisian bohemian life like a duck to water, Doheny was just passing through. When his family joined him, he sailed from Le Havre, bound for New York. Doheny soon dug into Irish-American affairs and was admitted to the New York bar. In 1855, he brought together, in his law offices, the men who founded the Fenian Brotherhood. Doheny, Michael Corcoran and John O'Mahony were the Brotherhood's earliest leading lights in New York.

The Felon's Track is fascinating because of its jolting honesty. Doheny eschews the conventional nationalist (and socialist) rhetorical style which insists that 'the people' were totally supportive of the revolutionaries seeking to improve their lot. The peasantry of famine-blighted Ireland emerge from Doheny's recollections as a craven lot, terrified of their foreign rulers and of the state apparatus which maintained that rule. Doheny and Stephens' journey seems to have brought them into contact with an incessant stream of informers, users, cowards and blackguards.

With disarming self-deprecation, Doheny writes about his inability to pronounce Tottenham Court Road. Equally disarming is his obvious liking for food. Almost every meal, no matter how modest, is diligently chronicled. It is clear that, on the run, he often had to sleep in horrible places and was used to much better accommodation. It is equally obvious that he sometimes had to sup on rotten food, and that he liked good grub. His vivid portraits of the lives of the agricultural classes make it clear that he did not have too much in common, socially, with those whom he sought to liberate.

In keeping with the Romantic vision which informed the entire Young Ireland escapade, *The Felon's Track* is full of splendid descriptions of vast mountain ranges, awe-inspiring lakes and primitive nature in all its beauty. An account of a venal peasant woman who gives Doheny and Stephens shelter near Glengariff is particularly racy and redolent of a subdued eroticism. Doheny continually encounters situations where women seem to be in charge or, at least, to be in charge of their own affairs.

One tends to think of James Stephens, one of the most contentious and divisive of the Fenian leaders, as a bald and bearded man of middle years. Back in 1848, he was an attractive 24 years old, brimming with songs and good spirits. Doheny amusingly recalls Stephens' ability to charm, and exploit, young women. He writes of a plan to send Stephens to England disguised as a servant maid, so tender were his features. Stephens stoutly rejected this idea. Doheny's fond portrayal of the future revolutionary leader and conspirator brings to life the human side of a sometimes seemingly difficult and enigmatic personality.

There is about *The Felon's Track* an air of wry disappointment. It recounts the period in the author's life during which he threw away a good career in his native place in return for a conspiratorial life of exile in New York.

These extracts from *The Felon's Track* take up the story at the point when Doheny, on the run in 1848, had already made his way into County Waterford.

THE FELON'S TRACK[*]

My host was the chief of one of the fierce factions of County Waterford, and bore many a mark of desperate fray. I do not remember having met any man, before or since, who felt so acutely the fate of the country. He procured the best fare he could, and prepared my bed with his own hands. After I retired to rest, he continued pacing the room for several hours, sometimes sighing deeply, sometimes muttering curses between his clenched teeth, and sometimes suggesting plans which he thought might be even then available to redeem the past. These plans were all of a character more or less desperate; but some were exceedingly ingenious. A truer type of a Celt could not easily be found; his very caution was stamped with vehemence.

Next day but one I proceeded to meet [John] O'Mahony ... I was unable to meet him; but encountered a faithful follower of Thomas Francis Meagher, who was the bearer of a message to the effect that if he could be prevailed upon to attempt escaping, means could be procured for him. I expressed at once my entire concurrence, and desired the messenger should return to say that on condition the same means would be made available for those who were not yet arrested, we would all gladly accept them ...

I sought out my friend to learn his success and prospects. He came, according to appointment, to a farmer's house in the direction of Rathgormack, bringing with him James Stephens, who was destined to be thenceforth the companion of my wanderings, privations and dangers. He detailed to us the affair at Ballingarry. When he reached the village of Urlingford, he found some difficulty in escaping from the very men he hoped to lead back to the conflict. After vainly making every effort first to urge

* *The Felon's Track or History of the Attempted Outbreak in Ireland* (1920), Michael Doheny. Extract abridged by Joe Ambrose.

them on, and secondly to satisfy them of his own identity, he travelled a distance of thirty miles, and took shelter in the house of a private friend, where he hoped he could remain until something definite would be known of his comrades' fate. That his stay was not of long duration, his appearance with us on Thursday, forty miles from the place of his concealment, amply testifies. That distance he travelled on foot on the preceding day, after having slept a night with a drunken man in a brake.

He was even more averse than we were to giving up the struggle, and it was agreed on finally that he should be allowed to rest in a place of safety; that the messenger who had come from Mr Meagher's friend should be despatched with my proposal, and meantime, that I should betake me to the Comeragh Mountains in search of Mr Meagher, while our other comrade should make a final effort to rally the remaining strength of the people. We would then be in a position to determine finally what we should do. Stephens and myself proceeded together as far as my former host's in the mountains, where I left him, and continued my route as far as the Comeraghs, I rested that evening at a place called Sradavalla, and early next day recommenced my search around and over the mountains. After crossing several minor hills, I ascended the summit of the Comeraghs, called Cuimshinane, which commands a prospect of nearly the whole counties of Waterford and Kilkenny, with a great part of Tipperary. That prospect was at once grand, beautiful and mournful. The corn crop began to be tinged with coming ripeness; but the potato was blighted, and presented a spectacle as black and dismal as the country's hopes ...

I discharged my stomach more than once, while descending the ranges of the Comeraghs. I again took up my station for the night at the village of Sradavalla. It was deemed prudent I should not sleep in the same house as on the previous night, and about eleven o'clock, accompanied by five or six men of the village, I proceeded to a house farther up the mountain. Here the accommodation was not such as we expected, and we were forced to return. On our arrival, I found my sister-in-law who was escorted by two boatmen from Carrick-on-Suir, and who reached this wild sequestered and almost inaccessible mountain village, after a journey of fifty miles. A sad change had come over our circumstances since last we parted ...

We spent that night together at the house of a woman who had been lately confined. She endeavoured to provide tea and eggs, and we enjoyed our supper with as keen a relish and as high a zest as possible. I learned that Meagher was in the other extremity of County Tipperary, and she [Doheny's sister-in-law] undertook to convey my message to his friend a second time, while his faithful scout would endeavour to discover his retreat, and induce him to join us. She departed on her mission, having to walk ten miles over the mountain roads. I returned to the place where I parted from Stephens, whom I found greatly recovered. We remained that night at the house of his entertainer, where we were joined the following morning by O'Mahony. We spent the three succeeding days in and about the woods at Coolnamuck. Three more anxious days and nights never darkened the destiny of baffled rebels. Every morning arose upon a new hope which was blasted ere night came on by some sad intelligence. The news that reached us was partly true and partly false: of the former character was the account of our beloved chief's arrest, which took place on the evening of Sunday, the 6th of August.[*] We heard Mr Meagher also was arrested, and we resolved, in order to satisfy ourselves of the correctness of this and other reports, to put ourselves in direct communication with some person in the town of Clonmel.[†] We accordingly proceeded to the neighbourhood of that town, within a mile of which, at the Waterford side, we established ourselves, and remained two days. Each day we sent in a

---

[*] *Beloved chief's arrest:* William Smith O'Brien was arrested at Thurles Railway Station.
[†] *Clonmel:* the Young Irelander trials took place in Clonmel, County Tipperary.

messenger who brought us correct intelligence of what occurred; and satisfied us not alone that Mr O'Brien was then in gaol, but that he was allowed to be torn from the midst of a people for whom he had imperilled his life, without a hand being raised in his defence. We then returned to the scene of our former meetings, and met, for the last time, beside a little brook near the Waterford slate-quarries. My ambassadress [sister-in-law] had also returned, and there were present three or four others. The reunion was gloomy. But one question remained for discussion: Was there any hope left? The message I received as to the means of escape was dark and discouraging. Nothing remained but the hazards of some desperate enterprise ...

The place which presented the greatest facilities for escape was the town of Dungarvan. Thither we resolved to repair; and about three o'clock, on the 13th day of August, we set off across the nearest range of the Comeraghs – Stephens and myself, accompanied by my sister-in-law, whom we hoped to employ in negotiating for a passage to France. A farmer and two women of the place undertook to conduct us the shortest way across the mountains, and provide us an asylum for the night, which we reached after a forced journey of six hours. We there parted from our guides; and the people to whom they recommended us were exceedingly kind, and much more hospitable than their means would permit.

On the following day our host became our guide for several miles across the declining Comeraghs, until we came in view of Dungarvan. We purchased some bread, eggs and tea at a village called Tubbernaheena; but while in the village we learned that the military and police were scouring the country far and wide, in search of arms, which compelled us to change our route and take an easterly direction. We crossed several miles of bog, and had to pass many a ravine; but the worst trial was before us. We applied in several houses for the means of preparing our dinner, having travelled at least twenty miles over moor and mountain. We applied in twenty places in vain. At last, half by force and half by entreaty, we prevailed on a woman, whose circumstances seemed comfortable ...

During the progress of our meal we established ourselves in the good graces of the housewife, but she obstinately refused to allow us to remain for the night. She directed us to a public house, where we found a proclamation menacing anyone who entertained, harboured or assisted us, with the direst punishment. In answer to our inquiry the owner, who was a woman, pointed to the proclamation. We made three or four other attempts equally fruitless. I determined to call on the Roman Catholic priest, and state who we were; for while, if alone, we would infinitely prefer taking such rest as we could in the nearest brake, or under shelter of a wall, we could not think of submitting our delicate companion [Doheny's sister-in-law] to the trials of a night in the open air, during an exceedingly inclement season. With some hesitation and great alarm, he procured lodging for us at a farmer's house in the neighbourhood. We saw him next morning, and his most earnest injunction was that we should leave the locality, which, according to him, was altogether unsafe. To escape arrest there for twelve hours was, he said, impossible. Similar advice was pressed on us afterwards in many a safer asylum ...

Before venturing nearer to Dungarvan, we determined to seek the services of another clergyman, who lived a distance of six or seven miles in the direction of Waterford. A ridge of the Comeraghs lay between us and his lonely dwelling. Along this ridge lay a winding bridle-road, skirted by patches of grassland and occasionally crossed by a sparkling mountain stream ... The day was brilliant; above us the clear, blue, unfathomable sky; around us the bracing mountain air, laden with the breath of hare-bell and heather, and far below the calm sea, sleeping in the morning light; and weariness, hunger and apprehension yielded to the influence of the scene ...

We reached the mansion of the clergyman, wayworn and half-famished. He, whom we sought, had won a character for truth, manliness and courage, and we calculated upon his unrestrained sympathies, if not generous hospitality. He was absent from his house ...

We awaited his arrival for more than an hour, and, through delicacy for his position, we remained concealed in a grove some distance from the door. He at length appeared, and I proceeded alone to meet him and make known my name. He started involuntarily and retreated a few paces from me. After repeating my name for a few seconds, he said, 'Surely you are not so unmanly as to compromise me?' I replied, that so sensible was I of the danger of committing him that I refused to enter his house, though we all, and particularly my female companion, sadly needed rest and shelter. After some time, he began to pace up and down in front of his door, repeating at every turn that it was indiscreet and dishonourable to compromise him ... I never felt a pang so keen as that which those unfeeling words sent through my heart. For a while I was unable to articulate, but at length I said: 'You are one of those who urged us to this fate. You gave us every assurance that, in any crisis, you would be at our side. We made the desperate trial which you recommended. We have failed, because we were abandoned by those who were foremost in urging us on; and even now – here, where God alone sees us – you meet with reproaches one who has sacrificed his all on earth in a cause you pretended to bless. Is not that fate worse than defeat – than flight – than death?' ''Tis a sad fate, no doubt,' said he. My object, I said, was to escape to France, and I called on him, believing he could assist me, as he must be acquainted with the boatmen around that part of the coast. He answered it was possible he could, but not then; asked how he could communicate with me; he pointed to a shorter route across the mountains than that by which we had descended, and turned in to his dinner, which was just announced.

We faced towards the mountain, hungry and exhausted, without being asked to taste food or drink ... It was already evening. We had no resource but to return to the house where we had slept two nights before, which we supposed might be distant about seven miles. To obtain some food, of whatever kind, was an indispensable preliminary. The house nearest to the mountain appeared to be that of a comfortable farmer. We entered it trembling and found our expectations not disappointed. But the housewife peremptorily refused our first request, evidently suspecting there was something wrong, and unable to reconcile our appearance with the idea of hunger or distress. She bestowed a peculiarly sinister scrutiny on my poor sister. After some parley, we said we should have something to eat, either for love or money, and while saying so, we began to examine the locks of our pistols ... She replied we should have what we asked for, but only for love. Her daughters, of whom there were two, busied themselves in producing new barley bread and skimmed milk, of which we partook unrestrainedly. We parted on better terms, and my friend Stephens was greeted with a smile from each of the lovely girls, which so influenced him that he insisted upon revealing our character and asking their hospitality for the night.

After a good deal of discussion it was agreed he should make the experiment alone. He returned and produced the military cap which he always wore inside his shirt. This at once produced the desired effect, and one of the young girls came bounding up the hill to invite us to return. It was arranged, however, that we should remain in a hay-loft until quite dusk, which we gladly agreed to ...

As night fell, we were introduced into a comfortable parlour. There we had tea and eggs, with some punch. The family felt the warmest interest in us; but at the same time they occasionally manifested evident alarm. The utmost precaution was observed so as to prevent our being noticed, and we only retired to bed when the hour of midnight had struck. During all that night the storm roared pitilessly and the rain fell heavily ... Next day the storm did not cease to howl or the rain to sweep on the angry winds. About five o'clock, during a brief pause of the rain, preparations were made which significantly intimated that we were expected to leave. Our host was well acquainted with the fishermen of Dungarvan and he solemnly warned us against treating with any of them. Betrayal, he said, would be certain. But he promised to accompany my sister next day to the town, where he would make every inquiry; and if he failed, as he anticipated, would see her away on the car; in which case we were to try another and a far remote sea-board ...

A hasty dinner was prepared, and we arranged to meet our host next day within a mile of Dungarvan ... I went forth into the recommencing storm, utterly unconscious of its rage and equally indifferent to fate. My comrade, who had no life to lose but his own ... provided he could dispose of it to good account, stepped blithely along and uttered no complaint, although he left behind him traces marked with blood. His terrible indifference soon restored my self-possession, and we found shelter for the night in a house near the spot designated for the next day's interview. Just as we arrived there, the chief magistrate and police had completed a search of the house. We entered as they retired, told who we were, and claimed hospitality, which we readily obtained.

The night passed as many a similar one did afterwards. Let our hardships be what they might during the day, we invariably enjoyed ourselves at night, and went to bed without a fear. On the following morning we sent our hostess into the town for shoes and other matters which were indispensable to our further progress. She returned, evidently alarmed to death, having read on the walls the Vice-regal threats against all who harboured the 'traitors.' She scarcely allowed us to remain until the time appointed for the interview, which was of short duration. We were informed that there was no hope from that quarter, and that our safety for one hour was extremely precarious ...

We set out on our long journey, about four o'clock in the evening, under very heavy rain. Our first effort was at the public house, already mentioned, where we again failed. We had some bread and punch, while drying our clothes at the fire. My comrade became very ill; but even this did not overcome the obstinate repugnance of the hostess to receive us. We were compelled to leave at about nine o'clock; and having travelled some miles, 'midst cold and rain, my comrade shivering from fever and suffering, we determined to sleep in freshly-saved hay. While making ourselves a resting-place in the hay, we were surprised by some countrymen who recognised us as the persons who dined on a former evening, but were coldly received and rudely expelled. Upon consulting with the women, who had seen us, they conjectured we were some of the fugitives, and followed for the purpose of inviting us to the hospitalities of their home. We accepted the offer gladly, and were received with the warmest welcome.

The principal apartment contained two beds, one of which was usually occupied by the man and his wife, and the other by their grown daughters. They gave both up to us ... and the whole family, men, women and children, watched over our sleep until morning. The eldest son displayed considerable information and still greater energy of character. He evinced the deepest interest in our fate, and accompanied us for several miles next morning. It was Sunday; the cold and wet of the previous evening had given way to calm and sunshine; and we made rapid way along the slopes of the Comeraghs – thence to the Knockmealdown Mountains, having one main object in view – to place the greatest distance possible between where we were to rest that night and where we had last slept. The greatest difficulty we experienced was in passing deep ravines. The steep ascent and descent were usually wooded and covered with furze and briars. Far below gurgled a rapid and swollen mountain stream, which we crossed without undressing and always experienced the greatest relief from the cold running water ...

About three o'clock in the evening we reached the picturesque grounds of Mount Melleray Abbey. We had then travelled thirty miles of mountain without any refreshments. The well-known hospitality of the good brothers was a great temptation to men in our situation, pressed by toil and hunger. But we felt that we possibly might compromise the Abbot and the brethren, and determined on not making ourselves known.* We entered the beautiful chapel of the Abbey, and ascended the gallery while vespers were sung. We were alone on the gallery, and had an opportunity of changing our stockings and wiping the blood from our feet. We remained upwards of an hour, and then set out, but little refreshed. We hoped to find refreshments in a small public house, on the road leading from Clogheen to Lismore. I entered the house rather hurriedly, and the first object that met my view was a policeman. I turned quickly round and disappeared. The rapidity of my movement attracted his attention, and, calling to his comrades and some countrymen who were in the house, they commenced a pursuit. We accordingly quickened our pace, and they, in turn, began to run, when it became a regular chase, which continued four miles, until we disappeared in the blue mists of the Mitchelstown Mountains, as night was falling around us. When we saw our pursuers retiring, we ventured to descend, and entered a cabin where we found a few cold half-formed new potatoes and some sour milk which we ravenously devoured. I do not remember ever enjoying a dinner as I did this. My comrade, who had suffered much from illness, was unable to eat with the same relish. It was night when we finished our repast, and we set off in search of some place to lay our heads. We met several refusals, and succeeded, with great difficulty at last, in a very poor cabin. We saw a lone hen on a cross-beam, which we proposed to purchase, and bought at last for two shillings. In less than an hour she was disposed of; and, as was invariably the case, we got the only bed in the house, where we slept a long and dream-

---

* Doheny may have been exercising discretion here. Many Melleray monks were exceptionally sympathetic to Irish nationalism and it seems likely that, given their traditions of Christian hospitality, they would have looked after the fleeing rebels. Perhaps, having identified the monastery, Doheny was anxious not to bring the place to the attention of the British authorities.

less sleep. It rained incessantly the next day, and we were forced repeatedly to take shelter in cabins by the wayside. But, being excessively anxious to get as far as possible beyond the circle enclosed by our foes, we descended several miles along the Kilworth Mountains. Towards the close of evening we crossed the River Funcheon, near Kilworth, by means of a fir-tree, the roots of which had been undermined by the rapid flood. We had spent the whole day in wet clothes. We mounted this tree, Indian-like, in the midst of rain, and dropped in the shallow part of the river from the branches.

We were unable to procure lodgings afterwards until nearly eleven o'clock, and then not without difficulty. We succeeded, at length, within about a quarter of a mile of Kilworth, whence we were able to procure bread, tea and beefsteaks. We were very kindly treated, and next day accompanied to the Blackwater, at Castle Hyde, by the eldest brother of the family.

This day I think, August the 20th, we travelled over forty miles, along bog and mountain, passed within a few miles of the city of Cork, and then, taking a north-western direction, proceeded to the village of Blarney; where we slept on a loft with a number of carmen who were on their way to Cork with corn ...

We could scarcely sleep, owing to the noise and bustle of the carmen, as they came and went, and loudly snored in various parts of our dormitory. But we were allowed to rest until seven in the morning, when we took a hasty breakfast and departed. It was a point with us never to walk along a road, and never to ask our way. We were now travelling through an open corn country, and our progress was accordingly slow. We felt, too, the necessity of not departing far from our intended route, and accordingly we called in occasionally to national schools to make the necessary observations on the maps.

We crossed the Lee undressed, near the village of 'Cross', and slept soundly in a churchyard on a neighbouring hill ... Our destination was Dunmanway, near which a friend of mine lived, in whose house I hoped we might remain concealed, while means of escape would be procured somewhere among the western headlands ...

My friend was absent, but daughters of his, whom I had not seen since childhood, recognised and welcomed us. We had then travelled 150 miles, and fancied that, as no one could think of our making such a journey without walking one half-mile of road, we would be safe there for many days. In this we were disappointed. It was communicated to us next morning early that our persons were recognised, and that half the inhabitants of Dunmanway were by that time aware of our whereabouts. It was added, that the people were venal and treacherous; a character which the inhabitants of that region of Cork invariably attribute to each other. We remained a second and most of a third day, notwithstanding, and enjoyed ourselves heartily, although our little festivities had all the air of a wake.

Over the next few weeks, Stephens and Doheny moved around from one location to another in Cork and Kerry seeking in vain to escape from Ireland. At one stage, they washed up in Glengarriff, a notable beauty spot on Bantry Bay.

We took shelter in a wretched hut, directly over the bay, and within about one mile of an hotel of great fame, frequented by travellers who are attracted to these districts to view the magnificent bay and the singular beauty of Glengarriff. Here we spent the remainder of the day. Eggs and potatoes were provided for us; and when, as evening approached, we prepared to depart to the hotel, the woman pressed us to remain, and produced clean sheets, telling us they would give up their bed, and adding that she would be satisfied with the fifth of what we should pay in the hotel, where, she slyly hinted, our reception would be very doubtful in our then trim. We readily consented to her arrangement; and it was further agreed that her husband should go to the hotel and provide some bacon, bread, tea, and whisky ...

The cabin was ten feet square, with no window and no chimney. The floor, except where the bed was propped in a corner, was composed of a sloping mountain rock, somewhat polished by human feet and the constant tread of sheep, which were always shut up with the inmates at night. The fire, which could be said to burn and smoke, but not to light, consisted of heath sods, dug fresh from the mountain. A splinter of bog-wood, lurid through the smoke, supplied us with light for our nightly meal. The tea was drawn in a broken pot, and drunk from wooden vessels, while the sheep chewed the cud in calm and happy indifference. They were about twelve in number, and occupied the whole space of the cabin between the bed and the fire-place ...

The rain continued to pour without abatement during the whole night and until sunset the succeeding day. The next night passed nearly in the same way as the first, save that I could not rest from a vague sense of apprehension with which this woman inspired me. Both the people of the house slept on the hearth-stone, without any bed, or, as far as I know, any covering, save their rags. I had an opportunity of overhearing their connubial colloquy, which was in Irish, and had reference solely to conjectures respecting us, our character, our object and our money. It convinced me that our safety would be compromised by any longer delay ...

I was awakened next morning by a strange voice, with an accent, as I thought, different from that which we had been accustomed to. Our immediate conclusion was that we were betrayed. But a short time convinced us that our visitor had come to warn us that if we remained many hours where we were, our fate would be sealed. He represented 'Finey' (as our hostess was familiarly called, in derision of her affected pride) in colours not very flattering to her virtue. He said he could positively furnish us with the means of escape; described his resources as unlimited, and his interest in us as paramount to every consideration he had on earth. He was an ecclesiastical student, and had left college to take part in the struggle of his country. He bitterly lamented that Dillon and O'Gorman were not in the way, that he might have the happiness of assisting in saving them also.* Agreeable to his advice, we left our den and proceeded up the mountain ... The sun rose majestically, broad, unclouded, full of effulgence, and shed his yellow beams, on a scene as lovely as ever met his burning eye. The mountains around the bay form very nearly a complete circle; the numerous peaks, from south to north, range at an average height of about 500 feet above the water's level, while a few ascend as high as 1,000. We stood on the loftiest of all. Immediately below us, a little to the right, embosomed in the mountains, lay the unmatched beauties of Glengarriff. There are few spots on earth of wilder attractions ...

Doheny found the people of Kerry and Cork to be more sympathetic to their cause than the people of Tipperary and Waterford had been. They formed a half-baked plan to kidnap Prime Minister Lord John Russell, then rumoured to be visiting Killarney.

In the remote regions of the counties of Cork and Kerry, the people seemed possessed of no political information. They had a vague notion that an effort was made to free the country from foreign thrall, and that the patriots and their cause were lost through the Catholic priests ... We calculated on collecting between fifty and one hundred of the hardiest and most desperate mountaineers, whom we could easily place in ambush near the lakes, to seize on Lord John Russell, who was at the time announced as a visitor to Killarney. Once in our possession, we could have him conveyed to some inaccessible fastness where we

---

* *Dillon and O'Gorman:* two Young Irelanders who went on to enjoy distinguished legal careers. They were at one time partners in a New York law firm. O'Gorman escaped to France after '48. A major figure in the life of New York, he was appointed a Judge of the Superior Court in 1881. Dillon had opposed the '48 rising but was arrested, convicted of High Treason, and sentenced to death. He escaped and made his way to France before heading for New York where he went into business with O'Gorman. He returned to Ireland in 1855 and was eventually elected as MP for Tipperary. His son, John Dillon, was a major figure in the Parliamentary Party and his grandson was James Dillon, who led Fine Gael.

could dictate terms to him concerning our imprisoned comrades. We had scarcely a doubt of putting our plan into execution, and our sojourn near Killarney was prolonged for the purpose of becoming more familiar with the pathways whereby to escape to the mountains with our prisoner ... The project was marred by the Premier's abandonment of his intention ...

We remained several days in the neighbourhood of Kenmare, where we had daily interviews with the friend to whom I have already alluded. He spent all his time in endeavouring to devise some means of escape, and intermediately provided resting-places for us at various distances. We had the guidance of a young country lad of fine intelligence and true fidelity, who was acquainted with every foot of bog and mountain for miles around ...

We were most kindly received and cared for wherever our friend or his guide bespoke a night's hospitality but we felt the circle of our armed foes was closing around us, and it became indispensable to break through it. It was clear that our steps were tracked, for every night a search was made for us in one or other of the houses over which the influence of our friend extended ... During this interval when, although we travelled an average of fifteen miles a day, we considered ourselves resting, we received the kindest attentions everywhere; frequently finding a rude mountain cabin furnished with excellent beds and every delicacy ...

It was proposed to my comrade to accompany a lady – who was just about to leave for London – in the dress and character of a servant-maid. He was well fitted for such disguise, being extremely young and having very delicate features. Besides this, he was supposed to be dead, having received a slight wound in the skirmish at Ballingarry. He obstinately refused to adopt the disguise, but consented to that of a servant boy. When the matter was finally arranged, it was proposed to us to sleep at Templenoe, on the north side of Kenmare Bay, where he was to be furnished with suitable clothes. Since the commencement, I did not feel the same sense of desolation as when these arrangements were completed, and an hour was appointed for his departure next morning. It was on the evening of the 23rd of September ... A cloud of sadness, and I believe chagrin, enveloped all my senses. I could not help feeling myself utterly abandoned ...

Stephens sang as usual, and endeavoured to rally me; but my mind had set in impenetrable gloom ... We parted before daylight, and I immediately determined on my own course. It was this: to assume the disguise of a clergyman and attempt to cross to France. The trials at Clonmel were approaching, and I concluded that they would engross the entire attention of Government, and would even require the presence of the whole corps of detectives who were acquainted with my person and were then on my track.

Doheny then moved decisively and swiftly, and was finally smuggled onto a Bristol-bound boat, the Juverna.

I walked on board the *Juverna*, just as she was losing her cables ... The few moments that intervened were fraught with most intense suspense. I stood on the fore deck among cattle, covered with rags and dirt, my eyes fixed on two detectives who stood at the cabin entrance, scrutinising narrowly the figure and features of every cabin passenger. The bell rang, the detectives stepped on shore, one of my friends who watched my movements from a distance waved a kind adieu, the *Juverna* slipped her cables, and by one bound was out in the river. The first motion of her paddles sounded to me like the assurance of fate, and I looked on the curling foam with measureless exultation. The *Juverna* made a momentary halt at Passage, and then glanced gaily through Cove Harbour out into the sea. As she cleared the road I turned back to look for the last time upon my fatherland. Her prospects, her promise, her strength, her hopes, her failure and her fall rushed in burning memory through my brain ... I looked upon my country's shores for, it may be, the last time and thought of her hopes, her misery and fall ...

Night soon fell drearily upon the water. I engaged a berth from one of the sailors, and before half an hour, lost all consciousness of country and friends, of wind and tide, and hope, and shame, and peril, in tranquil repose. On ascending next morning, the shores of England were in view, and we sailed up the channel to the mouth of the Avon under a calm and mellow sky. I had some breakfast with one of the cowherds. Night had fallen before we reached Bristol, and I slipped away from the boat, amid the confusion and bustle which checked the progress of the gay and rich, around whose footsteps avarice had gathered an eager and jostling crowd.

The next morning Doheny caught a London-bound train. In London, he was befriended by a London Bobby who rescued him from a good-humoured racist mob.

On arriving at the Paddington terminus, an unlooked-for difficulty presented itself. My costume attracted universal attention. It was, in fact, *outré* even in comparison with the most outlandish; for every article had been carefully selected for its singularity. My 'caubeen' especially excited the risibility of the merry boys who thronged the streets.* I was soon followed by an uproarious crowd of most incorrigible young rascals, who made lunges at my unfortunate head-gear. They peered at me round lamp-posts, and occasionally, 'Teigue' and 'Phelim', pronounced in a broad English accent, grated on my ear.† Although not indisposed to be merry, I grasped one of my tormentors and handed him over to a policeman. The sentinel of city morals dismissed him with a harsh rebuke, and threatened to 'haul up' whoever gave me further annoyance. We were then near Oxford Street. I told him I wanted to go to Tottenham Court road; but after making several fruitless attempts to pronounce the name, his own fertile

---

* *Caubeen:* cap.

† *Teigue and Phelim:* sectarian terms used to describe a Catholic. Taig is still used in this context.

genius had to supply my deficiency. He walked with me until the last unruly boy had disappeared, and then he sent me on my way rejoicing, after having spent some minutes in teaching me to articulate distinctly 'Tottenham Court Road'. It was already nightfall. I felt as if all danger were passed.

More let-downs, however, awaited Doheny in London before, eventually, he made his way to Paris accompanied by a sympathiser and disguised as a priest.

On our arrival at the Paris terminus, we got into an English omnibus which brought us to an English hotel – the Hotel de Louvre in the Rue St Thomas. There we dined together, some dozen or so of the passengers. After dinner my friend and I had champagne. While discussing its merits the conversation turned on Ireland. Opinions, of course, varied. Mine, it need scarcely be added, to an Englishman's ear sounded bloodily, and I urged them with the vehemence of baffled hope. An old English gentleman of that quiet school which affects liberality and moderation, but entertains the deepest animosity, deprecated the violence of my language and sentiments, and expressed his painful astonishment at hearing such opinions from the mouth of a clergyman; 'They would not be unbecoming,' added he, with great bitterness of tone, 'in that sanguinary brigand, Doheny'.‡

Involuntarily and simultaneously my friend and myself burst into an immoderate fit of laughter, the gentleman could not at all comprehend our mirth. He had travelled much, he said, and met men of many lands, of whom Irishmen were ever the most polite and best bred gentlemen; a fact which rendered our laughing in his face rather inexplicable. The conversation was again resumed and again waxed warm. I expressed my opinion of English paupers in Ireland, and said they ought to be transported in a convict ship back to Liverpool, in the same fashion

‡ *Sanguinary:* optimistic.

as Irish paupers of a different class are transmitted to Dublin by the Liverpool guardians. To this he replied by saying that there would be no peace in Ireland until the Mitchels and Dohenys were hanged, a fate which the latter was hastening to with irresistible impetus. At this self-satisfied prophecy we laughed louder than before, whereupon he waxed wrathful, and repeating his experience of the world in general, and of Irishmen in particular, demanded an explanation of the laugh. I said, 'That is a straightforward question, and demands a direct answer. It shall be given, although you have refused to answer, as all Englishmen of your class invariably do, to several direct questions which I have put to you. I laughed because I am that same sanguinary Doheny': and, pulling off my wig, I added, 'Me – *voila* – at your service.' Chairs tumbled in every direction, and their occupiers fled the room, leaving myself and my friend ample space to enjoy the joke and the champagne in undisturbed quiet …

THE FENIANS

THE EMERGENCE OF FENIANISM[*]

Philosophically judged, Young Ireland achieved a notable and fruitful victory. On the one land it compelled England to show the ruffian hand by which the 'sister island' was governed. On the other land it bestowed a new literature on the country, which commanded even the admiration of its enemies, and is the touchstone of all literary endeavour in Ireland since. Irishmen who could not embrace the politics of Young Ireland, welcomed the literature which seemed to combine the best characteristics of all that had gone before, with an informing spirit emanating from pure hearts and able heads.

Even in the disruption of the party, its scattered elements were destined to do wondrous service in testimony of the national faith and character of Irishmen, and of continued tribulation to the Government of Ireland. Those who were kept in jail under the suspension of the Habeas Corpus act, like Fintan Lalor, were no sooner released than they were planning and projecting, with other untiring spirits, a renewal of armed hostilities in 1849. The exiles who were in France took advantage of the disrupted state of that country to study successful means of revolution, and to interest many able Frenchmen in the Irish cause – no very difficult matter to be sure, as in addition to the sympathy between the Irish and French, anything against England is attractive to a true Frenchman.

The exiles in America, in the press, the lecture hall, the drill-room, possessed welcome vehicles for the expression of the doctrines which had driven them from home. It would be impossible, even were all the materials at hand, to present at this date anything like a fair record of the unceasing efforts made

---

[*] *Fenian Heroes and Martyrs* (1868), John Savage.

in Ireland and America to keep alive one organisation after the other for the encouragement and indoctrination of Irish national principles.

Distracted, now by differences of able men, now by the jealousies of weak ones, again by the want of means, it is remarkable that someone was always found to encourage a nucleus of nationalists. I have chiefly referred to the societies in New York, with which fraternal societies in Ireland were in communication. One great source of dissatisfaction arose from the very hopefulness which kept the cause alive in Ireland, and which led men there to exaggerate the means at their disposal. The mistaken idea, also prevailing in Ireland, of the position of the exiles in America who, it was thought, could control any amount of money and war material, caused the demands made on them to be of an equally extensive character. The existence of those societies was always precarious, sometimes exciting.

The Fenian organisation was the result of the societies which had preceded it. The most imposing of them had fallen away, and the nucleus from which sprung this formidable power was composed of Michael Doheny, Michael Corcoran, John O'Mahony, and one or two others. From small numerical dimensions it slowly but steadily expanded to the form in which it has arrested the attention of the world.

When O'Mahony was elected president of the society, and at the same time received his commission as Head Centre from elsewhere, toward the end of 1858, it numbered forty members, all of whom resided in New York. It had a great struggle for existence, but ultimately succeeded beyond the most sanguine hopes of its projectors. In five years it put forth its branches from the Atlantic to the Pacific. Stretching northward, it had crossed the St Lawrence and the great lakes, spreading widely over the British provinces. Toward the south it had reached the mouth of the Mississippi, before the great rebellion cut off communication with the southern circles.

Up to 1863, the Fenian Brotherhood was little understood outside of the circles composing it. Its representatives had never been summoned together to adopt such a constitution and rules for general government such as an association of its extent might have warranted. It had more the nature of a military organisation than a civil and self-governing body; and while this suited its infancy, many disadvantages became apparent when it had grown in numbers, intelligence and power. These disadvantages suggested to the Head Centre that the organisation should be reconstituted on the model of the institutions of the [American] Republic, governing itself on the elective principle. It was then decided to call a National Congress.

Other matters pertaining to the welfare of the Brotherhood demanded the consideration of its assembled wisdom. Thousands of the most ardent and best working members had rushed to the defence of the Union. Many whole circles had entered the army in a body. No less than fifty branches had become extinct or dormant, and the rest had lost considerably in ardour and efficiency through the absence of their choicest spirits in the field.

The revolutionary Brotherhood in Ireland demanded aid and sympathy; so the call for the first National Congress was issued. This body assembled at Chicago, in the Fenian Hall of that city, on the 3rd November, 1863. Sixty-three circles were represented, having a constituency of fifteen thousand men, half of whom at least were in the armies of the Union. 'We no longer need generals of our own blood,' said Mr O'Mahony, in the opening session, 'to lead us to battle for Ireland, nor veteran soldiers to follow them.' The Congress met to place the Organisation on a basis in accordance with the habits and customs of the United States, and to declare its position and objects before the world, so that all the friends of Irish freedom could understand them.

The organisation was declared to be –

'An Association having for its object the national freedom of Ireland, and composed for the most part of citizens of the

United States of America, of Irish birth or descent, but open to such other dwellers on the American continent as are friendly to the liberation of Ireland from the domination of England, by every honourable means within our reach, collectively and individually, save and except such means as may be in violation of the constitution and laws under which we live, and to which all of us, who are citizens of the United States, owe our allegiance.'

Deeming the preservation and success of the Union of supreme importance to the extension of democratic institutions, and to the well-being and social elevation of the whole human race, it was:

'Resolved, That we, the Representatives of the Fenian Brotherhood in the United States, do hereby solemnly declare, without limit or reservation, our entire allegiance, to the Constitution and Laws of the United States of America.'

All subjects pertaining to partisan American politics and religion were ignored.

The hostile assertions that the Brotherhood was 'a "Secret Society", bound together by an oath, and, as such, distinctly condemned by the Catholic Church' were repudiated and denied by resolution –

'That we, the members of this Convention, declare that the Fenian Brotherhood is not a Secret Society, inasmuch as no pledge of secrecy, expressed or implied, is demanded from the candidates for membership thereof; neither is it an oath-bound Society, for no oath whatever is required in order to entitle a man to all the privileges of the association.'

The following embraces the objects sought, and the means by which it may be accomplished:

'Resolved, That it is the special duty of the members of the Fenian Brotherhood to strive with all their might, and with their whole heart, to create and foster amongst Irishmen everywhere, feelings of fraternal harmony and kindly love of each other, unity of counsel, and a common policy upon the Irish question, with mutual forbearance upon all others, so that their efforts may be unanimously directed towards the common objects of their universal wishes after a common preconcerted plan. Thus will their force become irresistible, guided by one will and one purpose, in one undeviating system of action, and thus will they give shape and life, direction and movement to that love of Ireland, and that hatred of her oppressors, which are the predominant passions of every true Irish heart.'

The well-trained Irish-American soldiers were besought to rally round the organisation, and the men in Ireland exhorted to stand by it to the last extremity, nor flee from it to foreign countries. The Irish people were declared to constitute one of the distinct nationalities of the earth. The Irish Republic was acknowledged as virtually established, with James Stephens as its Chief Executive. Sympathy with the Poles was expressed and a resolution passed expressing:[*]

'Reverential gratitude and filial respect towards his Holiness Pope Pius the Ninth, for his paternal solicitude in the cause of suffering Poland, up in arms for her liberty, and for the anxious care with which he offers up to Heaven his ardent aspirations for her success, and recommends her brave sons, battling for "right against might", to the prayers and support of the Catholic world.'

The direction of the organisation was vested in a Head Centre, elected annually by a General Congress. State Centres, to direct State Organisations, Centres to direct Circle and sub-Centres, for sub-Circles. The Head Centre to be assisted by a Central Council of five, a Central Treasurer, Assistant Treasurer, nominated by him and elected by Congress, and Corresponding and Recording Secretaries.

'In order,' said O'Mahony, 'that the Fenian Brotherhood be in reality what your legislation has made it this day – a thoroughly democratic, self governing institution – it still remains for me to

---

[*] The Poles, in the 1860s, were seeking independence from Russia, which occupied the country.

divest myself of the almost absolute authority which, with your assent, I have held for nearly five years, and by so doing to place the government and direction of the Fenian Brotherhood in the guardianship of this General Convention.'

The resignation of John O'Mahony was accepted and he was immediately unanimously elected Head Centre, under the new Constitution. An address to Ireland was issued by this Congress, and messages of fraternity and encouragement received from, among others, General T. F. Meagher, General M. Corcoran, and Colonel Matthew Murphy of the Irish Legion.

The transactions of this Congress added great vitality to the Fenian cause. The second National Congress assembled in Cincinnati, Ohio, on the 17th of January 1865. In the interim the sixty-three branches had grown to be three hundred, while the financial receipts exceeded those of the whole seven years since the Brotherhood had been established.

Among the subjects brought before the Second Congress was a lengthy report by Mr Philip Coyne, of Missouri, Central Envoy to Ireland, of his examination and inspection of revolutionary affairs in Ireland. He reported the masses of the people as desirous for revolution, and that the middle class, though hesitating to pass into a career of trial and labour, would in the extremity of a revolutionary outbreak, act boldly with the patriots. The national journal, the *Irish People*, was recommended for sustainment, for the courage and ability it displayed, and the mode of organisation of the IRB was declared to be as nearly perfect as possible, being so arranged as to defy the strongest power or finest subtlety to penetrate it.

On the recommendation of the Head Centre, the Constitution was amended so that the Central Council was enlarged to ten members, with a President chosen by and from themselves. He was to act on occasions for the Head Centre; and the powers of the Council were materially extended. O'Mahony was unanimously re-elected.

Meanwhile so great a flame could not exist in America without some smoke becoming visible in Ireland. The newspaper reports of the progress of Fenianism in America were regarded as astounding developments, and being reprinted in England and Ireland, excited the anxiety, and enlisted all the resources of the Irish Government to watch and explode the counterpart Revolutionary Brotherhood, on that side of the Atlantic. But the Irish Brotherhood was manipulated with exceeding skill and foresight, and baffled the keenest scent of the authorities, while it spread widely among the people. James Stephens, one of the youthful participators in the '48 rising, had undertaken the organisation of Ireland. Certain envoys having been sent to Ireland from New York for the purpose of seeing upon what basis a new revolutionary organisation could be started in that country, carried letters from O'Mahony to Stephens, who had returned from France. In the early part of 1858, one of these envoys, Mr Joseph Deniffe, returned to America with a written document from Stephens, showing already a formidable basis for action, and engaging, if he were sustained with certain funds, to greatly increase the number by harvest time. The Directory of '48 was appealed to in vain by Meagher; who, if he did not actively enter into the movement afterwards, would never wilfully hinder any measure undertaken for Irish liberty. The money, although not amounting to more than two thousand dollars, was raised with difficulty. With the first instalment of it, Deniffe was sent back, also carrying with him a Commission for Stephens as Chief Director, signed by Doheny, O'Mahony, and others.

Having enrolled some thirty-five thousand men, Stephens came to America in the fall of 1858, to report progress, and solicit more generous subsidies than he had received from America. At a meeting of the friends of Ireland at Tammany Hall, New York, the collection of a fund was inaugurated; and at the request of Stephens, O'Mahony was created Head Centre. The arrest in Ireland at this time of the members of the 'Phoenix Society', which showed that some active disloyalty existed there, gave the cause here a much needed impetus, and aided the purposes of Stephens' visit.

Attention had been directed to him on the Phoenix trials; and for a couple of years following, during which time he was in France, the revolutionary party did not seem to make much progress in Ireland. This partly arose from the fact that remittances from America were not of that character to keep it in working order. In December, 1860, Mr O'Mahony went to Ireland himself, to be personally satisfied on the state of affairs. The most important districts were inspected, and a meeting of certain leaders held in Dublin, at which definite plans were laid down. Stephens returned to Ireland and O'Mahony to America, and the organisations on both sides of the ocean progressed with powerfully effective strides. That Stephens was successful to a degree without parallel in Ireland for half a century cannot be questioned. With special qualifications as an organiser, he travelled throughout the island under various names and in many disguises, making the personal acquaintance of the people, and was to them for some years an object of wonder, almost of worship. That O'Mahony had also done wonders in organising the Brotherhood in America and Canada, was attested by the thankful Congress of Chicago, which passed resolutions recording his wisdom, genius, eminent purity and heroic virtues, during the five trying years through which the organisation had struggled.

The mystery which baffled the Government in Ireland, and the might which the auxiliary Fenian Society of America represented, combined to bewilder and exasperate the authorities. At the close of the Civil War many officers of the Irish Brigade, Irish Legion, and other Irish-American commands, which had seen much service, found their way into Ireland. Of these not a few regarded their preservation in the great conflicts of the war as a providential sign that they were destined to lead their countrymen to victory on their native soil.

James Stephens
Hawk, Braggart and Blackguard?[*]

Educated at St Kieran's College, Kilkenny, Stephens qualified as a civil engineer and worked on the Limerick and north Waterford railway in 1843. He was William Smith O'Brien's sidekick during the 1848 Ballingarry rising. Suffering minor injuries, he gained a reputation for being plucky, brave and decisive. This reputation stood him in good stead during the early years of Fenianism, but it turned against him later on when he came to be regarded as an unreliable blusterer. It is clear from the testimonies of his comrades that they were initially charmed by him but, subsequently, came to question his *bona fides*.

Escaping to Paris after '48, he was a 'participant observer' during the Paris Commune and, with other Young Ireland refugees like John O'Mahony and Michael Doheny, he instigated the conversations and debates which gave rise, a few years later, to Fenianism. He was much persuaded and beguiled by the French conspiratorial style; he fell in love with subterranean revolutionary methods.

In 1856, he returned to Ireland on a fact-finding mission, disguised as a tramp. Known as *An Seabhac* (The Hawk), over the next two years he is said to have travelled over 3,000 miles, recruiting men who were sympathetic to 'the cause', i.e. the use of physical force to remove the British administration from Ireland. In 1857, interested parties from New York who wanted to get a new organisation going approached him. He sent an emissary to New York, seeking funding for this new movement. On St Patrick's Day 1858, the Irish Revolutionary Brotherhood, later known as the Irish Republican Brotherhood, was founded as a secret oath-bound pseudo-military body with The Hawk as 'Head Centre'.

[*] Joe Ambrose.

John O'Mahony founded, in New York, the American Brotherhood, soon known as the Fenian Brotherhood. Forced by the British authorities to maintain a very low profile in Ireland, Stephens spent a great deal of time over the next few years in Paris and New York, seizing nominal control of the American organisation early in 1859.

In 1863, in Dublin, he established a Fenian paper, *The Irish People*. In 1864, cracks began to appear in his relationship with O'Mahony and the American Fenians. Some were irritated or worse by his arrogance, exaggerated claims and dictatorial instincts. In 1865 he cancelled a planned Irish rising and *The Irish People*'s offices were raided. Most of the leading lights in the Irish movement were arrested on treason-felony charges and given stiff sentences. Stephens was arrested but made a spectacular escape from Richmond prison.

In 1866, in New York, he secretly completed plans to invade Canada. This invasion took place but was such a farce that it substantially diminished Stephen's standing.

In the following years, there were a variety of skirmishes involving the Fenians, a number of splits within the organisation, and Stephens' influence gradually ebbed away. He spent a great deal of time in Paris, attempted to regain control over the organisation which he'd helped found, and eventually withdrew completely from political life.

When he died in 1901 the *New York Times* reported that, 'In recent years he had been living on a fund which was collected for him in this country by Patrick Ford of the *Irish World* and Michael Davitt. The British government evidently thought that his career as a leader was ended by the two fiascos which he organised as it allowed him to return to Ireland.'

James Stephen's Personality[*]

No one was left in the slightest doubt that to be the greatest smith, salesman, and the like was to be something very small indeed compared to being the great organiser Stephens was allowed to be, or the great philosopher, poet, general, or the Lord knows what he in his own esteem potentially was. For to his mind the great man could do anything – and he had not the shadow of a doubt but that he was himself a great man.

But though I have a vivid picture of this man always before both my mental and physical eye, I feel as if I could only convey the faintest shadow of that picture to those who have not seen or known the original. It may be as well too to let such a picture as I can give grow upon the reader as I go on to tell what Stephens did or failed to do, especially as this must involve from time to time more or less of what he said and thought and what I myself thought of him at varying times and under various circumstances.

It was often impossible to disentangle fact from fancy in his talk. You often could not in the least believe what he said, but you mostly felt that he believed it himself, and could seldom or ever know that he didn't. Now, after nearly half a lifetime, when the glamour of Stephens' influence has quite left me, I know not any more than most of us knew in the case of Mohammed or of Oliver Cromwell, to what extent he was consciously untruthful.

Towards the end of the year '58 or the beginning of '59 came my first direct connection with Fenianism. Stephens called upon me before he left for America, telling me of his plans and hopes He had got a letter of introduction and, I believe, of strong recommendation from Father Kenyon to John Mitchel, but had finally been refused letters by John Dillon, after, as he alleged, having

---

* Extracted from *Recollections of Fenians and Fenianism* (1896), John O'Leary.

been let to think he would get them. How this may be I know not but it matters little. I received the statement with some grains of salt at the time. Dillon may have easily, from the properest motives, have changed his mind; and Stephens may have equally easily thought that Dillon was about to do what he wanted, simply because he did not altogether refuse at first. Stephens, after telling me all this, and no doubt much more that is of little consequence now, went on to ask me to meet him at a certain date at Boulogne. I scarcely remember quite accurately now what were the special reasons he assigned for desiring my presence at that time but certainly one amongst them was something he wanted done in connection with the custody of certain moneys he expected to bring over with him. Anyway, I assented to this request, though probably with reluctance. The assent of mine did not necessarily involve much more than the temporary cessation of my medical studies, which could only be regarded as some slight material or money loss, and a somewhat more direct meddling with matters treasonable than I had been guilty of since Lalor's time

Stephens I continued to see constantly, with ever-increasing belief and confidence in the man himself, if still with but little trust in the practicability of his plans. There was always a great bond of sympathy between us in a past crowded with common memories, both public and private and, if afterwards my feelings towards him became considerably modified, still my clear recollection is that during all this time they grew stronger and stronger, if not warmer and warmer. Not that there were not many things about him which were extremely distasteful to me, and some which were to a measure repulsive. He had eminently what the French call the defect of his qualities. His strong will, which was the greatest of all his qualities, was accompanied, as it is in most strong men, by great arrogance and dogmatism, rendered the less tolerable by his supreme contempt for the world in general, including some very big people in it and among them almost all the '48 leaders. Without a trace of charity or humility in his composition, he was necessarily habitually intolerant and unamiable, though he could be occasionally, and sometimes with some persons – notably Luby and myself – for considerable periods, very agreeable and even genial.

SOWING THE FENIAN SEED[*]

James Stephens sowed the seed of his movement in Skibbereen in May '58, and before September there was a crop of sworn rebels in every parish around that celebrated city. Nearly all the members of the Phoenix Society became members of the IRB and took the oath.

I suppose, at this hour of day, I will not be charged with giving away to the enemy any very important secret when I say that every man took an oath renouncing allegiance to the Queen of Great Britain and Ireland, swearing to take up arms at a moment's warning to fight to make Ireland an independent democratic republic, to obey as a soldier the commands of his superior officer, to be faithful and not to betray any comrade or any trust connected with the organisation.

After a year or two, when the organisation spread extensively, the first part of the oath was changed, and instead of renouncing allegiance to the Queen of England the recruit swore 'allegiance to the Irish republic now virtually established'.

The man who swore me in got the chance of working himself up to a colonelcy if he could enrol a regiment of men. He told me I could work myself into a captaincy if I enrolled a company. The first man I swore in was Patrick J. Downing, a first cousin of my own. He is now living in Washington. He earned a colonelcy by working in the Irish Revolutionary Brotherhood

* *Rossa's Recollections, 1838 to 1898* (1898), Jeremiah O'Donovan Rossa.

in Ireland, but coming to America, after his release from prison in Ireland, he joined the army here, was lieutenant colonel of John O'Mahony's regiment in 1861, went through the war and came out of the war colonel of the Forty-Second Tammany Regiment – a full colonel in America many years, and here am I a full private still. His brother Denis was sworn in in Ireland; he came to America after his imprisonment in Ireland, went into the war here, lost a leg at Gettysburg, went to Ireland a few years afterward, and died there. His brother Simon was sworn into the organisation in Ireland, came to America, joined a cavalry regiment, and was killed in the war. The youngest brother, Dan, sworn in in Ireland, came to America, too, joined the army here, and died a soldier. Here were four brothers, all the boys that were in the family, sworn in an early youth to fight for the freedom of their native land, coming to America and fighting for freedom in their adopted land. I have known many another Irishman that learned his first drill in Ireland in the Fenian Brigade who drew his last breath in life on the battlefield of America. So that whoever are down on the Fenians, Americans ought not to be among them.

The several men I swore in worked with such energy that my command very soon exceeded the number sufficient for a company command, and I got promotion. I was told I could form a regiment. Mortimer Moynahan worked energetically also, and his command likewise grew into a colonelcy. There was another colonel or centre in the district – the man who swore me in – but as he lives in the old land, and I have no liberty to give his name, I let him rest in peace. But a good, bold, brave, daring man was he in his day.

James Stephens had been active. He had been travelling through all parts of Ireland, seldom staying more than a day in one place, getting an introduction from a good man in one town to a reliable man in the next town, sowing the seed, laying down the law and taking his departure.

A part of the law laid down to us was that when we had made fair progress in the enrolment of men, a military man would be sent to give us instructions in drill. This instructor came to us in August, and in old barns, in cellars, in the woods and on the mountains the drilling of the men was carried on night after night. This instructor remained a month, and when he left us the man who had been most expert in learning the soldiers glorious trade was Patrick Downing (Colonel Downing, now of Washington). He took military charge of the district, and was out every night drilling the recruits. It is a penal offence against England in Ireland to learn drill or learn the use of arms, unless an Irishman is sworn into the English service there.

When we were in the woods or on the hills at night we had to have our guards posted around us so as to give warning of the approach of danger. We were in Loriga wood one night, an alarm was given that some people were approaching from a certain direction. We ran away in the opposite direction. Jerrie Cullinane leaped across a ditch at the other side of which was a big dyke. The dyke was broad, and not getting clearly across it he fell. I leaped after and fell upon him. Others leaped after me and in a minute some twenty or thirty of us were sprawling in the dyke. When we regained our footing we learned it was a false alarm startled us – the people who caused it were recruits who had not been to the rendezvous on time. This is one of the many incidents that used to occur to make us laugh and be merry while we were breaking English law learning how to fight for Ireland.

As I am writing this sketch of Fenianism in a free country, and as some free people may read it, I will step ahead of time a month or two and give one illustration of my experience of how terror stricken the English are at an Irishman's learning anything about military matters in Ireland.

Some thirty of us were in Cork jail in December '58. Denis Downing, who lost a leg at Gettysburg, was one of the prisoners. A policeman named Dove swore an information against him that he

127

saw him marching through the streets of Skibbereen 'in military order'. McCarthy Downing, our attorney, cross-examined the policeman, and asked who was with Denis Downing 'marching in military order'. Dove said, 'No one was with him, he was marching by himself, but he had a military step.'

McCarthy Downing laughed, the prisoners laughed, and Davis, the Castle magistrate, and Sir Matthew Barrington, the English Crown Prosecutor, looked dumbfounded. At the further prosecution of these trials at the ensuing Tralee Assizes, two coastguards were put in the witness chair to swear that with their spy glasses they saw men drilling on the summit of Cnoc Ouma. There is not such an entrancing view as can be had on the top of this mountain, environed by sea, lake and river. To the top of Cnoc Ouma the recruits of the Irish Revolutionary Brotherhood repaired every Sunday to learn their drill.

In organising the country James Stephens told the men there would be aid from the Irishmen of America. While we were to do all we could to arm ourselves, we would not be called into the field of battle until 10,000 men at least were landed from America. The assurance of aid from America put great spirit into us at home. It helped us to overcome many obstacles that were in the way of organisation. England and England's agents in Ireland were continually dinning into the people's ears that it would be nothing but madness for an unarmed people to think of rising against England – a nation that has conquered the world almost, a nation that had as many ships of war as could surround Ireland and burn every town and city on her coast.

Then there were the moral force patriots, who would have land and freedom from England without shedding a drop of blood, and without striking a blow. Upward and onward, the new recruits of the Irish Revolutionary Brotherhood had to fight their way against these. The toughest fight and the biggest victory that came to me while organising came to me one night I was at a harvest home at Fivemile Cross, outside of Newry. A farmer named Rice had gathered in all his crops and all neighbours around gathered at the house to enjoy the good things of the table, John Nolan, of Carlow, now dead and buried in Kansas City, was with me. We wanted to see a certain man in the district, and the man was at the harvest home of Mrs Rice. So we cut across the field to Mrs Rice's, met our men, and were received as honoured guests at the festive board. After supper the glasses came on the table and punch and lemonade and mulled porter were there in plenty. The chair was occupied by a very respectable looking old gentleman named Convery. At his right hand side sat John Nolan, at his left hand side was Mrs Rice, the widowed mother of the house, and I was seated next to her.

Mr Convery was a moral force patriot, an out and out O'Connellite; he had been an active man in the Repeal movement twenty years before that, and had also been an active worker in the movement for Catholic emancipation. He carried the whole countryside with him, and whatever he said to the people was law. In the course of conversation and speech making he pretty strongly condemned Fenianism. As John Nolan and I were there specially to propagate Fenianism, we decided our mission would be a failure unless we put a stop to the old gentleman's gallop. I was introduced to the company as a Mr Buckley, of America, who was home to Ireland on a visit and tour of pleasure, and, of course, could speak knowingly of the movements and aspirations of the Irish people who were far away from home.

Mr Convery had all the talk and seemed to be carrying the house with him. John Nolan was the only obstructionist at the table. I was saying nothing. At last Mrs Rice asked me what I thought of the subject they were discussing, and I had to speak. This was my speech: 'Mr Chairman and Mrs Rice and friends, for though a stranger among you, I feel I am at home among my Irish people and can call you all friends. I once had a home in Ireland, but in the part of the country in which I lived there were a class of people called landlords, and one day one of these landlords came,

129

bringing with him police and bailiffs, and forced myself and my mother and sister and two brothers out of the house, and then tore down the roof of it. That was in '47. We were all young, except my mother. We had neither house nor home, as the saying be. I don't know how she managed to provide for us, but shortly some relief came from an aunt and two cousins we had in Philadelphia, who heard we were evicted. After that, by degrees, the whole of us got to America. I have not lived there without knowing something of the feelings of our people, many of whom have experiences and recollections of Ireland such as I have, and I know they feel fondly for all belonging to them in Ireland, and feel very bitterly against landlords and English rule in their native home. I know many of them are engaged in a movement to free Ireland; I cannot claim the credit of belonging to that movement, but I know enough to be able to tell you that the men of every county are organised for work. Every county is to supply a ship and furnish that ship with men and arms; those thirty-two ships are to sail from different ports in America one particular day. The County Down ship will make for Newry, or some other port in your neighbourhood here; the Antrim ship will face Belfast, the Derry men will make for Derry; the Donegal men will make for Donegal, and so on all round Ireland. It is calculated that all the fleet England has – even if she could muster the whole of it around Ireland – could not prevent some of those ships from landing men and arms. I don't know how you would all feel tonight if you heard there was such a ship in Newry Bay, and that all the boys who had left the neighbourhood years ago were in it. Our good hostess here at my right was telling me a while ago that two of her sons, James and Pat, were in America; our worthy chairman himself was telling me that three of his brother's sons and four of his sister's sons were in America. It strikes me if the news came to us just now that the ship was below in the bay, that he would be as ready as any of us to run down to welcome the boys back, and maybe as ready as any of us to shoot down any one who would oppose their landing. I thank you for the hearty applause with which you have greeted my few remarks; and now I propose the health and the return to us again of our friends who tonight are far away from home.

Mrs Rice stood up and shook hands with me and kissed me. Mr Convery himself shook hands with me as the young men and young women crowded around me. On our way walking into Kerry next morning John Nolan would burst out into roars of laughter, thinking how we carried the day. The country was safe; Mr Convery was silenced, and as we afterward learned Fenianism prospered in the district.

Some four or five mouths after the starting of the organisation, the English began to suspect there was something mysterious going on; the people were showing a more independent spirit and were not so subservient to the will of the reigning powers. Some mishaps occurred in the swearing in of men that brought the work under the notice of the authorities. Patrick Mansfield Delaney and Martin Hawe, of Kilkenny, were arrested and put to prison, charged with attempting to administer oaths to men, and Denis Riordan of Macroom was arrested on a similar charge. While Mr Delaney was in prison a public demonstration for him was made on his farm. His crops were ripe and the men and women of Kilkenny came in hundreds one day and cut his wheat and oats, dug his potatoes, mowed his hay and did everything necessary to the saving of his harvest.

He was released from prison some months after. Martin Hawe and Denis Riordan were also released. But their arrest and what transpired at their trials in court made it evident to the public, that there was some kind of a conspiracy on foot to get rid of English rule in Ireland. The drillings that were going on at night in several parts of Ireland also came to be spoken of and, by and by, the newspapers began to speak of 'the state of the country'.

It is not so easy to write as many people think. I am already beginning to find it very hard to write the story now – well, not hard, but painful, because I have to write of things I would rather not write and of persons who are dead, of whom I would rather have nothing unpleasant to say. Mr Alexander M. Sullivan, who died in Dublin last year, was editor of the Dublin *Nation* in 1858. His native town was Bantry, a place some dozen miles distant from where I lived. He had the character there of being a good, trustworthy, patriotic Irishman, and I believe he was all that while he lived there. In the '48 movement he and his family acted a patriotic part. The people of his native town trusted him. Visiting Bantry in the autumn of '58 he got talking to James O'Shea and his brother William O'Shea and others who had been enrolled in the organisation. James is in New York today. William occupied the same prison with me in Cork from December 1858, to August 1859; he is the Captain William O'Shea who was killed in one of the battles here during the war.

When Mr Sullivan was in Bantry it seems he was told by someone that William Smith O'Brien was a sworn member of the secret organisation, and when he returned to Dublin he wrote Mr O'Brien asking him, was he? Mr O'Brien replied to him saying he was not, and he published the correspondence in *The Nation*. We were very angry with Mr Sullivan for doing this and, whether it brought trouble to us or not, it brought much trouble to him after I published a letter in the Dublin *Irishman* concerning it. I signed my name to the letter and he sued the *Irishman* for publishing it.

When I was in Chatham Prison the *Irishman* republished the letter, and he again took the *Irishman* into the law courts. He argued that what he did he did to correct misrepresentation and to save us who were young and ardent Nationalists from the consequence of our youthful folly. We argued that Ireland was like a house on fire with the family locked in, and if we clambered to the top of the walls trying to save the family and extinguish the flames, it was a poor way for Mr Sullivan to frighten us away from the risk and danger to fling stones at us and throw us into the fire. His exposure in his newspaper of the existence of a secret, oathbound, illegal society was directing the attention of the Government to the prosecution of the members of it. He asserted that the Government knew of its existence before he spoke, that a Kerry priest had given the information not with any bad intention, but with a view to arrest the spread of what he considered foolish work.

The English authorities were pretty certain that a dangerous movement was spreading, and they set to work to arrest it. They got hold in Kerry of a man named Daniel Sullivan (Goula) and they put him in training. A stipendiary magistrate, who had long experience among the Orange and Ribbon societies in the North of Ireland, was transferred from Belfast to Skibbereen and Goula was put in communication with him. Goula visited Skibbereen in November '58, under suspicious circumstances. Someone wrote to us saying he was bad and to beware of him, that no one would trust him in his own district, but that he was sworn in in Bantry by a man who did not know his true character. We had an eye on Goula, but he drew into his net everyone who was watching him, everyone who got acquainted with him. He was in my shop one day, and going out I followed him through the town at such a long distance so that I could just barely keep him in view. I saw him suddenly turn back towards me. I walked on, passed him by and had not gone far when I met the stipendiary magistrate. Goula had seen him and that is why he made the sudden turn back in the street. I reported what I saw to Morty Moynahan. It was Morty had communication with the Kerry men. Goula had laid the groundwork of having an excuse for visiting Skibbereen by writing a letter to Morty's employer, McCarthy Downing, prior to the visit. He applied to have his brother taken into the law office as apprentice clerk, and said he would come to town in a few days with letters of recommendation.

He came and put up to lodge at the home of a Kerry man, Mortimer Downing, from whom we rented the rooms of the

Phoenix Society. We told our men in town who Goula was and what he was suspected of, and it was agreed upon by some thirty of them that they would go to the rooms on a certain evening and satisfy their curiosity of taking a look at him and hearing him talk.

They satisfied their curiosity, but it came to be at the expense of their personal liberty because Goula swore every one of them into prison. He swore they were all drilling that night a mile outside the town and that O'Donovan Rossa was the drill master. The whole swearing was a lie. I never drilled any men. He never saw any drilling but he swore against the whole of us so that none of us would be able to contradict what he swore.

When I found myself kept nine months in jail on such a conspiracy as that, I felt that I had a personal grievance to feed the strength of what I felt on the question of the national grievances. I have many personal grievances of a like nature since then, and I have experiences too to confirm the opinion then formed, that when an Englishman governing Ireland suspects an Irishman of doing something that is quite natural for him to do in opposition to English rule, he has no scruple of conscience in employing a vagabond of some kind to swear he saw the thing done.

I knew poor men who were working for twenty cents a day to be offered hundreds of pounds to come forward to swear they saw us going to the woods or to the mountains where it was said the drilling was going on, and they would not take the bribe. I knew an unfortunate fallen woman – Kit Cadogan – to be offered money to swear she saw us going through the woods at night. She did see us often, and as she would hear us passing by we would hear her whisper through the trees '*Buadh De libh a Chuachalaidhe* – May God be victoriously with ye, boys'. One of the attorneys who was engaged by the English to assist in the prosecution of us that time, has his office today in the same building in which I have my office in the City of New York, and he can bear testimony that the poor 'unfortunates', as they are called – the poor, fallen women of the town – refused to take the bribe that would have made them comparatively wealthy.

Poor Kit Cadogan is an inmate of the Skibbereen Poor Law Union today. A bed in Heaven to her when she leaves it.

England encourages agitation so long as she is sure there is nothing else behind it. I have seen the time when she celebrated the national holiday of Ireland with all the parade, pomp and glory that it could be celebrated by a free and independent Ireland. I have seen a Patrick's Day celebration at Dublin Castle. The military bands played *The Wearing of the Green, Patrick's Day* and *Garryowen na Gloria.* The Lord Lieutenant and the Lady Lieutenant, the Lord's gentlemen and the Lady's ladies were on the balconies of the Castle bedecked with shamrock; one lady's maid had a lap dog in her arms, and around the lap dog's neck was a beautiful wreath of shamrocks.

Pagan O'Leary, who witnessed that display, came into a room where I was sitting an hour after. There were pots of shamrocks on the window sills. He raised up the windows and threw the pots into the yard below. 'If the national emblem of Ireland,' said he, 'is to be worn by an English dog, this is no place for it.' The same Pagan O'Leary is at present in a Soldiers' Home in Western Virginia; he had fought as an American soldier in the Mexican War.

I now come to the arrest of the Phoenix men. The English came down on us in the dead of night, broke down the doors of houses that were not readily opened to their knock, routed us out of bed and took us to the police barracks. When day broke and we looked at each other we saw that every man was a prisoner who, some evenings before, went out of curiosity to have a look at Goula. During the night police from outlying stations had been drafted into town. At nine in the morning every one of us were handcuffed to two policemen, and in coaches and cars we were driven from our homes amid the crying of wives and sisters and mothers, and the crying and cheering of the men and boys of the town.

The City of Cork seemed to be our destination, but nobody could tell where we were to rest. About nine at night we reached Bandon. The cars drove up to the jail door and this seemed to be our journey's end for that day. The jail door opened hospitably to receive us; we were ushered in, our chains were unbound and we were led to our apartments. I was lodged in a cell in which were three other men, William O'Shea, Jerry Cullinane and Tim McCarthy. Rain had been falling all the evening and the cell was flooded with water. We had to eat our supper perched on the plank bedstead. We had not much sleep, but we talked and tumbled all night till morning. Well, we did something more than talk too; we drank; we had whisky. One of the policemen, who was handcuffed to me all day, went out of the jail when he was released from me and purchased a bottle of whisky. He came back to the jail, made some excuse to the jailor for seeing me, and left the bottle in the cell. Some of these Irish policemen are Irishmen. I knew several of them to be sworn in, but they cannot be depended on as a body to do any revolutionary work for Ireland. But, what am I saying? Sure the Irishmen who are not policemen cannot be depended on as a body to work of that kind.

The Irishmen who are in the Irish police are not much different from the Irishmen who hold situations outside the police department. They are paid for doing a certain duty, they make their living by doing it, and they do it. If they could make their living in a decent manner, many would prefer to live the decent way. I say of them as I say of many Irishmen who are not policemen: they will never create or commence a revolution because they will never peril their way of living. But if Ireland once could take the field and hold the field for any time against the enemy, if Irishmen could fight and win one small battle, which would show the Irish police they meant fight and were in earnest and would give protection and co-operation to any one who would side with them, then I say you would have the great majority of the Irish police fighting at the side of Ireland instead of at the side of England.

DINNER WITH JAMES STEPHENS[*]

Coming on the year 1860, the men of Skibbereen took up the threads of the organisation that were let slip through the arrest of the Phoenix men of '58. We met James Stephens in Bantry, and Mr Dan McCartie, Morty Moynahan, and I with the Bantry men, Denis Cullinane, and some others went in Denis O'Sullivan's yacht to Glengarry, where we had dinner at Eccles' Hotel. Stephens paid for the dinner. Sailing through Bantry bay, Stephens was smoking a pipe. I remember his taking the pipe in his hand and saying he would not give the value of that dudeen for the worth of Ireland to England after the death of the Queen Victoria; that she, in fact, would be the last English reigning monarch of Ireland.

I don't know if he is of that opinion today. I do not know did he speak that way that day in Bantry bay from the strong faith he had in the success of his own movement. Anyway, the way he always spoke to his men seemed to give them confidence that he was able to go successfully through the work that was before him, and before them. That was one of his strong points, as an organiser.

---

* *Rossa's Recollections, 1838 to 1898* (1898), Jeremiah O'Donovan Rossa.

JAMES STEPHENS AND JOHN O'MAHONY[*]

On the banks of the Suir, at a place called Mullough, in the County Tipperary, there lived, in the beginning of '48, a gentle-man farmer of ample means and thorough education, of un-assuming manners and devoted patriotism, in whose warm southern nature a deep knowledge of the ancient Celtic tongue and misfortunes brooded with a silent but lofty enthusiasm, the hopes and aspirations which at the period manifested themselves in the Young Ireland party – who, in a word, was a 'rebel', a pure-souled, high-hearted, courageous, and in his district – which en-compassed the counties of Tipperary, Waterford, and Kilkenny – most powerful rebel. His name was John O'Mahony.

When the leaders took 'to the hills', he succoured, aided, and cheered them, and when they were arrested, wandering outlawed through the island, or seeking the shores of America and France, O'Mahony still brooded over the wrongs and sorrows of the fatherland. He could not leave his native hills. He looked down the golden valley of the Suir, and said, as Cromwell said when gloating over the same scene, 'This is a country worth fighting for.' Looking for O'Brien and Meagher, John Savage[†] met O'Mahony, and they remained together, organising the country while any hope remained.

Doheny says, 'they spent many anxious nights in counsel to-gether, when it was supposed all spirit had left the country.' The first ostensible object that brought the people together under their immediate guidance and control was the reaping of a field of wheat belonging to O'Mahony. A vast crowd, amounting to several hundred stalwart men, assembled. They had scarcely en-tered on their labour when the approach of a troop of horse was announced. O'Mahony and Savage were compelled to leave. The

---

[*] *Fenian Heroes and Martyrs* (1868), John Savage.
[†] The author of this account.

138

military cavalcade rode through the people and the corn, but the reapers desisted not, giving no pretext for any arrests or further outrage from the soldiers.' The time for defiance and resistance was yet some weeks ahead.

The organisation of the disaffected districts resulted in the insurrectionary movements in Tipperary and Waterford, which commenced on the 12th September. O'Mahony, by a series of really startling adventures, eluded the vigilance of the police. He was in Clonmel during the trial of O'Brien, organising a force to attack the Court House, when he was discovered, and saved himself by leaping from a back window. He ultimately escaped from Island Castle, between Bunmahon and Dungarvan, in the County Waterford, in a collier [coal boat], and was landed in Wales, where he remained for six weeks, until an opportunity offered for his conveyance to France. He resided in Paris for five years.

James Stephens is a native of the City of Kilkenny, and is now, probably, between forty-three and forty-four years of age. He received a good education, which he has continued to enlarge and improve. He was by profession a surveyor and civil engineer, and during the latter years of O'Connell's repeal agitation he was engaged on the great Southern and Western Railway works, at Inchicore, Dublin. About this time politics commenced to throw their fascination over the young engineer. In the early part of '48 his professional duties brought him from Dublin to Thurles and in the summer he took advantage of his proximity to Kilkenny to visit his parents. While in Kilkenny an incident occurred which changed the whole current of his life – that was the arrest in that city of Mr Patrick O'Donohoe, who was entrusted with dispatches from Dublin to Mr O'Brien. 'He proceeded on his mission to Kilkenny,' says Doheny, 'and there applied to one of the [Confederate] clubs. He was known to none of the members, and became at once the object of suspicion. It was, accordingly, determined to send him the rest of his journey under arrest, and Stephens and another member were appointed to that duty. They proceeded to Cashel, where Mr O'Donohoe was warmly welcomed by Mr O'Brien. Mr Stephens came to the same resolution; but the other guard refused to commit himself to fortunes which appeared so desperate. With Stephens and O'Donohoe this very desperation acted as the most ennobling and irresistible inducement. They clung to O'Brien to the last.'

All through O'Brien's movements Stephens exhibited an earnestness which won the approval of all who witnessed it. At Killenaule, when O'Brien's party threw up some barricades to intercept the passage of a troop of dragoons, young Stephens suddenly raised his rifle and covered the officer in command, his finger was on the trigger. 'One moment,' says Mitchel, 'and Ireland was in insurrection.' At the Ballingarry affair, Stephens was clear-sighted and efficient. After the failure of O'Brien's movement, he had many adventures with O'Mahony and finally escaped to France.

At this period, the Continent of Europe generally, and Paris particularly, was inwoven with a network of secret political societies. They had peculiar fascinations for those whose former attempts at rebellion had proved failures, simply for the want of previous organisation of the revolutionary elements. O'Mahony and Stephens soon conceived the idea of entering the most powerful of those societies, and acquiring the means by which an undisciplined mob can be most readily and effectually marched against an army of 'professional cut-throats'.

Accordingly, they became enrolled members and pupils of some of the ablest masters of revolutionary science which the nineteenth century has produced. In one point alone they neglected to copy from their continental instructors – they devised no means of visiting with summary chastisement such members of their organisation as were led by ambition, arrogance or cupidity, into the unpardonable crimes of treason and insubordination.

Stephens was an accomplished linguist, and, in time, his knowledge of the French language enabled him to contribute to the *feuilleton* columns of the Paris newspapers, every succeeding effort of his astonished those who were aware of his foreign birth and education.* His great triumph was his success in translating Dickens into French. Those translations, which were published, we believe, in *La Presse*, attracted the attention of the Paris literary world, and were a source of extreme surprise and gratification to the distinguished author of *David Copperfield*. His efforts as a *litterateur* thus brought Stephens a handsome compensation, which, added to certain remittances which O'Mahony received from time to time out of the remains of his Irish patrimony and the product of his exertions as instructor of Gaelic to some students of the Irish College, enabled our exiles to live comfortably enough.

After working night and day at their tuitions, translations, and above all, their revolutionary schemes, it was decided to make another attempt, and on a practical basis, to organise the Irish race at home and abroad, and continue, on a foundation of discipline, the struggle for national independence.

O'Mahony came to America towards the close of 1853, and Stephens went to Ireland. Using the pseudonym of Shook, Stephens, in 1858 and in 1859, was an active participator in the 'Phoenix Conspiracy', and during the prosecutions in Tralee and Cork which followed he was constantly referred to in the evidence given by the informer, O'Sullivan. He disappeared at the time of the trials, but returned subsequently.

Stephens became widely known, and the authorities were eager for his capture, which was at last effected between five and six on the morning of the 11th November, 1865, by Colonel Lake, attended by over thirty police and detectives, who surrounded his residence, Fairfield House, Sandymount. Scaling the garden walls, they knocked at the back door. Almost immediately Stephens came to the door, and inquired 'Who was there?' The constables announced themselves as police officers authorised by warrant to enter and search the house. Stephens

* *Feuilleton columns:* regular journalistic columns.

hesitated in opening the door, stating that he was undressed. The police promised not to resort to force or violence if he complied with their request. Stephens endeavoured to close the door. Mr Superintendent Ryan and Acting Inspectors Hughes and Dawson drove it in. Stephens rushed up stairs, followed by Hughes, who took him into custody in his own bedroom, his wife being in the apartment at the time.

Mrs Stephens started out of the bed, alarmed at seeing the police, and said, 'Are you going to take my husband from me?' Inspector Hughes then sent down for Constable Dawson to identify the prisoner. Dawson proceeded to the bedroom, and on entering said, 'How are you, Stephens?' Stephens replied, 'Who the devil are you, sir?' Dawson then told him who he was, and Stephens replied, 'Oh, I have read enough about you – I want no favour. Wife, you will never see me again.' The house was then searched, and in the adjoining bedrooms were arrested Kickham, Duffy and Brophy, who were all in bed at the time. The police, 'over thirty in number, were well armed, and entered with pistols in their hands, but the prisoners offered no resistance. Pistols were, however, lying about their rooms, and the police found immense quantities of bacon, flour, bread, etc. – enough, in fact, to feed all the parties for near a twelvemonth.'

On some of them, too, £45 in gold was found, and a bank check for a larger amount, and others of them were likewise well provided with cash. The prisoners were placed in separate cabs, each in charge of three officers, and were lodged in the Lower Castle yard at half-past six o'clock.

On Tuesday the 14th, the prisoners were brought before the Magistrate, under the Treason-felony Act. After some further identification, the hearing was adjourned to the next day, when Stephens acted in a very bold manner. In reply to the Magistrates, he said: 'I feel bound to say, in justification of, or rather with a view to, my own reputation, that I have employed no attorney or lawyer in this case, and that I mean to employ none, because, in making a plea of any kind, or filing any defence – I am not particularly well up in these legal terms – I should be recognising British law in Ireland. Now, I deliberately and conscientiously repudiate the existence of that law in Ireland – its right, or even its existence. I repudiate the right of its existence in Ireland. I defy and despise any punishment it can inflict on me. I have spoken.'

Stephens' repudiation of British law in Ireland tantalised the English press exceedingly. They sneered at his assumption and ridiculed his 'I have spoken'. They had not ceased levelling their shafts of satire at their prisoner, when the three kingdoms were startled by the news of his escape from prison. A howl of mingled indignation and trepidation went forth, and the conviction forced itself upon those who'd sneered at him that Stephens 'knew what he was about'.

The fear into which the authorities were thrown sharpened their memory, and many threats and rumours were remembered, which did not add to their peace of mind. Among these was a statement, made some months before, that Stephens had, in various disguises, visited all the jails in Ireland, had tested their strength, and declared that none of them were strong enough to hold him. 'The extreme daring and cleverness of the conception and execution of this feat,' said the Dublin *Evening Mail,* 'calls to mind the fact – a strange one, to say the least – that the American Fenians have boasted of the knowledge they had acquired of Irish prisons, and the power they had to draw the strongest bolts by which they might be held.'

The escape of Stephens was effected on the early morning of November 24. The night was dark and tempestuous, and very favourable for the attempt, as the storm and rain prevented the incidental noises from being heard. The Richmond prison is situated in an isolated position, on the Circular Road. There are no houses in front, and the canal is in the rear. The locality is little frequented, especially at night. The cell occupied by Stephens was in the corridor leading to the eastern wing of the building and adjoining the Chapel. His cell door was composed of strong hammered iron, and secured by a massive stock lock, a huge padlock, and a thick swinging bar. The corridor on which the cell opened was guarded by another iron door of great strength and thickness, and also double-locked. But these were only the commencement of the obstacles that would prevent escape by the doors; and escape from the windows was absolutely impossible. After leaving his cell, the padlock of which had been opened by a skeleton key, he had to pass through about eight locked doors, three of which had two locks, and all of which were left open, except one, which was relocked to prevent pursuit.

At a quarter to four in the morning, Daniel Byrne, the watchman, gave the alarm, stating that he had discovered two tables, placed one above the other, near the south-western wall, adjoining the Governor's garden. It was found that these tables belonged to the lunatic dining-hall, and had to be brought a long distance. There were no footprints on the upper table, which should have been the case had it been stood on by any person who had walked through the open passages, which were wet and muddy, as torrents of rain were falling. The wall bore no marks whatever of any person having escaped by climbing over it. When the Governor and his assistants went to the section of the prison in which Stephens had been confined, they found the doors of the corridor open, and also the door of his cell. His bed looked as if he had not recently slept in it, and as if he had only rolled himself up in a railway rug which was found on the floor, and waited for the time that his deliverer was to arrive. A portion of the clothes which he wore on the morning of his arrest he left after him, and he must have put on a suit of black, which he had received a few days before. His books and papers were in the position they were last seen in by the warders.

The searchers for the fugitive were not left long in doubt as to the means by which the many doors were opened, as a master-key, quite bright, as if it had been only recently made, was found in the lock of the corridor door. While the detectives were scouring the city and suburbs, far and near, watching the early steamer vessels going to sea, and making active use of the telegraph wires, the search and inquiries were continued in the prison and its neighbourhood.

It was quite evident that Stephens was under the guidance of a person who knew the prison well, as the winding and difficult route from one extreme of the prison to the other was accomplished without a single blunder. This added to the anxiety of the officials, which was destined to be still further increased and excited on learning that Daniel Byrne, who had formerly been a policeman, had left that force to join the Battalion of St Patrick in the Pope's army, had returned to Ireland, and that papers were found among his effects associating him with the Fenian Brotherhood.

'With such facts before us,' said the London *Times*, 'it may be asked, What stronghold of the Government is safe from the treachery of men who eat the Queen's bread? Are the arsenals and magazines? Is the Bank of Ireland?'

Byrne was at once arrested, and a proclamation issued, offering a reward of £1,000 for information leading to the arrest of Stephens, and of £300 for the arrest of any person who harboured, received or assisted him, with a free pardon, in addition to the reward, to any persons concerned in the escape who would give information to lead to his arrest.

Outside the prison Stephens was met by Colonel T. J. Kelly and John Flood, who has since had a still more thrilling, though less mysterious, escape from the hands of the authorities in Manchester on the 18th September 1867.

Of O'Mahony's labours up to his retiring from a leading part in the Fenians, on the arrival of Mr Stephens in America, the position, then and since, has been defined by himself and it is due to his services to give his own words. Of the past, he says:

For more than eight years I held the position of Chief Officer of the Fenian Brotherhood in America. By excessive labour and ceaseless vigilance, I built it up till it became the most extensive, if not the most effective, revolutionary organisation of Irishmen that ever existed. I may also assert that it would not, with its other surroundings, have ever reached its late magnitude, either at home or in this country, but for my persevering exertions. During all my administrative career, I am not conscious to myself of having committed one dishonest or one selfish act. From the first to the last, I have had around me, cognisant of my official conduct, many men who have since become my bitterest enemies. Not one of these persons has ever come forward openly to charge me specifically with such an act, though several of them have betrayed my most secret confidence in other matters. They cannot do it. During the same time I have had official communication, both by word and letter, with many thousands, hundreds of whom are also my bitterest enemies now. Not one of these has, up to this, charged me with ever having deceived him by wilful falsehood. It cannot be done.

In reply to the statement that his retirement was compulsory, Mr O'Mahony says:

My resignation was not alone altogether voluntary on my part, but I had resolved on that step for some months before it actually took place. My principal reasons were, because, after the 1st of January '66, I could not understand Mr Stephens' perseverance in his war programme in Ireland, and because I felt that there was no prospect of an united Fenian Brotherhood in this country, which I believed to be an indispensable requisite to success whilst I held my office in it. Surrounded and undermined, as I had been for some time, by treacherous and wily opponents and personal enemies of all kinds.

Of his position since retirement, he remarks:

With respect to my present connection with the Fenian Brotherhood, I beg to state that I am still a private member of that body, and in what is technically called 'good standing', in the Corcoran Circle in this city [New York]. But further than this I have had no connection with either Mr James Stephens or with his successors in the government of the organisation for now nearly twelve months. Since last May I have taken no part, public or private, in directing their acts or counsels. From its commencement I totally dissented from that reckless and haphazard course of action of which Mr Stephens gave notice in the now notorious promise made by him at the Jones' Wood meeting last summer.* I condemned the whole tenor of his conduct in the management of Fenian affairs from that time up to the hour of his departure for Europe. Had I been consulted on the subject in time, and had my opinion prevailed, no attempt at a rising would have been made in Ireland this Spring.

Of the rising in March, and the men connected with it, he says:

Their late action had indeed become indispensable to the present honour and ultimate success of the Fenian cause, as well as to their own characters as honest and devoted patriots. Theirs was a desperate venture, but it had become both a moral and military necessity upon their parts by reason of the severe pressure that was upon the organisation and themselves. Should it fail for the present, it has even already advanced and elevated the cause of Ireland immensely before the world, and has opened the road for others to her fast approaching liberation. Our gallant

* On 28 October 1866 some 100,000 people attended the Jones' Wood Fenian rally and heard Stephens speak. This was the last in a series of meetings which the Chief Organiser addressed during his visit to New York. The others had been poorly attended but the *New York Times* attributed this to the fact that an admission fee of 50 cents had been demanded for the earlier events. The paper declared the gathering to be 'a most decided success'. Stephens said, 'I said I would begin the fight in Ireland this year. I assure you that I shall be there and that our battle flags shall be unfurled on Irish soil before the New Year dawns [great applause]. I have had hard work to convince you of my integrity and of the integrity of the men at home; but at last you believe, and this meeting shows that you put confidence in me. The great trouble with Irishmen in America has been their want of faith in their brothers at home, and you have been led astray by false representations.' He assured the crowd that, after certain setbacks, the Fenian organisation in Ireland was stronger than it had ever been.

brothers who have lately left us must be considered the hardy pioneers of Ireland's freedom in any case.

THE FUNERAL OF TERENCE BELLEW MCMANUS[*]

In the year 1861 came the funeral of Terence Bellew McManus in Ireland.[†] He was one of the '48 men who died in San Francisco. His body was brought to Ireland. I had a letter from James Stephens asking me to be one of the delegation who would accompany the remains from Cork to Dublin.

The funeral procession in Cork City was on a Sunday. There was an immense gathering of people. Passing along the quay, a ship in the river was flying the English flag, and a little boy caused a little commotion by running and clambering up the ship's ropes and poles and tearing down that flag.

Coming on nightfall we were on board the train for Dublin. The delegation having charge of the coffin was in the train compartment next to the coffin. We were armed with pistols, as it was rumoured that there might be some necessity for using them. Some men were, it seems, in favour of making the funeral the occasion of a 'rising'; they thought it would arouse the country if the remains were taken to Slievenamon or some such historic place on the way between Cork and Dublin, and the people called upon to rally around, for God and for country. James Stephens was averse to that being done, and this is why he thought it well to have an armed guard to prevent its being done. I saw, a few nights after, that one of the men who favoured the project

---

[*] *Rossa's Recollections, 1838 to 1898 (*1898), Jeremiah O'Donovan Rossa.
[†] The McManus funeral, a hugely orchestrated Fenian affair, was the first of many such political obsequies. The corpse was paraded all over the States before being dragged across Ireland to be buried in Glasnevin. James Stephens masterminded the Irish end of the affair and it may well have been the most successful operation that he supervised.

was James Roche of Monaghan, who came from New York to Ireland at the time of the funeral. The delegation from America and some others went to the Shelbourne hotel in Dublin to see William Smith O'Brien on some matter. Smith O'Brien was not in when we called. We were waiting in the coffee-room; the subject of the 'rising' came to be spoken of; Maurice O'Donoghue, of Kilmallock, one of the Dublin Centres, charged James Roche with being the prime mover in the project of the 'rising'. Hot words passed between them. Maurice moved angrily toward Roche; Roche drew a cane sword. Some of us rushed between the two angry men and matters were soon quieted down.

But on the railway route between Cork and Dublin, something occurred that I may make note of. When the train came to Limerick Junction, there was a stop there of several minutes. A large crowd was on the platform. If there was an attempt to be made anywhere to take away the body, it was thought that would be the place most likely for it. James Stephens was in the coach with us. He had previously given orders that the men of Tipperary town be there to prevent such a thing being done. As the bell rang for the starting of the train, Stephens called on the men to kneel down and say a *Pater* and *Ave* for the dead; and, while the whole crowd was on their knees, the train rolled out from the depot.

Arriving in Dublin I attended a banquet given to Colonel Smith, Colonel O'Reilly, Colonel Doheny, Michael Cavanaugh, Jerrie Cavanaugh, and Captain Frank Welpley, the members of the American delegation, and I called upon some friends I had been in correspondence with. The dinner had been at Coffey's or Carey's Hotel in Bridge Street. Father Conway of Mayo, who was staying at the hotel, attended it. When the toasts and speech-making commenced, he was called upon to speak. He spoke of the sad state of his part of the country, and said that he was then travelling on a mission to collect funds for some parishioners of his who were under sentence of evictions – dwelling particularly upon one case, that of a man and his wife who had eight young children. 'Put my name down for ten pounds,' said Michael Doheny. The priest taking his notebook, commenced to write. 'Hold', said Doheny. 'The ten pounds is to buy a gun, powder, and a ball for the man who is evicted, that he may shoot whoever comes to put him out of his house.' The priest shut up his notebook.

AMONG THE FENIANS[*]

Wishing to post myself on one of the most current topics of the day, I, Mark, hunted up an old friend, Dennis McCarthy, who is editor of the new Fenian journal in San Francisco, *The Irish People*. I found him sitting on a sumptuous candle-box, in his shirt-sleeves, solacing himself with a whiff at the national dhudeen or caubeen or whatever they call it – a clay pipe with no stem to speak of. I thought it might flatter him to address him in his native tongue, and so I bowed with considerable grace and said:

'Arrah!'

And he said, 'Be jabers!'

'Och hone!' said I.

'Mavourneen dheelish, acushla machree,' replied The Mc-Carthy.

'Erin go bragh,' I continued with vivacity.

'Asthore!' responded The McCarthy.

'Tare an' ouns!' said I.

'Bhe dha husth; fag a rogarah lums!' said the bold Fenian.

'Ye have me there, be me sowl!' said I (for I am not 'up' in the niceties of the language, you understand; I only know enough of it to enable me to 'keep my end up' in an ordinary conversation).

* *The Celebrated Jumping Frog of Calaveras and other sketches* (1867), Mark Twain.

ON JOHN O'MAHONY[†]

He made the impression on me that he was a man proud of his name and of his race. And I liked him for that. I liked to see an Irishman proud of his people. It is seldom you will find such a man doing anything that would disgrace anyone belonging to him. In my work of organising in Ireland, I felt myself perfectly safe in dealing with men who were proud – no matter how poor they were – of belonging to the 'Old Stock'. I trusted them, and would trust them again.

Three years ago, in the summer of 1894, I was travelling with Michael Cusack, John Sarsfield Casey (since dead), and some others, by the Galtee Mountains, from Mitchelstown to Knocklong. We stopped at a village called Kilbehenny. We strolled into the graveyard, and there I saw a large tomb, on the top slab of which were cut the words:

'THIS IS THE TOMB OF THE O'MAHONYS'

That was the tomb of John O'Mahony's family. Some days after, I stood within the walls of the ruins of Muckross Abbey in Killarney, and there I saw another tomb (just like the one in Kilbehenny) on which were graven the words:

'THIS IS THE TOMB OF THE O'DONOGHUES'

That was the tomb of the family of the O'Donoghue of the Glens. That showed me that in old Irish times John O'Mahony's family had the same standing among the people as the other family. In those graveyards, I thought of Shane O'Neill of Tyrone who, when offered an English title, said he was prouder of the title of 'The O'Neill' than of any title England could give him.

[†] *Rossa's Recollections, 1838 to 1898* (1898), Jeremiah O'Donovan Rossa.

THE DEATH OF MICHAEL DOHENY, 1862[*]

Michael Doheny kept 'the whiteness of his soul'. The same star that shone over his hopes in Ireland and led him into exile, was his beacon and his glory in it. His brain was ever illuminated by it. It was to him the eternal and unquenchable lamp in his temple of immortality.

The hopes and feelings which bent in homage to it found vent in participation in various Irish societies and military organisations, and in the constant use of his pen and tongue, whenever opportunity presented, to expound or give aid and comfort to the darling projects of his manhood; in all of which he was lovingly and enthusiastically seconded and animated by a devoted wife, and by a sister-in-law – now, alas, no more – to whose untiring solicitude, under all circumstances of his career, he has left us most touching and ennobling testimony.

He was a member of every society started in New York for the dissemination of Irish principles, or the aid of those who kept alive the patriotic fire in Ireland. His connection with the Fenian Brotherhood has already been noticed. His soul was centred on it. It presented to him a prospect which would more than repay his lifelong labours – under every change of fortune – to the great cause. But he passed away before it had assumed the gigantic proportions which set the world wondering.

After a brief illness, Doheny departed this life at his residence, Eighteenth Street and Ninth Avenue, South Brooklyn, at half-past nine o'clock, on the night of the 1st of April. The suddenness of his decease sent a thrill through the hearts of his comrades and friends, as well as the community at large, which has not yet, even after five years, been tempered down to a calm comprehension of the sorrowful fact. Those who knew and loved him, those who had such hopes in his faith, can scarcely yet re-

[*] *Fenian Heroes and Martyrs* (1868), John Savage.

alise that Michael Doheny is no more – that the hearty energy and eloquent tongue, which once indicated so stalwart a physique and so luxuriant an intellect, can no more come within our circle to enliven us with his brilliant and loving reminiscences, and exalt us with the holy purposes in which he alone lived, moved, and had a being.

Doheny was one of those firmly-knit, hearty men, whose departure to the 'shadowy land' we rarely permit ourselves to think of, much less to dwell on. In his instance, the love and affection his purity and innocence of heart instigated and won placed at a still more remote distance any anticipations of so sad a reality. The officers of the Sixty-Ninth Regiment, and those of the Phoenix Brigade, attended his remains to the Calvary cemetery, where all that was mortal of the exiled orator, poet, patriot and man, Michael Doheny, was lowered into the grave by John O'Mahony, Richard O'Gorman, John Savage, Captain John Kavanagh, Patrick O'Dea, and John Hughes, who were his associates in Ireland.

THE FENIAN RAIDS ON CANADA[†]

The seceders from the Stephens faction met in Convention in Cincinnati, Ohio, in September 1865, a very large number of delegates being present from all of the States in the Union. After the usual preliminary oratory and the adoption of several resolutions, the delegates formed themselves into a body which they termed 'the Senate Wing of the Fenian Brotherhood'. They ridiculed the idea of invading Ireland successfully, and changed their base of operations.

'On to Canada' became their slogan, and the idea was so popular that they quickly secured the allegiance of thousands of

† Capt. John A. Macdonald in *Troublesome Times in Canada, A history of the Fenian raids of 1866 and 1870* (1910).

disappointed Irishmen who were anxious and ready to strike a blow at England in any quarter. In order that there should be some recognised source from which all orders, proclamations and edicts could be officially promulgated, it was resolved to form an Irish Republic (on paper), as the Fenians were without territory until they captured it. This was accomplished by the adoption of a constitution framed on the model of that used by the United States. Its provisions included the usual regulations (both civil and military) for a Republican form of government, and its unanimous acceptance by the delegates was received with glad acclaim.

Col Wm. R. Roberts was chosen as President of the new Republic and Gen. T. W. Sweeny (who was then commanding officer of the 16th United States Infantry) as Secretary of War. The other Cabinet portfolios were handed out to 'lesser lights' in the Fenian fold.

As even Republican governments cannot be maintained, or military campaigns conducted without the expenditure of money, the Irish Republic could prove no exception to the rule, and therefore the work of collecting funds and gathering munitions of war for the invasion of Canada was immediately commenced. Fenian 'circles', or lodges, were organised in every possible corner of the United States for the purpose of stirring up the enthusiasm of the Irish people and securing money to purchase arms and ammunition. Military companies and regiments were formed wherever practicable and drilling and parading was pursued openly during the fall of 1865 and winter of 1866, getting ready for the coming fray.

Funds were raised in various ways – by voluntary subscriptions, by holding picnics, excursions, fairs, bazaars and other methods. But the largest source of revenue was derived by imposing upon the credulity of the sons and daughters of Erin by the sale to them of bonds of the Irish Republic, a chimerical dream which was painted in such glowing colours and presented with such stirring appeals to their patriotism that hard-earned dollars were pulled out from every nook and cranny in many Irish homes to invest in these 'securities' and thus help along the cause. The following is a copy of the bond, which will serve to show its wording:

It is Hereby Certified that
The Irish Republic is indebted to .... or bearer in the sum of TEN DOLLARS, redeemable six months after the acknowledgment of THE IRISH NATION, with interest from the date hereof inclusive, at six per cent, per annum, payable on presentation of this Bond at the Treasury of the Irish Republic.

Date ...... [Stamp Office of the Treasury.]
John O'Neill: Agent for the Irish Republic

In the light of subsequent events, when the dreams of the visionary enthusiasts have been so rudely dispelled, the sight of one of these bonds must present as much sadness and pathos to the beholder as the vision of an old Confederate bank note does to the erstwhile defenders of the 'Lost Cause' of the Southern States.

As the coffers of the Irish Republic began to fill rapidly, the Fenian leaders became more hopeful and bombastic, while enthusiasm among the rank and file continued to be worked up to fever pitch. President Roberts gathered a select coterie about him at his headquarters in New York to assist in upholding his dignity, and incidentally help to boost the cause. Plots and plans of all kinds were hatched against Great Britain, and loudmouthed orators were kept busy for several months fanning the embers of Irish patriotism into flame.

General Sweeny was very active during the winter of 1865 and 1866 in getting his 'War Department' fully organised and his field forces ready for the spring campaign against Canada. His staff was composed of the following officers, all of whom had seen active service in the Civil War:

Chief of Staff – Brigadier-General C. Carroll Tavish.
Chief of Engineer Corps – Col. John Meehan.

Chief of Ordnance – Col. C. H. Rundell.
Engineer Corps – Lieut.-Col. C. H. Tresiliar.
Assistant Adjutant-General – Major E. J. Courtney.
Ordnance Department – Major M. O'Reilly.
Quartermaster – Major M. H. Van Brunt.
Aide-de-Camps – Capt. D. W. Greely and Capt. Daniel O'Connell.

This galaxy of officers strutted majestically around Headquarters garbed in the gorgeous green and gold uniforms of the Fenian Army, looked wise, and promised all enquirers that important movements would be made in the spring. Secret meetings were held almost daily at Headquarters, when the plan of campaign would be discussed over and over again, and amendments made wherever necessary. Finally the following plan of operations was given out in March, 1866, as the gist of one evolved by the Council, which is said to have embodied Gen. Sweeny's whole strategic programme:–

'Expeditions for the invasion of Canada will rendezvous at Detroit and Rochester, and at Ogdensburg and Plattsburg, and at Portland. The forces assembled at the two first-named points are to operate conjointly against Toronto, Hamilton, and the west of Upper Canada. From Ogdensburg and Plattsburg demonstrations will be made against Montreal, and ultimately Quebec; Kingston will be approached by Cape Vincent, while Portland will be the general place of embarkation for expeditions against the capitals of New Brunswick and Nova Scotia.

'The Canadian and provincial borders once crossed, bases of operations will be established in the enemy's country, so that international quarrels with the Washington Government may be evaded. There are to be lands chosen at the head of Passamaquoddy Bay, Saint John's, on the Chambly, close to the foot of Lake Champlain; Prescott, on the Saint Lawrence; Wolfe Island, at the foot of Lake Ontario; Hamilton, Cobourg, Goderich, and Windsor, in Upper Canada. These places are all within convenient distances of the United States, and afford by water an easy retreat, as well as cunning receptacles for fresh American levies.

'The Irish Republic calculates to have, by the first of April, fifteen millions of dollars at its disposal in ready cash. This will give transportation and maintenance for one month to thirty thousand men, a greater number than were ever before mustered to the conquest of the Canadian possessions. Of this force, eight thousand will carry the line of the Grand Trunk road west of Hamilton; five thousand, crossing from Rochester to Cobourg, will be prepared to move either east, in time to act jointly with three thousand men from Wolfe Island, upon Kingston, or to take part with the western detachment in the capture of Toronto. All this, it is believed, will be the work of two weeks. Thus entrenched securely in Upper Canada, holding all the routes of the Grand Trunk, sufficient rolling stock secured to control the main line, the Fenians hope to attract to their colours fifty thousand American Irishmen, and equip a navy on Lakes Huron, Erie and Ontario. The avenues to return so being secured, thirty thousand men, under General Sweeny, will move down the Saint Lawrence, upon Kingston, simultaneously with ten thousand men by the lines of the Chambly, and these will converge upon Montreal; in the meantime isolated expeditions from the rendezvous at Saint Andrews will reduce Saint John and Halifax, these furnishing depots for privateers and ocean men-of-war to intercept British transports and effectually close the Saint Lawrence. Quebec will thus fall by the slow conquest of time; or, if the resources of the garrison should be greater than the patience of the invaders, the same heights which two Irishmen have scaled before, will again give foothold to the columns of the brotherhood.

'At Chicago the Fenians already possess five sailing vessels, a tug, and two steam transports; at Buffalo they are negotiating for vessels; at Bay City, Michigan, and at Cleveland they have other craft in the process of refitting; these will simultaneously raise the green flag and stand ready to succour the land forces. Goderich, Sarnia and Windsor will be simultaneously occupied; all the available rolling stock seized, and the main line of the Grand Trunk cut at Grand River to prevent the passage of cars and locomotives to Hamilton. The geographical configuration of the western half of Upper Canada will permit of a few thousand men holding the entire section of the country between Cobourg and the Georgian Bay. These are connected by a chain of lakes and water courses, and the country affords subsistence for a vast army. Horses sufficient to mount as many cavalry as the Brotherhood can muster, quartermasters' teams in quantity, and a vast amount of lake shipping will at once be reduced to a grand military department, with Hamilton for the capital, and a loan advertised for.

'While this is being negotiated, Gen. Sweeny will push rapidly forward on the line of the Grand Trunk, in time to superintend the fall of Montreal, where ocean shipping will be found in great quantity. With the reduction of Montreal a demand will be made upon the United States for a formal recognition of Canada, whose name is to be changed at once to New Ireland. While this is being urged, the green flag will scour all the bays and gulfs in Canada; a Fenian fleet from San Francisco will carry Vancouver and the Fraser River country to give security to the Pacific squadron, rendezvousing at San Juan, and the rights of belligerents will be enforced from the British Government by prompt retaliation for the cruelties of British court-martials.

'The population of the British provinces is little above two and a half millions, and the military resources of the united provinces fall short of sixty thousand men. Of these nearly ten thousand are of Irish birth or descent. The States will furnish for the subjugation of these, eighty thousand veteran troops. With the single exception of Quebec, it is believed the whole of the British provinces will fall in a single campaign. During the ensuing winter diversions will be put in motion in Ireland, and while it is believed the Brotherhood can defy the Queen's war transports to land an army in the west, arrangements will be developed to equip a powerful navy for aggressive operations on the sea. Before the 1st of June, it is thought, fifty commissioned vessels of war and privateers, carrying three hundred guns, will be afloat, and to maintain these a tremendous moral influence will be exerted upon every Irish-American citizen to contribute the utmost to the general fund for the support of the war.

'By the tempting offer of a surrender of Canada to the United States, Mr Seward, it is hoped, will wink at connivance between American citizens and the Fenian conquerors, and by another summer it is thought the dominion of the Brotherhood north of the St Lawrence will be formally acknowledged by the United States, Russia, and each of the American republics.' The third year of Irish tenure in Canada will, it is believed, array two of the great powers against Great Britain.

'John Mitchel, at Paris, will organise the bureau of foreign agents; and Ireland, maintaining a position of perpetual revolt, will engage for her own suppression a considerable part of the regular British levies.

'At the present time a bureau of operations is being quietly organised in Paris, where the opposition press has already proclaimed for Irish nationality. It is Mr Mitchel who sees that the funds of the Brotherhood are distributed in Ireland; he also is in correspondence with liberal statesmen in Great Britain, and conducts the disintegration of the British army by touching the loyalty of the Irish troops, who constitute one-third of the Queen's service.

'Among the earliest aggressive operations will be the overhauling of a Cunard steamer between New York and Cape Race,

---

* William Henry Seward was a senator from New York, Governor of New York 1838–1842, unsuccessful candidate for the 1860 Republican presidential nomination; secretary of state under Presidents Lincoln and Johnson 1861–1869. While secretary of state he concluded a treaty with Russia for the purchase of Alaska.

with her usual allotment of specie.* In like manner the British lines of steamers proceeding from England to Quebec, Portland, Boston and Halifax, will be arrested and their funds secured.

'Military operations in Ireland must, of necessity, be confined to the interior. Three military departments will be organised – the Shannon, the Liffey, and the Foyle – and the campaign will be entirely predatory or guerrilla in its conduct. The British Coast Guard stations will fall easy conquests, their number and isolation contributing to their ruin; while from the Wicklow Mountains, through all the rocky fastnesses of Ireland, the cottagers will descend upon the British garrisons, maintaining perpetual and bloody rebellion till the better news comes across the sea or the patience of England is quite worn out.'

This was a mighty and stupendous programme truly, but oh how visionary! It embraced the extreme aspirations of the boldest and most sanguinary Fenians, and its publication no doubt served to bring more money into their treasury. But, alas for human hopes, its execution never happened.

Yet it fired the hearts of the soldiers of the Irish Republican Army, and they eagerly awaited the summons to march 'On to Canada.' All through that winter drilling and preparation continued, and the enthusiasm of the men was kept warm by fervid oratory appealing to their patriotism, while they boldly chanted their song:

We are a Fenian Brotherhood,
skilled in the arts of war.
And we're going to fight for Ireland,
the land that we adore.
Many battles we have won,
along with the boys in blue.
And we'll go and capture Canada,
for we've nothing else to do.

* *Cape Race:* a landmark located on Newfoundland, Canada.

160

Fenian Informers[†]

Patrick Condon, alias Godfrey Massey, was called. On the witness ascending the table, the prisoner, General Bourke, changed his position in the dock, and looked Massey straight in the face, but the latter turned his eye aside. The witness stated that he was a colonel in the 2nd Texas regiment, Confederate service, afterwards a canvasser for a commercial house in New Orleans; that he became connected with the Fenian Brotherhood about August, 1865, and went to New York in October, 1866. He first saw Bourke, whom he now identified, in the Central Fenian Office, New York. He met Stephens there also.

He continued: I was at a Fenian meeting in Philadelphia. Steps were there taken for the purpose of collecting war materials and money. An officer was appointed to take charge of the materials. The materials were to be sent to New York for shipment to Ireland. Stephens and I left Philadelphia and went to Washington. We there met some men belonging to the organisation, and consulted them. I know that James Stephens was connected with the Fenian Brotherhood. That portion of it which began with John O'Mahony was under his direction. I have known the prisoner, Bourke, as Colonel Thomas Bourke, in America. I gave money to Colonel Thomas Bourke. I gave him about £10 in London. I stated to him when I gave him the money, the purpose of which was that he should come with me to Ireland to join the rising, that was some weeks previous to the 11th February last. He said that he had to leave London for Ireland on the evening of the day in which he would receive the money. After I left Washington, I went to New York. I arrived there before Stephens by a few days.

On Stephens' return, there was a meeting of the Fenians held

† *Fenian Heroes and Martyrs* (1886), John Savage.

at New York about the middle of December, 1866. Some of the Irish Centres were present. I cannot think of the names of all, but about thirty were present. I am not sure whether the prisoner, Colonel Bourke, was there. Stephens presided at the meeting. Stephens made a statement, showing the amount of war material held by the Brotherhood at New York. He said that the amount was not one-seventh of the minimum fixed by himself. He said that the minimum was thirty thousand rifles. He objected to opening the fight, as he had promised, but to prove his fidelity to Ireland, he offered to come over and put himself in the hands of the police authorities, and to be hanged.

That proposition was scouted by every one, and it was determined that the fight should be opened. I knew a person named Captain McCafferty. He was at that meeting. Some evenings after that, Stephens convened another meeting. About twenty officials were present at that meeting. It was purely a military one. McCafferty wanted to know the plan of the campaign. Stephens did not like to mention it. I said that McCafferty was right, and supported his motion to divulge the plan of the campaign to his officers. That was what turned out afterwards to be the campaign for Ireland. At that meeting several of the officers said that they would leave on the next day, Saturday, for Ireland, and they did. There was a list of names of officers who were to go to Ireland made out. I got that list of names from Colonel Kelly. Some of the officers left for Ireland. I do not remember the names of those who left for Ireland.

After that meeting I attended a meeting at Stephens' lodgings. James Stephens was present, so were Colonel Kelly and others. At a subsequent meeting, Stephens was deposed and repudiated, and Colonel Kelly was put in his stead. I left New York on 11th January of the present year. I took shipping for England. Before leaving New York, I received from Colonel Kelly £550 in gold (British money) to be distributed among the officers in Ireland. The list I referred to a few minutes ago, I destroyed. When I arrived here I met the officers whose names Colonel Kelly disclosed to me, and in accordance with instructions I gave them the moneys. I arrived in Liverpool on the 20th January, in the present year. I remained there for a day, and then proceeded to London, where I stopped at private lodgings until the 11th February. Amongst the officers whose names Colonel Kelly disclosed to me, and whom I met in London, was the prisoner, Thomas Bourke, who was appointed to the Tipperary district. Captain O'Brien and Dominick O'Mahony were officers for Cork. Captain Deasy was for the Millstreet district. A man named Joyce was officer for Fermoy. General Halpin was for the Dublin district. I do not know that there was any one mentioned for Louth or Drogheda. Colonel Kelly lodged in 5 Upper Creswell Street, London. I saw there General Fariola, a Franco-Italian, and a person named Cluseret. I knew General Halpin well. I saw there Beirne or O'Beirne, from Dublin, Mahony from Cork, and Harbison from Belfast, who said they were delegates or representatives of the Fenian Brotherhood in Ireland. I gave them money; £30 would cover what each got. I stated to them that the money was given for the support of the organisation.

At that meeting an address was drawn up. It was discussed as they went along – that is, paragraph by paragraph. It spoke about the wrongs of Ireland, and called upon the people to take up arms, and invoking the sympathy and aid of the working men of England. I came to Dublin on the 11th February. There was a meeting of Centres held the next day. O'Beirne was there. The Centres stated the numerical strength, material of war, and the number of arms held by each. I took the returns myself of the respective Centres then and there assembled.

What did they state the numerical strength was? About fourteen thousand. And the material of war and arms? About three thousand stand of arms – to consist of rifles, guns and pikes. The next day I went into the county Mayo, first to Castlebar, then to Westport, where I stopped one night. I then returned to Dublin, thence to Cork, where a Fenian meeting was held on the out-skirts of the town, convened by O'Mahony, the same I gave the money to in London. The numerical strength given me in Cork was twenty thousand men, and about one thousand five hundred weapons, the vast majority of them pikes. I left Cork the next day for the town of Tipperary, for the purpose of acquiring knowledge of the country for military purposes. I next returned to Dublin, and then left for London. I went to Colonel Kelly's lodgings. Kelly gave me some more money to be distributed. He told me the rising was fixed for the 5th of March, that being the anniversary of the day on which some of the persons taken in Canada were sentenced to be executed. He told me that the railroad centres were to be destroyed if they could not be held by the insurgents. A guerrilla war was to be maintained, and the railways destroyed by the insurgents.

I left London on the morning after my arrival, and returned to Dublin, for a day or two. I then went to Mullingar, for military purposes. On my return to Dublin a meeting of Fenian Centres was held, at some distance from Portobello Barracks. O'Beirne was there. Told him the night of the 5th March was fixed for the rising. On the next day I went to Cork, where I saw O'Mahony, to whom I said that the 5th of March had been fixed upon for the rising. Soon after I left Cork, and went to Limerick Junction, where I was arrested, on the railway platform, on the night of the 4th March.

On the cross-examination, Counsellor Butt forced Massey to acknowledge the disgrace both of his mother and wife. He proved he was the illegitimate son of the former by one Massey, and that the latter pressed him to become an informer.*

The statement of the other wretch, Corydon, whose brazen nonchalance was quite in keeping with his degradation, was as follows:

I was a lieutenant in the Federal army; I became a member

* Isaac Butt, *de facto* founder of the Irish Parliamentary Party.

164

of the Fenian Brotherhood in the summer of 1862. I was then in the Federal army. I took an oath when I joined the [Fenian] organisation. I remained nearly four years in the Federal army. I left it in July 1865. I attended Fenian meetings while I was in the Federal army. I remained in New York about a month after the army was disbanded. I attended the Fenian headquarters nearly every day while I was in New York; they were in Duane street; John O'Mahony was the head of the organisation; I was sent by John O'Mahony to James Stephens in August. I was not the bearer of any despatches; I was accompanied by four other persons connected with the Fenian organisation; we went to Liverpool, and from that we came to Dublin.

In Dublin I attended a Fenian meeting at North Anne Street; it was attended by James Stephens, O'Donovan Rossa and others; I said to Stephens we were desired by John O'Mahony to report ourselves to him – he told us to find lodgings, and that he would know where to find us; I remained in Dublin till November, 1865; while here I heard of James Stephen's arrest.

Colonel Kelly told me that the purport of the dispatches was that Stephens would be out of jail in five or six days. I went to New York by the *Scotia* on the 19th November; I saw O'Mahony and many other Fenian officers. We had a meeting when I arrived, and we gave the tidings of the expected escape of Stephens; the prisoner Bourke was there. I had been introduced to him on Union Square. I came back to Ireland. The announcement of Stephen's escape was made while I was there. Bourke was an organiser for Manhattan, and he urged the men to unity and said when Stephens could get out of an English jail what could not people outside do in accomplishing the objects for which they were banded.

I came to Queenstown [Cobh] on the 22nd December; I went to Cork and from thence to Dublin. I remained in Ireland one night. I delivered my dispatches to Colonel Kelly in Heytesbury Street. I got dispatches from Kelly to O'Mahony, and went to New York again, where I saw Bourke in January, 1866. I came to Liverpool, and thence to Dublin. I remained here until April. In April, 1866, I went to Liverpool and remained there until February last; I received pay from the funds of the Fenian Brotherhood. We received orders to be prepared to move on to Chester. Our orders were at first to remain quiet until we would be told to move. I next saw the prisoner in the early part of January, 1867, in Liverpool; it was then stated that he came from America. I met persons who had come from America with him. The prisoner Bourke stated that they came over for the purpose of fighting and it was useless to think any longer that Stephens would fight, for he would not.

A few days before the Chester affair all the American officers in Liverpool were at a meeting. McCafferty and Flood said they were sent from the directory in London, with money to pay their way to Chester. They said that the American officers in Liverpool would go to Chester, that the castle there was to be attacked, the arms seized, a train seized, and the arms put into it. The rails were to be taken up and the wires also, and they were to proceed by train to Holyhead, where they would seize the mail boat and land in Ireland. That plan was agreed to at the meeting. No arrangements for carrying it out were made. After the meeting separated, and on the Sunday before the Monday, I gave information to the authorities in Liverpool, I made arrangements to go to Chester; all the American officers, about twenty, went to Chester. I saw them at Birkenhead. I went there with them. I met Austin Gibbons, one of the American officers at Birkenhead. A countermand of the order to march on Chester was given by Gibbons. He told me that someone had informed.

After that, late in February, I got orders to come to Dublin. I remained there until the intended rising. I knew Colonel Godfrey Massey – I saw him after I came to Ireland. I was told to go to Millstreet and see the 'Centre' there, a man named Kearney, that he would give me instructions how to act, and through him to find my way to Colonel O'Connor in Kerry. I was desired to tell O'Connor about the rising to take place on the 5th of March. In case I could not see O'Connor, Kearney was to get me introduced to the 'Centre', near Milltown, county Kerry, and I was to take the command. My party was to blow up bridges, tear up the rails and telegraph wires, and 'break banks' and if possible, we were to go as far as Rathkeale, Limerick. I went to Millstreet on the 4th of March. I saw Kearney, he told me to go back to Cork city and see a man named Michael Murphy, who would probably give me instructions. I went to Cork that night. I saw Michael Murphy. He sent me to Dominick Mahony, the Head Centre for Cork. I did not see Massey in Cork. Captain Condon was in military command at Cork – he told me to go to Midleton. I remained in Cork till Monday, the 4th of March. I left by the morning train. I met Massey's messenger who told me that Massey was coming by the 12 o'clock train to Limerick Junction. I came to Dublin, and arrived about 4 o'clock. I went to the Lower Castle Yard, and gave information to the authorities. I saw Massey next a prisoner. I first began to give information to the authorities in Liverpool in September, 1866.

THE IRISH PEOPLE*

By the early 1860s, Michael Doheny was dead from a fever and John O'Mahony was temporarily the undisputed leader of the Fenian Brotherhood in New York. The Brotherhood, despite having Irish-born leaders, came to perceive Irish separatism through the prisms of American ideology, American capital, and American requirements. This set in train the vague and ultimately negative influence of right-wing American thinking upon Irish nationalist politics.

* *Seán Treacy and the Tan War,* Joe Ambrose.

167

Over in Ireland Stephens travelled the land, disguised as a hobo, secretly recruiting Fenians. Kevin B. Nowlan has estimated that, by 1864–5, the Chief Organiser's efforts resulted in there being maybe 80,000 Fenians in Ireland and England, plus thousands of secret followers who were members of the British army.

Stephens was behind the foundation of a Dublin-based Fenian weekly newspaper, *The Irish People*, in 1863. The ambitions which informed this venture were a desire to emulate the influence which *The Nation* had exerted over public opinion and the hope that it'd raise badly-needed funds. Stephens felt that a conspiracy shouldn't publicise itself by putting out a paper but he was convinced by others. His caution, in this regard, proved justifiable. It was their involvement with *The Irish People* which, indirectly, destroyed the lives of quite a few leading Fenians.

The first issue appeared on 28 November 1863. John O'Leary was editor-in-chief. O'Donovan Rossa, Thomas Clarke Luby, and Charles J. Kickham were his editorial staff. It never had any real influence, but it did successfully propagate the rebel Fenian agenda.

Once the paper was gone to the printers the team would usually retire to some tranquil surroundings to unwind and discuss the matters of the day. These gatherings tended to be frugal affairs, as befitted those living a revolutionary life, but for one such soiree a Cork supporter sent up a veritable banquet for the relaxing radicals. 'After the wild duck and snipe, which had come all the way from Cape Clear,' wrote Kickham, 'there came walnuts and oranges. It is fair to admit that there was also a decanter of what seemed to be the very best Irish whisky, as Luby and O'Leary appreciated a stiff tumbler of whiskey punch … The "Chief Organiser" did not affect the more national beverage, but seemed to have a decided relish for a glass of Guinness' porter. Methinks I see him now – Shakespearian head, flowing auburn beard, lady hand, and all – as he takes his meerschaum from his lips, and pointing with the amber-tipped cherrywood tube to the table, says "If some people saw us now, what noise there would be about our luxurious habits!"'

A few weeks after the launch of *The Irish People*, O'Leary was left in complete charge when Stephens, despite the wild duck, the Guinness, and the walnuts, withdrew from active day-to-day involvement.

John O'Leary was born into a Tipperary town merchant family in 1820 and educated there at the Abbey School before being sent to Carlow College. A.M. Sullivan said that he belonged, 'to one of the most worthy, amiable, and respectable families in Tipperary'. He studied law at Trinity College, Dublin, in 1847. It was at this time that he met up with like-minded activists such as Charles Gavan Duffy, Lalor and Meagher.

When he got out of prison after his involvement in 1848, he momentarily attended Cork University under the pretext of studying medicine. By 1855, he'd drifted over to Paris where he socialised with bohemians such as the American painter Whistler before running into Stephens while visiting a boarding-house where his cousin lived. Despite Stephens' ardent promptings, O'Leary was pessimistic about the revolutionary possibilities provided by Ireland. He had inherited an income of several hundred pounds a year from his father and was quite content to potter around Paris buying rare books. Someone who didn't much like O'Leary said that he was, 'reserved, sententious, almost cynical; keenly observant, sharply critical, full of restrained passion.'

When word got around Ireland that *The Irish People* was coming out, the paper's offices were inundated with that which all editors fear – unsolicited manuscripts. Sheaves of patriotic verse which appalled the exceptionally well read O'Leary poured in. He said that, 'patriotism seems to take a peculiar delight in the manufacture of bad verse, while those who make a good article are too often not over patriotic.' In the twelfth issue of the paper he wrote: 'We have received this week such a pile of verses that, though very tired, we are tempted to give what we were going to call our poetical contributors a few hints. We confess we do this chiefly to save our own time; for though we are usually told that the authors are hard worked, and only write in the intervals of labour, we are afraid they must have too much time to spare, or rather to waste.'

The burden of editorship rested heavily on O'Leary's shoulders. Something of a literary snob, he felt that the 'talking and writing people' in Ireland were neither particularly rebellious nor much in favour of armed struggles. Ambitious about what he was doing, he put a great deal of his intellectual energies into finding semi-decent professional writers who might emulate the salon of bright and vivid prose stylists that *The Nation* had access to during its halcyon days. One of the few 'proper' writers that he could rely on was Charles J. Kickham.

Kickham was born at Mullinahone in 1828. His father was a wealthy storekeeper and Charles was related on his mother's side to John O'Mahony. When he was fourteen a shooting accident left him practically deaf and blind. He had organised the Mullinahone Confederate Club, playing minor roles in both the '48 rising and in the Tenant League. It fell to Kickham to fight, on behalf of the Fenians, a rhetorical war of attrition against their mortal foes, the Irish Catholic Church establishment.

What might be the feelings in a decent Christian's heart, Kickham once enquired in print, when he discovered that 'the dignitaries of his church, who know not want and nakedness themselves' were friendly with his oppressors? He wrote that, 'those who would prepare to grapple with the despoiler, and save a suffering people from destruction, are vilified and denounced' while at the same time, 'the place-beggar, the political mountebank, the ermined perjurer, the very exterminator – all these are courted and smiled upon and blessed.' Kickham said that he tended to agree with the Franciscan Luke Wadding who wrote: 'Time was when we had wooden chalices and golden priests, but now we have golden chalices and wooden priests.'

E. R. R. Green, in his essay 'Charles Joseph Kickham and John O'Leary', gives a delicately calibrated pen portrait of the two literary-minded Fenians: 'Charles Kickham and John O'Leary are the only literary figures produced by the Fenian movement who are at all deserving of the name, and even in their case there was no very striking achievement. O'Leary published one book, *Recollections of Fenians and Fenianism* which it must be admitted was well padded with material provided by his old comrade, Luby. Kickham's fame rests on a single novel, and although no book has enjoyed more popularity in Ireland, *Knocknagow* is by no means the greatest Irish work of fiction. Yet it must not be forgotten that these were men of action to whom the writing of books was not a primary concern. They were marked out by an identity of purpose, upheld with an integrity that typified the Fenian spirit to a younger generation ... They had a good deal in common to start with; there was only about two years' difference between their ages and they were both Tipperary men of the same prosperous shop-keeping stock.'

Pierce Nagle, a traitor working in their midst at *The Irish People*'s offices, destroyed them. Nagle had been a teacher near Clonmel – he was recruited by the Irish Constabulary as a spy and provided them with a list containing the names of all the people who distributed the paper throughout the country and also the names of those who were in touch with the Fenian leadership.

According to Malcolm Brown, writing in *The Politics of Irish Literature*, Nagle 'felt his sensibilities bruised by Stephens' domineering manner. He sailed to New York and called on the British consulate officials to offer his services as a spy. A business arrangement was agreed upon, beginning with the payment of his fare back to Dublin, where he was hired by *The Irish People* as a wrapper in the mail room.'

In September 1865, he got his chance. A Tipperary Fenian visited *The Irish People*'s offices with a letter for Stephens, who gave the courier a typically hyperbolic message to take back to Tipperary: 'There is no time to be lost. This year must be the year of action. I speak with a knowledge and authority to which no other man could pretend, and I repeat the flag of Ireland – of the Irish Republic – must this year be raised.'

Stephens allegedly also gave the visitor some cash. As a result, later that same day, the Tipperary man returned to the offices in a drunken condition. Nagle seized the moment and, under the guise of taking care of the drunkard, got hold of Stephens' message to Tipperary. On 15 September, detectives raided *The Irish People*'s offices, seized their files, and arrested everybody found there. Twenty-three Fenians were arrested including O'Leary and, some time later, Kickham.

Many years later Nagle was beaten up on a London street and died in hospital as a result of his injuries.

Stephens' message did not constitute proof that the paper's staff was engaged in a criminal conspiracy, so files and rubbish bins were trawled in the search for more solid evidence. Eventually an unpublished 'letter to the editor' was unearthed. In it the writer, regarded by O'Leary and the others as being half-cracked, said: 'The French exterminated their aristocracy, and every honest revolution must imitate that of France. We must do the same … the Irish aristocracy must be hounded down by the liberal press and slain afterwards by the hands of an aroused and infuriated people.'

As Kickham was led away to his cell, sentence having been passed on him, he noticed on the ground, and picked up, a picture of the Blessed Virgin. He piously kissed it and said to his warder: 'I have been accustomed to have the likeness of the Mother of God morning and evening before my eyes since I was a child. Will you ask the governor if I may keep this?'

O'Leary, Kickham, and O'Donovan Rossa got long and cruelly enforced sentences. Rossa came out of prison a broken man; O'Leary and Kickham emerged into freedom, in their different ways, as damaged goods. O'Leary never liked to talk about his time in prison. Movingly, and with some dignity, he later said, 'I was in the hands of my enemy'.

Fragile Kickham's health collapsed during his incarceration. His abuse at the hands of his captors was raised in parliament in 1867. He was held in solitary confinement at Pentonville, subsequently transferred to Woking's hospital prison, and finally released in 1869. By then, he was almost totally blind.

JOHN O'LEARY'S SPEECH FROM THE DOCK[*]

While the jury in the case of Thomas Clarke Luby were absent from the court deliberating on and framing their verdict, John O'Leary was put forward to the bar. He stepped boldly to the front, with a flash of fire in his dark eyes, and a scowl on his features, looking hatred and defiance on judges, lawyers, jurymen, and all the rest of them. All eyes were fixed on him, for he was one of those persons whose exterior attracts attention and indicates a character above the common. He was tall, slightly built, and of gentlemanly deportment; every feature of his thin angular face gave token of great intellectual energy and determination, and its pallid hue was rendered almost death-like by contrast with his long black hair and flowing moustache and beard. Easy it was to see that when the government placed John O'Leary in the dock they had caged a proud spirit, and an able and resolute enemy. He had come of a patriot stock, and from a part of Ireland where rebels to English rule were never either few or faint-hearted. He was born in the town of Tipperary, of parents whose circumstances were comfortable, and who, at the time of their decease, left him in possession of property worth a couple of hundred

* *Speeches from the Dock, or Protests of Irish Patriotism: Speeches Delivered After Conviction* (1868), A.M. Sullivan.

pounds per annum. He was educated for the medical profession in the Queen's College, Cork, spent some time in France, and subsequently visited America, where he made the acquaintance of the chief organisers of the Fenian movement, by whom he was regarded as a most valuable acquisition to the ranks of the brotherhood. After his return to Ireland he continued to render the Fenian cause such services as lay in his power, and when James Stephens, who knew his courage and ability, invited him to take the post of chief editor of the Fenian organ which he was about to establish in Dublin, O'Leary readily obeyed the call, and accepted the dangerous position. In the columns of *The Irish People* he laboured hard to defend and extend the principles of the Fenian organisation until the date of his arrest and the suppression of the paper.

The trial lasted from Friday, the 1st, up to Wednesday, the 6th of December, when it was closed with a verdict of guilty and a sentence of twenty years' penal servitude – Mr Justice Fitzgerald remarking that no distinction in the degree of criminality could be discovered between the case of the prisoner and that of the previous convict. The following is the address delivered by O'Leary, who appeared to labour under much excitement, when asked in the usual terms if he had any reason to show why sentence should not be passed upon him: –

'I was not wholly unprepared for this verdict, because I felt that the government which could so safely pack the bench could not fail to make sure of its verdict.'

Mr Justice Fitzgerald – 'We are willing to hear anything in reason from you, but we cannot allow language of that kind to be used.'

Mr O'Leary – 'My friend Mr Luby did not wish to touch on this matter from a natural fear lest he should do any harm to the other political prisoners; but there can be but little fear of that now, for a jury has been found to convict me of this conspiracy upon the evidence. Mr Luby admitted that he was technically guilty according to British law; but I say that it is only by the most torturing interpretation that these men could make out their case against me. With reference to this conspiracy there has been much misapprehension in Ireland, and serious misapprehension. Mr Justice Keogh said in his charge against Mr Luby that men would be always found ready for money, or for some other motive, to place themselves at the disposal of the government; but I think the men who have been generally bought in this way, and who certainly made the best of the bargain, were agitators and not rebels. I have to say one word in reference to the foul charge upon which that miserable man, Barry, has made me responsible.'

Mr Justice Fitzgerald – 'We cannot allow that tone of observation.'

Mr O'Leary continued – 'That man has charged me – I need not defend myself or my friends from the charge. I shall merely denounce the moral assassin. Mr Justice Keogh the other day spoke of revolutions, and administered a lecture to Mr Luby. He spoke of cattle being driven away, and of houses being burned down, that men would be killed, and so on. I would like to know if all that does not apply to war as well as to revolution?

'One word more and I shall have done. I have been found guilty of treason or treason-felony. Treason is a foul crime. The poet Dante consigned traitors to, I believe, the ninth circle of hell; but what kind of traitors? Traitors against king, against country, against friends and benefactors. England is not my country; I have betrayed no friend, no benefactor. I leave the matter there.'

One hour after the utterance of these words John O'Leary, dressed in convict garb, his hair clipped, and his beard shaved off, was the occupant of a cell in Mountjoy prison, commencing his long term of suffering in expiation of the crime of having sought to obtain self-government for his native land.

The Manchester Martyrs[*]

The Manchester Martyrs! Who were they? A few words will tell.

Two members of the Fenian organisation – Kelly and Deasy – were trapped in Manchester, and lay awaiting trial in an English prison. The Fenians in that city resolved to rescue them. This they did by stopping the prison van upon the road between Manchester and Salford, breaking open the van, shooting a policeman in the act, and carrying off their comrades under the very eyes of the English authorities.

Out of a number of men arrested for complicity in the deed, three were hanged. These three were ALLEN, LARKIN and O'BRIEN – the three Manchester Martyrs whose memory we honour today. Why do we honour them?

We honour them because of their heroic souls. Let us remember that by every test by which parties in Ireland to-day measure political wisdom, or personal prudence, the act of these men ought to be condemned. They were in a hostile city, surrounded by a hostile population; they were playing into the hands of the Government by bringing all the Fenians out in broad daylight to be spotted and remembered; they were discouraging the Irish people by giving them another failure to record; they had no hopes of foreign help even if their brothers in Ireland took the field spurred by their action; at the most their action would only be an Irish riot in an English city; and finally, they were imperilling the whole organisation for the sake of two men. These were all the sound sensible arguments of the prudent, practical politicians and theoretical revolutionists. But 'how beggarly appear words before a defiant deed!'

The Fenians of Manchester rose superior to all the whines about prudence, caution and restraint, and saw only two of their countrymen struck at for loyalty to freedom, and seeing this,

---

[*] James Connolly, *The Workers' Republic*, 20 November 1915.

struck back at the enemy with blows that are still resounding through the heart of the world. The echo of those blows has for a generation been as a baptismal dedication to the soul and life of thousands of Irish men and women, consecrating them to the service of freedom.

Had Kelly and Deasy been struck at in our time, we would not have startled the world by the vehemence of our blow in return; we would not have sent out the call for a muster of our hosts to peril all in their rescue. No, we would simply have instructed our typist to look up the office files and see if they had paid up their subscription in the Cumann Cosanta, and were entitled to their insurance benefit.

Thus we have progressed in the path of civilised methods, far, far away from the undisciplined hatred and reckless fighting of the '67 men. MORYAH![†]

ALLEN, LARKIN and O'BRIEN died that the right of their small nationality to independence might be attested by their blood – died that some day an Irish Republic might live. The song of their martyrdom was written by a man who had laboured hard to prevent the fruition of their hopes; the prayer of their last moments has become the hackneyed catch word of every political Judas seeking to betray their cause. Everything associated with them has been stolen or corrupted, except the imperishable example of their 'defiant deed'. Of that neither men, devils, nor doubters can deprive us.

Oh, the British Empire is great and strong and powerful compared with Ireland. 'Tis true that compared with Germany the Empire is a doddering old miser confronted with a lusty youth, a miser whose only hope is to purchase the limbs and bodies of others to protect her stolen properties. 'Tis true that the Empire cannot stand up alone to any European power, that she must have allies or perish. 'Tis true that even with allies her military and financial system is cracking at every point, sweating

† *Moryah:* as if, like fun.

blood in fear at every pore. But still all the stolen property that England possesses our Irish forefathers have helped to steal and we are helping to defend.

Was it wise then, or commendable, for the men of '67 to rebel against the Empire that their and our fathers have helped to build or steal? There are thousands of answers to that question, but let the European battlefields of today provide the one all-sufficient answer.

All these mountains of Irish dead, all these corpses mangled beyond recognition, all these arms, legs, eyes, ears, fingers, toes, hands, all these shivering putrefying bodies and portions of bodies – once warm living and tender parts of Irish men and youths – all these horrors buried in Flanders or the Gallipoli Peninsula, are all items in the price Ireland pays for being part of the British Empire. All these widows whose husbands were torn from their sides and forced to go to war, their prayers and tears for the ones who will return no more, are another part of the price of Empire. All those fatherless orphans, who for the last time have heard the cheery laugh of an affectionate father, and who must for years suffer all the bitter hardships of a childhood poorly provided for against want and hunger – all those and their misery are part of the price Ireland pays for Empire. All those shattered, maimed and diseased wrecks of humanity who for years will crowd our poorhouses and asylums, or crawl along our roads and streets affronting our health by their wounds, and our comfort by their appeals for charity – all, all are part of the price Ireland pays for the glory of being an integral part of the British Empire.

And for what do we pay this price? Answer, ye practical ones! Ye men of sense, of prudence, of moderation, of business capacity!

Ireland is rotten with slums, a legacy of Empire. The debt of this war will prevent us from getting money to replace them with sound clean, healthy homes. Every big gun fired in the

Dardanelles fired away at every shot the cost of building a home for a working class family. Ireland has the most inefficient educational system, and the poorest schools in Europe. Empire compels us to pay pounds for blowing out the brains of others for every farthing it allows us with which to train our own.

An Empire on which the sun never sets cannot guarantee its men and women as much comfort as is enjoyed by the every-day citizen of the smallest, least military nation in Europe. Nations that know not the power and possessions of Empire have happier, better educated, better housed, better equipped men and women than Ireland has ever known, or can ever know as an integral part of the British Empire.

The British Empire is a piratical enterprise in which the velour of slaves fights for the glory and profit of their masters. The Home Rule Party aspire to be trusted accomplices of that conspiracy, the Manchester Martyrs were its unyielding foes even to the dungeon and the scaffold. Therefore we honour the memory of the Manchester Martyrs. As future generations shall honour them.

The Wearing of the Green
The Manchester Martyrs[*]

The news of the Manchester executions on the morning of Saturday, 23rd November 1867, fell upon Ireland with sudden and dismal disillusion.

In time to come, when the generation now living shall have passed away, men will probably find it difficult to fully realise or understand the state of stupor and amazement which ensued in this country on the first tidings of that event; seeing that the victims had lain for weeks under sentence of death, to be ex-

[*] *Wearing of the Green or The Prosecuted Funeral Procession* (1868), A.M. Sullivan.

ecuted on this date. A great billow of grief rose and surged from end to end of the land. Political distinctions disappeared or were forgotten. The Manchester Victims – the Manchester Martyrs they were already called – belonged to the Fenian organisation; a conspiracy which the wisest and truest patriots of Ireland had condemned and resisted; yet men who had been prominent in withstanding that hopeless and disastrous scheme – priests and laymen – were now amongst the foremost in denouncing the savage act of vengeance perpetrated at Manchester. The Catholic clergy were the first to give articulate expression to the national emotion. The executions took place on Saturday; before night the telegraph had spread the news through the island and on the next morning, being Sunday, from a thousand altars the sad event was announced to the assembled worshippers.

Prayers were publicly offered for the souls of the victims. When the news was announced, a moan of sorrowful surprise burst from the congregation, followed by the wailing and sobbing of women. When the priest, his own voice broken with emotion, asked all to join with him in praying to the Merciful God to grant those young victims a place beside His throne, the assemblage with one voice responded, praying and weeping aloud!

No stormy 'indignation meetings' were held. No tumult, no violence, no cries for vengeance arose. In all probability all this would have happened had the victims not passed into eternity. But now, they were gone where prayer alone could follow and in the presence of this solemn fact the religious sentiment overbore all others with the Irish people.

Cries of anger and threats of vengeance could not avail the dead but, happily, religion gave a vent to the pent-up feelings of the living. By prayer and mourning they could at once demonstrate their horror of the guilty deed. Requiem Masses were announced and celebrated in several churches and were attended by crowds everywhere too vast for the sacred edifices to contain. The churches in several instances were draped with black, and the ceremonies conducted with more than ordinary solemnity. In every case, however, the authorities of the Catholic church were careful to ensure that the sacred functions were attended for spiritual considerations, not used for illegitimate political purposes.

Soon public feeling found yet another vent; a mode of manifesting itself; namely, funeral processions. The brutal vengeance of the law consigned the bodies of Allen, Larkin, and O'Brien to dishonoured graves and forbade the presence of sympathising friend or sorrowing relative who might drop a tear above their mutilated remains. Their countrymen, however, determined that ample atonement should be made to the memory of the dead for this denial of the decencies of sepulture.

On Sunday, 1st December, in Cork, Manchester, Mitchelstown, Midleton, Limerick, and Skibbereen, funeral processions, at which thousands of persons attended, were held. That in Cork being admittedly the most imposing, not only in point of numbers, but in the character of the demonstration and the demeanour of the people. For more than twenty years Cork city has held an advanced position in the Irish national struggle. In truth, it has been one of the great strongholds of the national cause since 1848. Nowhere else did the national spirit keep its hold so tenaciously amidst the people. In 1848 Cork city contained probably the most formidable organisation in the country; formidable, not merely in numbers, but in the superior intelligence, earnestness, and determination of the men. Even in the Fenian conspiracy, it is unquestionable that the southern capital contributed to that movement men – chiefly belonging to the mercantile and commercial classes – who, in personal worth and standing, as well as in courage, intelligence, and patriotism, were the flower of the organisation. Finally, it must be said, that it was Cork city by its funeral demonstration of the 1st December that struck the first great blow at the Manchester verdict, and set all Ireland in motion.

Meanwhile the Irish capital had moved, and was organising a demonstration destined to surpass all that had yet been witnessed. Early in the second week of December a committee was formed for the purpose of organising a funeral procession in Dublin worthy of the national metropolis. Dublin would have come forward sooner but the question of the legality of the processions that were announced to come off the previous week in Cork and other places, had been the subject of fierce discussion in the government press and the national leaders were determined to avoid the slightest infringement of the law or the least inroad on the public peace.

It was only when, on the 3rd of December, Lord Derby, the Prime Minister, declared the opinion of the crown that the projected processions were not illegal, that the national party in Dublin decided to form a committee and organise a procession. The following were Lord Derby's words:

> The government would continue to carry out the law with firmness and impartiality. The Party Processions Act, however, did not meet the case of the funeral processions, the parties engaged in them having, by not displaying banners or other emblems, kept within the law as far as his information went.

The Dublin funeral committee thereupon at once issued the following announcement, by placard and advertisement:

GOD SAVE IRELAND!
A PUBLIC FUNERAL PROCESSION

In honour of the Irish Patriots Executed at Manchester, 23rd November, Will take place in Dublin on Sunday next, the 8th inst.
The procession will assemble in Beresford Place, near the Custom House, and will start from thence at the hour of twelve o'clock noon.
No flags, banners, or party emblems will be allowed.

IRISHMEN
Assemble in your thousands, and show by your numbers and your orderly demeanour your sympathy with the fate of the executed patriots.

IRISHWOMEN

You are requested to lend the dignity of your presence to this important National Demonstration.

By Order of the Committee.
JOHN MARTIN, Chairman. J.C. WATERS, Hon. Secretary.
JAMES
SCANLAN, Hon. Secretary. J.J. LALOR, Hon. Secretary. DONAL
SULLIVAN, Up. Buckingham Street, Treasurer.

The appearance of the 'funeral procession placards' all over the city on Thursday, 5th December, increased the public excitement.* No other topic was discussed in any place of public resort, but the event forthcoming on Sunday. The first evidence of what it was about to be, was the appearance of the drapery establishments in the city on Saturday morning. The windows, exteriorly and interiorly, being one mass of crape and green ribbon – funeral knots, badges, scarves, hat-bands, neckties, etc.,

---

* Owen McGee, in his 2001 *Eire Ireland* essay '"God save Ireland": Manchester Martyr demonstrations in Dublin, 1867–1916', writes that, 'Only one of the four men on the organising committee was an IRB man, although IRB men played an important part in marshalling the procession. Immediately after the success of this demonstration Dublin Castle ordered the arrest of a handful of its participants and prohibited the holding of similar demonstrations throughout the United Kingdom.' McGee identifies Dr J. C. Waters as the IRB man. John Martin, who gave the speech at Glasnevin cemetery which ended the procession/protest, was a Young Ireland veteran hostile to the Fenians. Martin's family had been Presbyterian landlords near Newry, and the plight of his tenants during the Famine drove him towards John Mitchel. When Mitchel was arrested Martin founded a journal called *The Irish Felon* in which many of Fintan Lalor's polemics appeared. In May 1848 he was arrested and sent to Van Diemen's Land with a ten year sentence. Before he was sentenced he said, 'I thought there should be an end to that horrible system which while it lasted gave me no peace of mind, for I could not enjoy anything in my country so long as I saw my countrymen forced to be vicious, forced to hate each other, and degraded to the level of paupers and brutes. This is the reason I engaged in politics'. He served his sentence and in 1854 he moved to Paris before returning to Ireland in 1856. He became active in the Tenant Right League, wrote for *The Nation*, and established the National League which brought him into conflict with the Fenians. He was one of those briefly arrested after the Dublin Manchester Martyrs funeral procession. In 1871 Martin was elected Home Rule MP for Meath. Known as Honest John Martin, he was regarded in his locality as being a good landlord. He died in 1875, effectively broke and homeless, having declined to collect rents from his tenants when times were tough. His seat went, after a by-election, to Charles Stewart Parnell.

exposed for sale.* Before noon most of the retail, and several of the wholesale houses had their entire stock of green ribbon and crape exhausted, it being computed that nearly one hundred thousand yards had been sold up to midnight of Saturday! Meantime the committee appointing stewards, marshals, etc. – in a word, completing the numerous details on the perfection of which it greatly depended whether Sunday was to witness a successful demonstration or a scene of disastrous disorder. The trades of Dublin, Kingstown, and Dalkey exhibited that spirit of patriotism for which they have been proverbial in our generation. From their ranks came the most efficient aids in every department of the preparations. On Saturday evening the carpenters, in a body, immediately after their day's work was over, instead of seeking home and rest, turned into *The Nation* office machine rooms, which they quickly improvised into a vast workshop, and there, as volunteers, laboured away till near midnight, manufacturing 'wands' for the stewards of next morning's procession.

Sunday, 8th December 1867, dawned through watery skies. From shortly after daybreak, rain, or rather half-melted sleet, continued to fall. Many persons concluded that there would be no attempt to hold the procession under such inclement weather. This circumstance was, no doubt, a grievous discouragement but so far from preventing the procession, it was destined to add a hundredfold to the significance and importance of the demonstration. Had the day been fine, tens of thousands of persons who eventually only lined the streets, wearing the funeral emblems, would have marched in the procession as they had originally intended but hostile critics would in this case have said that the fineness of the day and the excitement of the pageant had merely caused a hundred thousand persons to come out for a holiday.

Now, however, the depth, reality, and intensity of the popular feeling was about to be keenly tested. The subjoined account of this

* *Crape*: from the French crêpe. A silk fabric dyed black and widely used at funerals.

memorable demonstration is summarised from the Dublin daily papers, the report of the *Freeman's Journal* being chiefly used:

As early as ten o'clock crowds began to gather in Beresford Place, and in an hour about ten thousand men were present. Drizzling rain fell with persistence. The early trains from Kingstown and Dalkey and all the townlands brought large numbers into Dublin. Westland Row, Brunswick, D'Olier, and Sackville Streets streamed with masses of humanity. A great number of the processionists met in Earlsfort Terrace, and at twelve o'clock some thousands had collected. It was not easy to learn the object of this gathering. It may have been a mistake, and most probably it was, as they fell in with the great body in the course of half an hour. The space from the quays, including the great sweep in front of the Custom House, was swarming with men, and women, and small children, and the big ungainly crowd bulged out in Gardiner Street and the broad space leading up Talbot Street.

The ranks began to be formed at eleven o'clock amid a downpour of cold rain. The mud was deep and aqueous, and great pools ran through the streets almost level with the paths. Some of the more prominent of the men, and several of the committee, rode about directing and organising the crowd, which presented a most extraordinary appearance. A couple of thousand young children stood quietly in the rain and slush for over an hour while behind them, in close-packed numbers, were over two thousand young women.

Not the least blame can be attached to those who managed the affairs of the day, inasmuch as the throng must have far exceeded even their most optimistic expectations. Long before twelve o'clock, the streets converging on the square were packed with spectators or intending processionists. Cabs struggled hopelessly to yield up the large number of highly respectable and well-attired ladies who had come to walk. Those who had hired vehicles for the day to join the procession were convinced of the impracticable character of their intention and many delicate old men, who would not give up the design, braved the terrors of asthma and bronchitis and joined the rain-defying throng. All the windows in Beresford Place were filled with spectators, and the rain and cold seemed to have no saddening effect on the numerous multitude. The various bands of the trade were being disposed in their respective positions, and the hearses were a long way off and altogether in the background, when, at a quarter to twelve, the first rank of men moved forward. Almost everyone had an umbrella, but they were thoroughly saturated with the never-ceasing downpour. As the steady, well-kept, twelve-deep ranks moved slowly out, some ease was given to those pent up behind and it was really wonderful to see the facility with which the people adapted themselves to the orders of their directors.

Every chance of falling in was seized, and soon the procession was in motion. The first five hundred men were of the artisan class. They were dressed very respectably, and each man wore upon his left shoulder a green rosette, and on his left arm a band of crape. Others had close crape intertwined carefully with green ribbon around their hats and the great majority of the better sort adhered to this plan, which was executed with a skill unmistakably feminine.

Here and there at intervals a man appeared with a broad green scarf around his shoulders, some embroidered with shamrocks, and others decorated with harps. There was not a man throughout the procession but was conspicuous by some emblem of nationality. Appointed officers walked at the sides with wands in their hands and gently kept back the interested crowd whose sympathy was certainly demonstrative. Behind the five hundred men came a couple of thousand young children. These excited, perhaps, the most considerable interest amongst the bystanders, whether sympathetic, neutral, or opposite. Of tender age and innocent of opinions on any subject, they were being marshalled by their parents in a demonstration which will probably give a tone to their career hereafter; and seeds in the juvenile mind ever bear fruit in due season. The presence of these shivering little ones gave a serious significance to the procession – they were hostages to the party who had organised the demonstration. Earnestness must indeed have been strong in the mind of the parent who directed his little son or daughter to walk in saturating rain and painful cold through five or six miles of mud and water, and all this merely to say 'I and my children were there'. It portends something more than sentiment. It is national education with a vengeance.

After the children came about one hundred young women who had been unable to gain their proper position, and accepted the place which chance assigned them. They were succeeded by a band dressed very respectably. These were followed by a number of rather elderly men, probably the parents of the children far ahead. At this portion of the procession, a mile from the point, they marched four deep, there having been a gradual decline from the front.

Next came the bricklayers' band all dressed in green caps, a very superior-looking body of men. Then followed a very imposing well-kept line, composed of young men of the better class, well attired and respectable looking. These wore crape hat-bands, and green rosettes with harps in the centre. Several had broad green body scarves, with gold tinsel shamrocks and harps intertwined. As this portion of the procession marched they attracted very considerable attention by their orderly, measured tread, and the almost soldierly precision with which they maintained the line. They numbered about four or five thousand, and there were few who were not young, sinewy, stalwart fellows. When they had reached the further end of Abbey Street, the ground about Beresford Place was gradually becoming clear.

All round the Custom House was still packed a dense throng, and large streams were flowing from the northern districts, Clontarf, the Strand, and the quays. The shipping was gaily decorated, and many of the masts were filled with young tars wearing green bands on their hats.* At half-past twelve the most interesting portion of the procession left the Custom House. About two thousand young women, who in attire, demeanour, and general appearance, certainly justified their title to be called ladies, walked in six-deep ranks. The general public kept pace with them for a great distance. The green was most demonstrative, every lady having shawl, bonnet, veil, dress, or mantle of the national hue. The mud made sad havoc of their attire, but notwithstanding all mishaps they maintained good order. They stretched for over half a mile, and added notably to the imposing appearance of the procession. So great was the pressure in Abbey Street, that for a very long time there were no less than three processions walking side-by-side.

One of the bands was about to play near the Abbey Street Wesleyan House, but when a policeman told them of the proximity of the place of worship, they immediately desisted. The first hearse was a very long way back in the line, and the foremost men must have been near Ormond Quay, when the four horses moved into Abbey Street. They were draped with black cloths and white plumes were at their heads. The hearse also had white plumes, and was covered with black palls. On the side was 'William P. Allen.' A number of men followed, and then came a band. In the earlier portion of the day there were seen but two hearses, the second one bearing Larkin's name. It was succeeded by four mourning coaches, drawn by two horses each.

In this throng were very many men of business, large employers, and members of the professions. Several of the trades were in great force. It had been arranged to have the trade banners carried in front of the artisans of every calling, but at the suggestion

* *Tar:* sailor.

of the chairman this design was abandoned. The men walked, however, in considerable strength. They marched from their various committee-rooms to the Custom House. The quay porters were present to the number of 500, and presented a very orderly, clean appearance. They were comfortably dressed, and walked close after the hearse bearing Larkin's name. Around this bier were a number of men bearing in their hands long and waving palms – emblems of martyrdom. The trades came next, and were led off by the various branches of the association known as the Amalgamated Trades. The plasterers made about 300, the painters 350, the boot and shoemakers mustered 1,000, the bricklayers 500, the carpenters 300, the slaters 450, the sawyers 200, and the skinners, coopers, tailors, bakers, and the other trades, made a very respectable show, both as to numbers and appearance.

The whole ground near the starting place was clear at half-past one, and by that time the demonstration was seen to a greater advantage than previously. All down Abbey Street the pathways were crowded by persons who were practically of it, though not in it. Very many young girls naturally enough preferred to stand on the pathways rather than to be saturated with mud and water. Cabs filled with ladies and gentlemen remained at the waysides all day watching the march. The horses' heads were gaily decorated with green ribbons, while every Jehu† in the city wore a rosette or a crape band. Nothing of special note occurred until the procession turned into Dame Street. The appearance of the demonstration was here far greater than at any other portion of the city. Both sides of the street, and as far as Carlisle Bridge, were lined with cabs and carriages filled with spectators who were prevented by the bitter day from taking an active part in proceedings. The procession was here grandly imposing, and after Larkin's hearse were no less than nine carriages, and several cabs.

The cavalry were in readiness for action, if necessary. Mounted military and police orderlies were stationed at various points of

† Jew.

the city. The constabulary at the depot, Phoenix Park, were also prepared. At police stations throughout the city large numbers of men were kept all day under arms. It is pleasant to state that no interference was necessary, as the great demonstration terminated without the slightest disturbance. The public houses generally remained closed until five o'clock, and the sobriety of the crowds was the subject of the general comment.[*]

From an early hour in the morning every possible position along the quays that afforded a good view of the procession was taken advantage of, and, despite the inclemency of the weather, the parapets of the various bridges, commencing at Capel Street, were crowded with adventurous youths who seemed to think nothing of the risks they ran in comparison with the opportunities they had of seeing the great sight in all its splendour. Sidewalks were crowded and impassable. The lower windows of the houses were made the most of by men who clutched the shutters and bars, whilst the upper windows were, as a general rule, filled with the fair sex. The women wore green ribbons and veils, and many entire dresses of the favourite colour. The numerous windows of the Four Courts accommodated hundreds of ladies and within the building were two pieces of artillery, a plentiful supply of rockets, and a number of policemen. It was arranged that the rockets should be fired from the roof in case military assistance was required.

The head of the procession appeared at Essex Bridge shortly before twelve. As it was expected to leave Beresford Place about that time, and as such gigantic arrangements are seldom carried out punctually, the thousands of people who congregated in this locality were pleasantly disappointed when a society band

---

[*] The author of this account, A. M. Sullivan, was a celebrated anti-liquor temperance campaigner. Sullivan was not exactly an impartial reporter upon this event. In fact he was one of the distinguished businessmen, mentioned here, who marched at the head of the demonstration. He was also the proprietor of *The Nation*, whose works were temporarily turned over to the funeral's organisers. The Fenians loathed Sullivan, and were not alone in this regard.

turned the corner of Mary Street and came towards the quays, with the processionists marching in slow and regular time. The order that prevailed was almost marvellous – not a sound was heard but the mournful strains of the music.

The procession passed along the quays as far as Kingsbridge. About one o'clock the head of the procession burst like confined water when relieved of restraint, on entering James Street, where every window and doorstep was crowded.

The music of the 'Dead March in Saul', heard in the distance, caused the people to break from the lines in which they had partially stood awaiting the arrival of the procession, which now, for the first time, began to assume its full proportions. As it moved along the quays at the north side of the river, every street, bridge, and laneway served to obstruct to a considerable extent its progress and its order, owing to interruption from carriage traffic and from the crowds that poured into it and swelled it in its onward course. In the vast multitudes that lined this great western artery of the city, the greatest order and propriety were observed, and all seemed to be impressed with the one solemn and all-pervading idea that they were assembled to express their deep sympathy with the fate of three men whom they believed had been condemned and had suffered death unjustly.

Even amongst the young there was not the slightest levity. The old characteristics of a great Irish gathering were not to be perceived anywhere. The wrong, whether real or imaginary, done to Allen, O'Brien, and Larkin, made their memory sacred with the thousands that stood for hours in the December wet and cold to testify by their presence their feelings and their sympathies. Horsemen wearing green rosettes, trimmed with crape, who rode in advance of the procession, kept back the crowds at either side that encroached on the space in the centre of the street required for the vast coming mass to move through. On it came, the advance with measured tread, to the music of the band in front, and notwithstanding the mire which had to be waded through, the line went on at a quiet pace, and with admirable order. There was no effort at anything like semi-military swagger or pompous demonstration.

The cortege at this point looked grand and solemn in the extreme because of its vastness. The gloomy, wet, and cheerless weather was quite in keeping with the funeral march of 35,000 people. The bands were placed at such proper distances that the playing of one did not interfere with the other.

After passing James' Gate the band in front ceased to perform, and on passing the house on Thomas Street every head was uncovered in honour of Lord Edward Fitzgerald, who was arrested and mortally wounded in the front bedroom of the second floor of that house.

When Allen, O'Brien, and Larkin were condemned to death as political offenders, some of the highest and the noblest in the land warned the government to pause before the extreme penalty pronounced on the condemned men would be carried into effect, but all remonstrance was in vain and last Saturday fortnight, three comparatively unknown men in their death passed into the ranks of heroes and martyrs, because it was believed, and believed generally, that their lives were sacrificed to expediency.

The spot where Robert Emmet closed his young life on a bloody scaffold was yesterday regarded by thousands upon thousands of his countrymen and women as a holy place, and all looked upon his fate as similar to that of the three men whose memory they had assembled to honour, and whose death they pronounced to be unjust. As if by some secret and uncontrollable impulse a mighty, ringing, and enthusiastic cheer, broke from the moving throng as the angle of the footway at the eastern end of St Catherine's church, where the scaffold on which Emmet was executed stood, was passed. In that cheer there appeared to be no fiction, as it evidently came straight from the hearts of thousands, who waved their hats. As the procession moved on, from every part of it the cheers rose again and again, men holding up their children, and pointing out the place where one who loved Ireland, 'not wisely but too well,' rendered up his life. When the hearse with white plumes came up bearing on the side draperies the words 'William P. Allen', all the enthusiasm and excitement ceased, and along the lines of spectators prayers for the repose of the soul of the departed man passed from mouth to mouth; and a sense of deep sadness seemed to settle down on the swaying multitude as the procession rolled along on its way. After this hearse came large numbers of females walking on bravely, apparently heedless of the muddy streets and the unceasing rain that came down without a moment's intermission. When the second hearse, bearing white plumes and the name of 'Michael O'Brien' on the side pendants, came up, again all heads were uncovered, and prayers recited by the people for the everlasting rest of the departed. As the third hearse, with sable plumes, came up bearing at either side the name of 'Michael Larkin', prayers for his soul's welfare were mingled with expressions of commiseration for his widow and children.

The procession again reached the quays, and moved along Wood Quay and Essex Quay, and into Parliament Street, which it reached at twenty minutes to two. Passing down Parliament Street, and approaching the O'Connell statue, a number of persons began to cheer, but this was promptly suppressed by the leaders, who galloped in advance for some distance with a view to the preservation of the mournful silence that had prevailed. The reverential manner in which many thousands of people passed the statue of the Liberator was very observable. A rather heavy rain was falling at the time, yet there were thousands who uncovered their heads as they looked up to the statue which expressed the noble attitude and features of O'Connell. As the procession moved along through Dame Street the footways became blocked up, and lines of cabs took up places in the middle of the carriageway, and the police exercised a wise discretion in preventing vehicles from the surrounding streets driving in amongst the crowds. By this means the danger of serious accident was prevented without any public inconvenience being occasioned, as a line parallel to that which the procession was taking was kept clear for all horse conveyances. Owing to the hour growing late, and a considerable distance still to be gone over, the procession moved at a quick pace.

In anticipation of its arrival great crowds collected in the vicinity of the Bank of Ireland and Trinity College, where the cortege was kept well together, notwithstanding the difficulty of such a vast mass passing on through the heart of the city filled at this point with immense masses of spectators. On passing the old Parliament House numbers of men in the procession took off their hats, but the disposition to cheer was suppressed, as it was at several other points along the route.

Turning down Westmoreland Street the procession passed slowly along between the thick files of people on each side. Passing the bridge, a glance to the right, down the river, revealed the fact that the ships, almost without exception, had their flags flying half mast high, and that the rigging of several were filled with seamen. Here the sight was imposing. A throng of spectators lined each side of the magnificent thoroughfare, and the lofty houses had their windows on each side occupied with spectators. Pressing onwards with measured, steady pace, regardless of the heavy rain, the cold wind, and the gloomy sky, the procession soon filled Sackville Street from end to end with its dense dark mass which, stretching away over Carlisle Bridge, seemed motionless in the distance.

It progressed towards Cavendish Row. Through this comparatively narrow thoroughfare the procession passed along into North Frederick Street and Blessington Street, and thence by Upper Berkeley Street to the Circular Road. As the first part of the array passed the Mater Hospital, and came in sight of the Mountjoy Prison, they gave a cheer, which was caught up by those behind, and as file after file passed the prison the cheers were repeated.

With unbroken and undiminished ranks the procession pressed on towards Glasnevin; but when the head had reached the cemetery, the closing section must have been far away in the city.

The first part of the procession halted outside the gate of the cemetery, the spacious area in front of which was in a few moments completely filled by the dense masses who came up. A move then became necessary, and accordingly the procession recommenced its journey by passing through the open gates of the cemetery down the pathways leading to the McManus grave, followed by some of the bands playing the *Adeste Fidelis*. As fast as the files passed through others marched up, and when, after some time, the carriage containing Mr John Martin arrived, the open ground fronting the cemetery was one enormous mass of the processionists, while behind on the road leading up to this point thousands were to be seen moving slowly forward to the strains of the 'Dead March', given out by the bands immediately in front of the hearses.

MR MARTIN'S ADDRESS

On the arrival of the procession at the cemetery Mr Martin was hailed with loud applause. It being understood he would make some observations, the multitude gathered together to hear him. He addressed the vast multitude from the window of a house overlooking the great open space in front of the cemetery. On presenting himself he was received with enthusiastic cheering. When silence was obtained he said:

Fellow countrymen – This is a strange kind of funeral procession in which we are engaged today. We are here, a vast multitude of men, women, and children in a very inclement season of the year, under rain and through mud. We are here escorting three empty hearses to the consecrated last resting place of those who die in the Lord (cheers). The three bodies that we would tenderly bear to the churchyard, and would bury in consecrated ground with all the solemn rites of religion, are not here. They are away in a foreign and hostile land (hear, hear) where they have been thrown into unconsecrated ground, branded by the triumphant hatred of our enemies as the vile remains of murderers (cries of 'no murderers', and cheers).

Those three men whose memories we are here today to honour – Allen, O'Brien, and Larkin – they were not murderers (great cheering). [A Voice – Lord have mercy on them.] Mr Martin: These men were pious men, virtuous men. They were men who feared God and loved their country. They sorrowed for the sorrows of the dear old native land of their love (hear, hear). They wished, if possible, to save her, and for that love and for that wish they were doomed to an ignominious death at the hands of the British hangman (hear, hear). It was as Irish patriots that these men were doomed to death (cheers). And it was as Irish patriots that they met their death (cheers). For these reasons, my countrymen, we here today have joined in this solemn procession to honour their memories (cheers). For that reason we say from our hearts, 'May their souls rest in peace' (cries of Amen, and cheers). For that reason, my countrymen, we join in their last prayer, 'God save Ireland' (enthusiastic cheering).

The death of these three men was an act of English policy. [Here there was some interruption caused by the fresh arrivals and the pushing forward.] I beg of all within reach of my voice to end this demonstration as we have carried it through to the present time, with admirable patience, in the best spirit, with respect, silence and solemnity, to the end (cheers, and cries of 'we will').

Through all these years the Irish people continued to pray for the restoration of their Irish national rule. They offered their forgiveness to England. They offered even their friendship to England if she would only give up her usurped power to tyrannise over us, and leave us to live in peace, and as honourable

196

neighbours. But in vain. England felt herself strong enough to continue to insult and rob us, and she was too greedy and too insolent to cease from robbing and insulting us (cheers).

Now it has come to pass as a consequence of that malignant policy pursued for so many long years – it has come to pass that the great body of the Irish people despair of obtaining peaceful restitution of our national rights (cheers). And it has also come to pass that vast numbers of Irishmen, whom the oppression of English rule forbade to live by honest industry in their own country, have in America learned to become soldiers (cheers). And those Irish soldiers seem resolved to make war against England (cheers). And England is in a panic of rage and fear in consequence of this (loud cheers). And being in a panic about Fenianism, she hopes to strike terror into her Irish malcontents by a legal murder (loud cheers). England wanted to show that she was not afraid of Fenianism [A Voice: 'She will be']. And she has only shown that she is not afraid to do injustice in the face of Heaven and of man. Many a wicked statute she has framed, many a jury she has packed, in order to dispose of her Irish political offenders but in the case of Allen, O'Brien, and Larkin, she has committed such an outrage on justice and decency as to make even many Englishmen stand aghast. When the three men – our dearly beloved Irish brethren – were forced to give up their innocent lives as a sacrifice for the cause of Ireland (loud cheers); and, fellow-countrymen, these three humble Irishmen who represented Ireland on that sad occasion behaved themselves as Christians, as patriots, modestly, courageously, piously, nobly (loud cheers). We need not blush for them. They bore themselves all through with a courage worthy of the greatest heroes that ever obtained glory upon earth. They behaved through all the trying scenes I referred to with Christian patience – with resignation to the will of God – (hear, hear) – with modest, yet proud and firm adherence to principle (cheers). They showed their love to Ireland and their fear of God from the first to the last (cheers).

You have behaved yourselves all through this day with most admirable spirit as good Irishmen and women, as good boys and girls of holy Ireland ought to be (cheers). You will return home with the same good order and inoffensiveness. You will join with me now in repeating the prayer of the three martyrs whom we mourn. 'God save Ireland!'

Mr Martin concluded amid enthusiastic cheering. Accompanied by a large body of the processionists, he proceeded to the cemetery, where he visited the grave of Terence Bellew McManus. The crowds walked around the grave as a mark of respect for the memory of McManus. Mr Martin left the cemetery soon after and went to his carriage. The people gathered about him and thanked him, and cheered him loudly. The vast assemblage dispersed in the most orderly and peaceful manner, and returned to their homes.

REBEL FENIAN SONGS[*]

Catalpa and *The Fenian Escape* celebrate the rescue of Fenian prisoners, exiled to Australia, by a boat, *Catalpa*, which was manned by Irish and American sailors. The IRB/Clan na Gael supremo John Devoy masterminded the rescue.

J. J. Breslin, a charismatic champion who organised James Stephens' escape from Richmond, was in charge of the Australian end of the *Catalpa* mission. A New England Quaker, Captain George Anthony and his first mate, Sam Smith, were in charge of the boat and the escape at sea. The six escapees included the future Invincible John Walsh.

Catalpa was collected in 1957 from a Perth journalist who said, 'I remember in my early days as a cadet hearing a band of old boys in a pub in Fremantle singing this song. It is said that

[*] Joe Ambrose.

the song became so popular that it was banned by the author-ity of the day and jail was threatened to anyone caught singing it. It was suggested, too, that the escape was made easy because there was plenty of American gold and some of it was placed in the hands of unscrupulous warders. The incident took place in April 1876.'

Peadar Kearney, IRB man, author of the Irish national an-them, and the uncle of writer Brendan Behan wrote *The Bold Fenian Men* around the time of the 1916 Rising; it was per-formed by the Sons of the Pioneers in John Ford's 1950 film, *Rio Grande*.

God Save Ireland was the unofficial Irish national anthem until Peadar Kearney's *Soldier's Song* was adopted in 1926. The song was written by T. D. Sullivan – A. M.'s brother and busi-ness partner – in 1867 to commemorate and immortalise the Manchester Martyrs. John McCormack recorded the song in 1906 and, in the 1960s, Luke Kelly and the Dubliners took it in hand. It remains hugely popular on football terraces and in the popular imagination.

Catalpa

A noble whale ship and commander
Called the *Catalpa*, they say,
Came out to Western Australia,
And took six poor Fenians away.

Chorus
So come all you screw warders and jailers,
Remember Perth regatta day,
Take care of the rest of your Fenians,
Or the Yankees will steal them away.

Seven long years they served here,
And seven long more had to stay,
For defending their country, Old Ireland,
For that they were banished away.

You kept them in Western Australia
Till their hair began to turn grey.
When a Yank from the States of America
Came out here and stole them away.

Now all the Perth boats were a-racing
And making short tacks for the spot.
But the Yankee she tacked into Fremantle,
And took the best prize of the lot.

The *Georgette* armed with bold warriors
Went out the poor Yanks to arrest.
But she hoisted her star-spangled banner
Saying you'll not board me I guess.

So remember those six Fenians colonial,
And sing o'er these few verses with skill,
And remember the Yankee that stole them,
And the home that they left on the hill.

Now they've landed safe in America,
And there will be able to cry.
Hoist up the green flag and shamrock,
Hurrah for old Ireland we'll die.

The Fenian Escape

Now boys, if you will listen, a story I'll relate,
I'll tell you of the noble men who from their foe escaped.

Though bound with Saxon fetters in the dark Australian jail,
They struck a blow for freedom and for Yankeeland set sail.

On the seventeenth of April last the Stars and Stripes did fly
On board the bark *Catalpa*, waving proudly to the sky;
She showed the green above the red as she did calmly lay
Prepared to take the Fenian boys in safety o'er the sea.

When Breslin and brave Desmond brought the prisoners to the
	shore,
They gave one shout for freedom; soon to bless them evermore.
And manned by gallant Irish hearts, pulled towards the Yankee
	shore,
For well they knew, from its proud folds, no tyrant could them
	drag.

They had nearly reached in safety the *Catalpa* taut and trim,
When fast approaching them they saw a vision dark and grim.
It was the gunboat *Georgette*, and on her deck there stood,
One hundred hired assassins, to shed each patriot's blood.

The gunboat reached the bounding bark and fired across her bow,
Then in loud voice commanded that the vessel should heave to.
But noble Captain Anthony in thunder tones did cry,
'You dare not fire a shot at that bright flag that floats on high.'

'My ship is sailing peacefully beneath that flag of stars,
It's manned by Irish hearts of oak and manly Yankee tars;
And that dear emblem near the fore, so plain to be seen,
Is the banner I'll protect, old Ireland's flag of green.'

The Britisher he sailed away, from the Stars and Stripes he ran,
He knew his chance was slim to fight the boys of Uncle Sam;
So Hogan, Wilson, Harrington, with Darragh off did go;
With Hassett and bold Cranston, soon to whip the Saxon foe.

Here's luck to Captain Anthony who well these men did free,
He dared the English man-o'-war to fight him on the sea;
And here's to that dear emblem which in triumph shall be seen
The flag for which our heroes fought, old Ireland's flag of green.

The Bold Fenian Men

'Twas down by the glenside, I met an old woman
A-plucking young nettles, she ne'er saw me coming.
I listened a while to the song she was humming:
Glory O, Glory O, to the bold Fenian men

'Tis fifty long years since I saw the moon beaming
On strong manly forms, on eyes with hope gleaming.
I see them again, sure, in all my sad dreaming,
Glory O, Glory O, to the bold Fenian men.

When I was a young girl, their marching and drilling
Awoke in the glenside sounds awesome and thrilling.
They loved poor old Ireland, to die they were willing,
Glory O, Glory O, to the bold Fenian men.

Some died on the glenside, some died near a stranger,
And wise men have told us their cause was a failure,
But they fought for old Ireland and never feared danger,
Glory O, Glory O, to the bold Fenian men.

I passed on my way, God be praised that I met her.
Be life long or short, sure I'll never forget her.
We may have brave men, but we'll never have better.
Glory O, Glory O, to the bold Fenian men

God Save Ireland

High upon the gallows tree swung the noble-hearted three.
By the vengeful tyrant stricken in their bloom;
But they met him face to face, with the courage of their race,
And they went with souls undaunted to their doom.

Chorus
'God save Ireland!' said the heroes;
'God save Ireland' said they all.
Whether on the scaffold high
Or the battlefield we die,
Oh, what matter when for Erin dear we fall!

Girt around with cruel foes, still their courage proudly rose,
For they thought of hearts that loved them far and near;
Of the millions true and brave o'er the ocean's swelling wave,
And the friends in holy Ireland ever dear.

Chorus

Climbed they up the rugged stair, rang their voices out in prayer,
Then with England's fatal cord around them cast,
Close beside the gallows tree kissed like brothers lovingly,
True to home and faith and freedom to the last.

Chorus

Never till the latest day shall the memory pass away,
Of the gallant lives thus given for our land;
But on the cause must go, amidst joy and weal and woe,
Till we make our Isle a nation free and grand.

Chorus

The Marx Family on the Fenians[*]

Karl Marx submitted *The English Government and the Fenian Prisoners* to *L'Internationale*, a Belgian worker's magazine published between 1869 and 1873 in Brussels. It was sent as a private letter to the editor and Marx – who was excited by and interested in Fenian activities – assumed that the text would be edited before being published. It appeared more or less exactly as Marx drafted it.

Marx's daughter Jenny was as enervated as her father by the plight of the Fenian prisoners. Married to a French veteran of the Paris Commune, she wrote a series of groundbreaking articles on O'Donovan Rossa and the other felons for a French paper, *La Marseillaise*.

Writing about Jenny Marx after her death, Friedrich Engels pointed out: 'When the Irish press disclosed the infamous treatment that the Fenians sentenced in 1866 and later had to suffer in jail, and the English papers stubbornly ignored the atrocities; and when the Gladstone Government, despite the promises it made during the election campaign, refused to amnesty them or even to ameliorate their conditions, Jenny Marx found a means to make the pious Mr Gladstone take immediate steps. She wrote two articles for Rochefort's *Marseillaise* vividly describing how political prisoners are treated in free England. This had an effect. The disclosures in a big Paris newspaper could not be endured. A few weeks later O'Donovan Rossa and most of the others were free and on their way to America.'

---

[*] Joe Ambrose.

THE ENGLISH GOVERNMENT
AND THE FENIAN PRISONERS[†]

I

The silence which is observed in the European press concerning the disgraceful acts committed by this oligarchical bourgeois government is due to a variety of reasons. Firstly, the English Government is rich and the press, as you know, is immaculate. Moreover, the English Government is the model government, recognised as such by the landlords, by the capitalists on the Continent and even by Garibaldi: consequently we should not revile this ideal government. Finally, the French Republicans are narrow-minded and selfish enough to reserve all their anger for the Empire. It would be an insult to free speech to inform their fellow countrymen that in the land of bourgeois freedom sentences of 20 years hard labour are given for offences which are punished by 6 months in prison in the land of barracks. The following information on the treatment of Fenian prisoners has been taken from English journals:

Mulcahy, sub-editor of the newspaper *The Irish People*, sentenced for taking part in the Fenian conspiracy, was harnessed to a cart loaded with stones with a metal band round his neck at Dartmoor.

O'Donovan Rossa, owner of *The Irish People*, was shut up for 35 days in a pitch-black dungeon with his hands tied behind his back day and night. They were not even untied to allow him to eat the miserable slops which were left for him on the earthen floor.

Kickham, one of the editors of *The Irish People*, although he was unable to use his right arm because of an abscess, was forced to sit with his fellow prisoners on a heap of rubble in the November cold and fog and break up stones and bricks with his

---

† *Marx and Engels on Ireland* (1971). Originally written in English and published in French in *L'Internationale*, 27 February and 6 March 1870.

left hand. He returned to his cell at night and had nothing to eat but 6 ounces of bread and a pint of hot water.

O'Leary, an old man of sixty or seventy who was sent to prison, was put on bread and water for three weeks because he would not renounce paganism (this, apparently, is what a jailer called free thinking) and become either Papist, Protestant, Presbyterian or even Quaker, or take up one of the many religions which the prison governor offered to the heathen Irish.*

Martin H. Carey is incarcerated in a lunatic asylum at Millbank. The silence and the other bad treatment which he has received have made him lose his reason.

Colonel Richard Burke is in no better condition. One of his friends writes that his mind is affected, he has lost his memory and his behaviour, manners and speech are those of a madman.

The political prisoners are dragged from one prison to the next as if they were wild animals. They are forced to keep company with the vilest knaves; they are obliged to clean the pans used by these wretches, to wear the shirts and flannels which have previously been worn by these criminals, many of whom are suffering from the foullest diseases, and to wash in the same water. Before the arrival of the Fenians at Portland all the criminals were allowed to talk with their visitors. A visiting cage was installed for the Fenian prisoners. It consists of three compartments divided by partitions of thick iron bars; the jailer occupies the central compartment and the prisoner and his friends can only see each other through this double row of bars.

In the docks you can find prisoners who eat all sorts of slugs, and frogs are considered dainties at Chatham. General Thomas Burke said he was not surprised to find a dead mouse floating in the soup. The convicts say that it was a bad day for them when the Fenians were sent to the prisons. (The prison regime has become much more severe.)

---

* *O'Leary, an old man of sixty or seventy:* this a reference to Pagan O'Leary, not to John O'Leary.

I should like to add a few words to these extracts.

Last year Mr Bruce, the Home Secretary, a great liberal, great policeman and great mine owner in Wales who cruelly exploits his workers, was questioned on the bad treatment of Fenian prisoners and O'Donovan Rossa in particular. At first he denied everything, but was later compelled to confess. Following this Mr Moore, an Irish member in the House of Commons, demanded an enquiry into the facts. This was flatly refused by the radical ministry of which the head is that demigod Mr Gladstone (he has been compared to Jesus Christ publicly) and that old bourgeois demagogue, John Bright, is one of the most influential members.[†]

The recent wave of reports concerning the bad treatment of the Fenians led several members of Parliament to request Mr Bruce for permission to visit the prisoners in order to be able to verify the falseness of these rumours. Mr Bruce refused this permission on the grounds that the prison governors were afraid that the prisoners would be too excited by visits of this kind.

Last week the Home Secretary was again submitted to questioning. He was asked whether it was true that O'Donovan Rossa received corporal punishment (i.e. whipping) after his election to Parliament as the member for Tipperary. The Minister confirmed that he had not received such treatment since 1868 (which is tantamount to saying that the political prisoner had been given the whip over a period of two to three years).

I am also sending you extracts (which we are going to publish in our next issue) concerning the case of Michael Terbert, a Fenian sentenced as such to forced labour, who was serving his sentence at Spike Island Convict Prison. You will see that the coroner himself attributes this man's death to the torture which was inflicted on him. This investigation was held last week.

In the course of two years more than twenty Fenian workers have died or gone insane thanks to the philanthropic natures of

† *Bright:* a British Radical and Liberal MP, associated with the Anti-Corn Law League. A great orator of his time and a critic of British foreign policy.

these honest bourgeois souls, backed by the honest landlords.

You are probably aware that the English press professes a chaste distaste for the dreadful general security laws which grace 'la belle France'. With the exception of a few short intervals, it is security laws which formed the Irish Charter. Since 1793 the English Government has taken advantage of any pretext to suspend the Habeas Corpus Act (which guarantees the liberty of the individual) regularly and periodically, in fact all laws, except that of brute force. In this way thousands of people have been arrested in Ireland on being suspected of Fenianism without ever having been tried, brought before a judge or court, or even charged. Not content with depriving them of their liberty, the English Government has had them tortured in the most savage way imaginable. The following is but one example.

One of the prisons where persons suspected of being Fenians were buried alive is Mountjoy Prison in Dublin. The prison inspector, Murray, is a despicable brute who maltreated the prisoners so cruelly that some of them went mad. The prison doctor, an excellent man called McDonnell (who also played a creditable part in the enquiry into Michael Terbert's death), spent several months writing letters of protest which he addressed in the first instance to Murray himself. When Murray did not reply he sent accusing letters to higher authorities, but being an expert jailer Murray intercepted these letters.

Finally McDonnell wrote directly to Lord Mayo who was then Viceroy of Ireland. This was during the period when the Tories were in power (Derby and Disraeli). What effect did his actions have? The documents relating to the case were published by order of Parliament and ... Dr McDonnell was dismissed from his post!!! Whereas Murray retained his.

Then the so-called radical government of Gladstone came to power, the warm-hearted, unctuous, magnanimous Gladstone who had wept so passionately and so sincerely before the eyes of the whole of Europe over the fate of Poerio and other members of the bourgeoisie who were badly treated by King Bomba.* What did this idol of the progressive bourgeoisie do? While insulting the Irish by his insolent replies to their demands for an amnesty, he not only confirmed the monster Murray in his post, but endowed the position of chief jailer with a nice fat sinecure as a token of his personal satisfaction! There's the apostle of the philanthropic bourgeoisie for you!

But something had to be done to pull the wool over the eyes of the public. It was essential to appear to be doing something for Ireland, and the Irish Land Bill was proclaimed with a great song and dance. All this is nothing but a pose with the ultimate aim of deceiving Europe, winning over the Irish judges and advocates with the prospect of endless disputes between landlords and farmers, conciliating the landlords with the promise of financial aid from the state and deluding the more prosperous farmers with a few mild concessions.

In the long introduction to his grandiloquent and confused speech Gladstone admits that even the 'benevolent' laws which liberal England bestowed on Ireland over the last hundred years have always led to the country's further decline. And after this naive confession the same man persists in torturing those who want to put an end to this harmful and stupid legislation.

II

The following is an account taken from an English newspaper of the results of an enquiry into the death of Michael Terbert, a Fenian prisoner who died at Spike Island Prison due to the bad treatment which he had received:

'On Thursday last Mr John Moore, Coroner of the Midleton district, held an inquest at Spike Island Convict Prison, on the

---

* *King Bomba:* nickname for King Ferdinand of the Two Sicilies, who ruled over his territory with tyranny and against the wishes of his subjects. British administrations were much opposed to him. Gladstone wrote a celebrated pamphlet denouncing Bomba's activities.

body of a convict ... named Michael Terbert, who had died in hospital.

'Peter Hay, governor of the prison, was called first. He deposed "The deceased, Michael Terbert, came to this prison in June, 1866; I can't say how his health was at the time; he had been convicted on the 12th of January, 1866, and his sentence was seven years' penal servitude; he appeared delicate for some time past, as will appear from one of the prison books, which states that he was removed on the recommendation of medical officers, as being unfit for cellular discipline." Witness then went into a detail of the frequent punishments inflicted on the deceased for breach of discipline, many of them for the use "of disrespectful language to the medical officer".

'Jeremiah Hubert Kelly deposed – "I remember when Michael Terbert came here from Mountjoy Prison; it was then stated that he was unfit for cellular discipline – that means being always confined to a cell; certificate to the effect was signed by Dr McDonnell; ... I found him, however, to be in good health, and I sent him to work; I find by the record that he was in hospital from the 31st January, 1869, until the 6th February, 1869; he suffered then from increased affection of the heart, and from that time he did not work on the public works, but indoors, at oakum;[*] from the 19th March, 1869, until the 24th March, 1869, he was in hospital, suffering from the same affection of heart; from the 24th April till the 5th May he was also in hospital from spitting of blood; from the 19th May till the 1st June he was in hospital for heart disease; from the 21st June till the 22nd June he was under hospital treatment for the same; he was also in hospital from the 22nd July till the 15th August, for the same – from 9th November till the 13th December for debility, and from 20th December to the 8th February, when he died from acute dropsy;[†]

---

* *Oakum:* a tarred fibre used in shipbuilding. It used to be made from old tarry ropes and its preparation was often undertaken in prisons.
† *Dropsy:* the swelling of soft tissues (perhaps around the feet and ankles) due to the accumulation of excess water. This might be caused by edema due to congestive heart failure.

on the 13th November he first appeared to suffer from dropsy, and it was then dissipated; I visit the cells every day, and I must have seen him when under punishment from time to time; it is my duty to remit, by recommendation, that punishment, if I consider the prisoner is not fit to bear it; I think I did so twice in his case.

"'As a medical man, did you consider that five days on bread and water per day was excessive punishment for him, notwithstanding his state of health in Mountjoy and here?"– "I did not; the deceased had a good appetite; I don't think that the treatment induced acute dropsy, of which he died"…

'Martin O'Connell, resident apothecary of Spike Island, was next examined – Witness mentioned to Dr Kelly last July that while the deceased was labouring under heart disease, he should not have been punished; … he was of opinion that such punishment as the deceased got was prejudicial to his health, considering that he was an invalid for the past twelve months … he could not say that invalids were so punished, as he only attended cells in Dr Kelly's absence; he was certain, considering the state of the deceased man's health, that five days continuously in cells would be injurious to his health; … The Coroner then … dealt forcibly with the treatment which the prisoner had received … alternating between the hospital and the punishment cell.

'The jury returned the following verdict: "We find that Michael Terbert died in hospital at Spike Island Convict Prison, on the 8th of February, 1870, of dropsy; he was twenty-five years of age, and unmarried. We have also to express in the strongest terms our total disapproval of the frequent punishment he suffered in cells on bread and water for several days in succession during his imprisonment in Spike Island, where he had been sent in June, 1866, from Mountjoy Prison, for the reason that in Dr McDonnell's opinion he was unfit for cellular discipline at Mountjoy; and we express our condemnation of such treatment".'

A Letter from Rossa:
The treatment of Fenian Prisoners*

London, March 5

During the meeting of the House of Commons on March 3 Mr Stackpoole questioned Mr Gladstone on the treatment of Fenian prisoners. He said, among other things, that Dr Lyons of Dublin had recently stated that 'the discipline, diet, personal restrictions and the other punishments were bound to cause permanent damage to the prisoners' health'.

After having expressed complete satisfaction with the way in which prisoners were treated, Mr Gladstone crowned his little speech with this brilliantly witty remark:

> As to the health of O'Donovan Rossa, I am glad to be able to say that during her last visit to her husband Mrs O'Donovan Rossa congratulated him on looking better.

Whereupon a burst of Homeric laughter broke out from all sides of that noble assembly. Her last visit! Note that Mrs O'Donovan Rossa had not only been separated from her husband for several years, but that she had travelled all over America earning money to feed her children by giving public lectures on English literature.

Is the profound satisfaction of the head jailer shared by his prisoners? Read the following extracts from a letter written by O'Donovan Rossa, which by some miracle was slipped out of the prison and arrived at its destination after an incredible delay:

Letter from Rossa:

I have already told you about the hypocrisy of these English masters who, after placing me in a position which forced me to

---

* Jenny Marx. First published in French in the newspaper *La Marseillaise* 1870.

get down on my knees and elbows to eat, are now depriving me of food and light and giving me chains and a Bible. I am not complaining of the penalties which my masters inflict on me – it is my job to suffer – but I insist that I have the right to inform the world of the treatment to which I am subjected, and that it is illegal to hold back my letters describing this treatment. The minute precautions taken by the prison authorities to prevent me writing letters are as disgusting as they are absurd. The most insulting method was to strip me once a day for several months and then examine my arms, legs and all other parts of my body.

This took place at Millbank daily from February to May 1867. One day I refused, whereupon five prison officers arrived, beat me mercilessly and tore off my clothes.

Once I succeeded in getting a letter to the outside, for which I was rewarded by a visit from Messrs Knox and Pollock, two police magistrates.

How ironical to send two government employees to find out the truth about the English prisons. These gentlemen refused to take note of anything important which I had to tell them. When I touched upon a subject which was not to their liking, they stopped me by saying that prison discipline was not their concern. Isn't that so, Messrs Pollock and Knox? When I told you that I had been forced to wash in water which had already been used by half a dozen English prisoners, did you not refuse to note my complaint? At Chatham I was given a certain amount of tow to pull out and told that I would go without food if I did not finish the work by a certain time.

'Perhaps you'll still punish me even if I do the job in time,' I shouted. 'That's what happened to me at Millbank.'

'How could it?' asked the jailer.

Then I told him that on July 4 I had finished my work ten minutes before the appointed time and picked up a book. The officer saw me do this, accused me of being lazy and I was put on bread and water and locked in a dark cell for forty-eight hours.

One day I caught sight of my friend Edward Duffy. He was extremely pale. A little later I heard that Duffy was seriously ill and that he had expressed the wish to see me (we had been very close in Ireland). I begged the governor to give me permission to visit him. He refused point-blank. This was round about Christmas '67 – and a few weeks later a prisoner whispered to me through the bars of my cell: 'Duffy is dead'.

How movingly this would have been described by the English if it had happened in Russia!

I must say a word in memory of John Lynch. In March 1866 I found myself together with him in the exercise yard. We were being watched so closely that he only managed to say to me, 'The cold is killing me.' But then what did the English do to us? They took us to London on Christmas Eve. When we arrived at the prison they took away our flannels and left us shivering in our cells for several months. Yes, they cannot deny that it was they who killed John Lynch. But nevertheless they managed to produce officials at the enquiry who were ready to prove that Lynch had been given very gentle treatment.

The lies of our English oppressors exceed one's wildest imagination.

If I am to die in prison I entreat my family and my friends not to believe a word of what these people say. Let me not be suspected of personal rancour against those who persecuted me with their lies. I accuse only tyranny which makes the use of such methods necessary.

Many a time the circumstances have reminded me of Machiavelli's words: 'that tyrants have a special interest in circulating the Bible so that the people understand its precepts and offer no resistance to being robbed by brigands.'

So long as an enslaved people follows the sermons on morality and obedience preached to them by the priests, the tyrants have nothing to fear.

If this letter reaches my fellow countrymen I have the right to demand that they raise their voices to insist that justice be done for their suffering brothers. Let these words whip up the blood that is moving sluggishly in their veins!

I was harnessed to a cart with a rope tied round my neck. This knot was fastened to a long shaft and two English prisoners received orders to prevent the cart from bouncing. But they refrained from doing this, the shaft rose up into the air and the knot came undone. If it had tightened I would be dead. I insist that they do not possess the right to put me in a situation where my life depends on the acts of other people.

A ray of light is penetrating through the bolts and bars of my prison. This is a reminder of the day at Newtownards where I met Orangemen and Ribbonmen who had forgotten their bigotry!

O'Donovan Rossa
Political prisoner sentenced to hard labour

A Fenian Prisoner Gone Insane[*]

A characteristic exchange of letters has taken place between Bruce [the Home Secretary] and Mr McCarthy Downing concerning Colonel Richard Burke. Before reproducing it I should like to remark in passing that Mr Downing is an Irish member of the House of Commons. This ambitious advocate joined the ministerial phalanx with the noble aim of making a career. Thus, we are not dealing here with a suspect witness.

February 22, 1870
Sir,
If my information is correct, Richard Burke, one of the Fenian prisoners formerly held in Chatham Prison, has been trans-

---

* Jenny Marx. First published in French in the newspaper *La Marseillaise*, 1870.

ferred to Woking in a state of insanity. In March 1869 I took the liberty of bringing his state of apparent ill-health to your notice, and in the following July Mr Blake, former member for Waterford, and I informed you of our opinion that if the system of his treatment were not changed, the worst consequences were to be feared. I received no reply to this letter. My object in writing to you is the cause of humanity and the hope of obtaining his release so that his family may have the consolation of seeing to his needs and mitigating his suffering. I have in my hand a letter from the prisoner to his brother dated December 3 in which he says that he has been systematically poisoned, this being, I imagine, one of the phases of his disease. I sincerely trust that the kind sentiments for which you are known will urge you to grant this request.

Yours, etc.,
McCarthy Downing
Home Office,

February 25, 1870
Sir,
Richard Burke was transferred from Chatham as a result of his illusion that he was poisoned or cruelly treated by the prison medical officers. At the same time, without him being positively ill, his health deteriorated. Consequently I gave orders for him to be moved to Woking and had him examined by Dr Meyer from Broadmoor Asylum, who was of the opinion that his illusion would disappear when his health improved. His health did, in fact, improve rapidly and an ordinary observer would not have noted any signs of his mental weakness. I should very much like to be in a position to give you an assurance of his early release, but am not able to do so. His crime and the consequences of the attempt to free him are too serious for me to be able to give you such an assurance. Meanwhile all that medical science and good

treatment can do to restore his mental and physical health will be done.

H. A. Bruce

February 28, 1870

Sir,

After receiving your letter of the 25th in reply to my request that Burke should be handed over to the care of his brother, I hoped to find an occasion to talk to you on this matter in the House of Commons, but you were so busy on Thursday and Friday that an interview was out of the question. I have received letters from a number of Burke's friends. They are waiting anxiously to hear whether my request has been successful. I have not yet informed them that it has not. Before disappointing them I felt 'justified' in writing to you again on the matter. I thought that as a person who has invariably and at some risk denounced Fenianism, I could permit myself to give a word of impartial, friendly advice to the government.

I have no hesitation in saying that the release of a political prisoner who has become mentally unbalanced would not be criticised and certainly not condemned by the general public. In Ireland people would say: 'Well, the government is not as cruel as we thought.' Whereas if, on the other hand, Burke is kept in prison this will provide new material for the national press to attack it as being even crueller than the Neapolitan governors in their worst days. And I confess that I cannot see how men of moderate views could defend the act of refusal in such a case ...

McCarthy Downing

Sir,

I regret that I am unable to recommend Burke's release. It is true that he has shown signs of insanity and that in ordinary cases I would be 'justified' in recommending him to the mercy of the Crown. But his case is not an ordinary one, because he was not only a hardened conspirator, but his participation in the attempt to blow up Clerkenwell which, if it had succeeded, would have been even more disastrous than it was, makes him an improper recipient of pardon.

H. A. Bruce

CHURCHILL AND THE FENIANS*

My nurse, Mrs Everest, was nervous about the Fenians. I gathered these were wicked people and there was no end to what they would do if they had their way. On one occasion when I was out riding on my donkey, we thought we saw a long dark procession of Fenians approaching. I am sure now it must have been the Rifle Brigade out for a route march. But we were all very much alarmed, particularly the donkey, who expressed his anxiety by kicking. I was thrown off and had concussion.

KNOCKNAGOW†

When Charles Kickham was released from prison he devoted himself to writing and, despite his disabilities, enjoyed phenomenal success. His novel *Knocknagow* became one of the most popular of all Irish novels, and was still being widely read in the 1950s. One critic has pointed out that, while it wasn't a great achievement as a work of literature, it was a political and polemical novel which

---

* *My Early Life: A Roving Commission* (1930), Winston Churchill.
† Joe Ambrose.

attacked that which it saw as being wrong. *Knocknagow* attacked the landlord system in Ireland and, by implication, British rule in Ireland which is perceived as underpinning that system. W.B. Yeats said that it was the most honest of Irish novels.

Sports writer Con Houlihan wrote that *Knocknagow* is 'like a great basket in to which Kickham threw observations and ideas and perceptions and whatever else came into his fertile mind. A novel, I suppose, should tell a story or at least have a central theme: *Knocknagow* does not tell a story but it certainly has a central theme. And that theme is introduced to us in the first chapter in *Knocknagow*: the struggle for the land was the central issue in Ireland in the nineteenth century.'

In his occasional writings and in his fiction, Kickham identified himself as being a Tipperary man. He signed his articles and poems 'K. Mullinahone', 'C.J.K.', and 'Slievenamon'. His hugely popular ballads and poems included *Rory of the Hill* and *The Irish Peasant Girl*, about the girl who 'lived beside the Anner at the foot of Slievenamon'. Popularly known as *She Lived beside the Anner*, this ballad is still part of the popular folk repertoire.

The Fenian movement was re-organised in the 1870s with a new constitution. Kickham headed the secret council that controlled it. He died in 1882.

The Spirit of '98[‡]

Father Hannigan and Maurice Kearney, with old Phil Morris and Phil Lahy, and a few more choice spirits, drew close together round the social board, and enjoyed themselves in their own way.

‡ *Knocknagow, or The Homes of Tipperary* (1879), Charles J. Kickham.

'I gave my daughter to Ned Brophy,' said old Larry Clancy, in reply to a question of Father Hannigan's – 'I gave my daughter to Ned Brophy, because he has a good lase.'*

'A good landlord is as good as a good lase,' said Maurice Kearney.

'I do not know that,' returned Larry Clancy, slowly and emphatically. 'For my own part, I'd rather have a good lase and the worst landlord, than no lase and the best landlord that ever broke bread. Security is the only thing to give a man courage.'

'He's right,' exclaimed old Phil Morris, striking his stick against the ground. 'Security is the only thing. But if every man was of my mind he'd have security or know for what.'

'Hold your tongue, you old sinner,' said Father Hannigan, who had often combated Phil Morris's views, as to how the land question could be brought to a speedy settlement.

'I have my old pike yet and maybe I'd want it yet!' he exclaimed, with a look of defiance at the priest.† 'And the man that'd come to turn me out on the road, as I see others turned out on the road, I'd give him the length of it, as sure as God made Moses.'

'And swing for it,' said Father Hannigan.

'Ay, and swing for it,' shouted the old Croppy; for it was a musket bullet that shattered Phil Morris's knee in '98. 'Ay, and swing for it.'

'And be damned,' added the priest. 'Don't you know 'tis murder – wilful murder?'

'I don't know that,' he replied. 'But the prayers of the congregation would carry the man's sowl to heaven, that'd do a manly act, and put a tyrant out of the country, and keep other tyrants from following his example. 'Tis self-defence,' he added, striking his stick against the ground; ''tis justice.'

---

* *Lase:* a lease. Most farmers were tenant farmers at this time and the possession of a long lease gave a farmer stability and some status.
† *My old pike:* pikes were the major weapon used by the peasantry during 1798 and the speaker is indicating that he was 'out' in '98.

''Tis bad work,' said Father Hannigan. 'And take my word, luck or grace will never come of it.'

'I agree with you,' Hugh Kearney observed, who had joined them during the latter part of the discussion.

'You do!' exclaimed old Phil, turning upon him with a scowl. 'And who the divil cares what you or the likes of you agree with? You're well off as you are, and little trouble it'd give you to see the people hunted like dogs.'

'You're wrong there, Phil,' replied Hugh. 'I'd like to see that old pike of yours taken from the thatch for a manly fight like that you fought in '98. But that's a different thing.'

'Well, I know that,' returned Phil Morris, letting his chin drop upon his chest, and seeming to brood over the subject for a minute or two. 'But five years ago,' he added, 'I could count three-an-twenty houses, big and little, between the cross of Liscorrig and Shanbally Bridge; and today you couldn't light your pipe along that whole piece of a road, barrin' at one house – and that's my own. And why am I left there? Because they knew I'd do it,' he muttered through his clenched teeth, as if he were speaking to himself.

'Let him alone,' said the priest. 'There's no use in talking to him.'

'There's raison in what he says,' says old Larry Clancy, in his slow, emphatic way. 'I say,' he added, looking at the priest, 'there's raison in what he says.'

'Don't be talking foolish,' returned Father Hannigan, who saw that the eyes of three or four small farmers were fixed inquiringly on his face. 'Good never came of it.'

'Do you hear him?' exclaimed old Phil Morris, turning to Hugh Kearney.

'Well, to a great extent,' said Hugh, after a short silence – for he saw they all expected he would speak – 'to a great extent I agree with Father Hannigan. But there is no use in denying that the dread of assassination is the only protection the people have against extermination in this part of Ireland.'

'I say 'tis justice in the eye of God,' exclaimed old Phil Morris, 'to punish the bloody tyrants – the robbers and murderers that rob the people of their little spots, and turn 'em out to perish.'

''Tis justice to punish the bloody robbers!' And as old Phil struck his stick against the ground and looked around, there was a murmur of applause from the bystanders, who by this time were pretty numerous.

'The man that believes he is robbed or persecuted,' said the priest, 'cannot be an impartial judge. If everyone was to take the law in his own hands, there would be nothing but violence and bloodshed.'

'Well, what do you say to giving the exterminators a fair trial before judge and jury?'

'What judge and jury?'

''Tisn't the judge and jury in the coorthouse,' returned Phil Morris, 'because they're all for the tyrants, and some of 'em tyrants themselves; but a fair jury of the people, and a fair judge.'

'I know what you mean,' said Father Hannigan. 'But if the judge and jury in the courthouse be all for the tyrant, don't you think your judge and jury would be as much for the victim?'

'No; they'd never condemn a man that didn't desarve it,' replied Phil.

'Ignorant men,' rejoined the priest, 'blinded by passion – perhaps smarting under wrong themselves, or dreading that their own turn might come next couldn't be a fair judge and jury, Phil, even if what you speak of were lawful or just in the sight of God. So hold your tongue.'

'Ay, that's the way always. "Howld your tongue" settles it.'

'There is Mr Lloyd,' continued Father Hannigan, as that gentleman returned to his seat, 'and if he put out a tenant would you shoot him?'

'The divil a hair of his head would be touched,' replied Phil. 'He gives good lases at a fair rent; and the man that does that

222

won't turn out a tenant unless he desarves to be turned out. Answer me this one question. Did you ever know of a good landlord to be shot, or a good agent? Answer me that.'

'Well, no,' replied the priest. 'I never did.'

'There it is,' observed Larry Clancy, as if that settled the question and Father Hannigan had thrown in the sponge.

'Well, now, Mr Lowe,' said Father Hannigan, 'what's your opinion of this matter?'

'I am almost entirely ignorant of it,' he replied. 'But I confess I came over to Ireland under the impression that the people were lawless and revengeful, particularly in your county.'

'You only saw the dark side of the picture,' returned Father Hannigan. 'We are not so black as we are painted.'

'I believe that. And a remark made by an Irish judge, with whom I had the honour of dining a few weeks ago, made a great impression on me, I confess.'

'What did he say?'

'He had sentenced several men to be hanged a short time before, and a gentleman present made some severe remarks, while discussing the subject of agrarian outrages, when the Judge said: "I never met an instance of a landlord being killed, who did not deserve – I won't say to be hanged, as I am a judge – but I do say, a case of the kind never came before me that the landlord did not deserve to be damned!"'

Old Phil Morris looked with astonishment at the speaker.

'Put it there,' he exclaimed, reaching his horny hand across the table. 'If you were the divil you're an honest man.'

'I don't despair of old Ireland yet,' said the priest. 'The people are good if they only get fair play.'

'Ireland will never do any good till we have trade and manufactures of our own,' observed Phil Lahy. And a certain thickness of utterance indicated that Phil had forgotten his resolution respecting the cordial long ago.*

---

* *Cordial:* soda or soft drink.

'Our rulers crushed our trade and manufactures,' said Father Hannigan.

'Yes,' returned Phil Lahy, 'but the people are too much given to farming. A beggarly farmer that's stuck in the mud from mornin' to night, and don't know beef from mutton – no, nor the taste of an egg; for if he dare look at a hen's tail, his wife would fling the dish-cloth at him. And that poor crawler, with his head bald from the rain droppin' on it from the eave from standin' outside his honour's window, waitin' till his honour condescended to talk to him – that beggar would despise the tradesman and look down on him. Tom Hogan comes in to me this mornin' to know was there any news in the paper. "There is," says I. "I'll read one of the best articles ever you heard for you," says I. "Look at the markets," says Tom Hogan. Ha! ha! ha!"* And Phil Lahy laughed quite sardonically, '"Look at the markets". Ha! ha! ha!'

'There's some truth in what you say,' said Father Hannigan.

'Ay,' continued Phil, 'and the big farmer will make doctors and attorneys of his sons, instead of setting 'em up in business.'

'I'm going to bind my youngest son to his uncle,' said Mr Kearney.

'For a wonder,' returned Phil Lahy, tasting his punch and, not considering it up to the mark, adding another glass of whiskey.

'That's what I call a double entendre, Phil,' said Father Hannigan.

'I fear you are forgetting your promise,' Hugh observed.

'What promise?' Phil asked.

'Not to drink anything stronger than cordial.'

Phil Lahy stared at the speaker for half a minute; and then stared at the double entendre for half a minute more.

In fact, Phil Lahy felt himself in a dilemma. Making a sudden dive, however, at the ginger cordial decanter, he filled his glass and carefully added the glass of cordial to the two glasses of whiskey in his tumbler.

---

* *The markets:* a reference to livestock markets, not stock markets.

'Will that please you?' he asked, turning to Hugh, as if that didn't satisfy him nothing could.

Hugh rubbed his hand over his face, and did his best to keep from laughing.

'Would you doubt Phil for getting out of a promise?' observed Father Hannigan. 'He'd drive a coach-and-six through any promise that ever was made – as old Dan used to say of an Act of Parliament.'[†]

'Old Dan said many a good thing,' rejoined Phil Lahy, not choosing to notice the reference to the 'promise'. 'But the best thing ever he said,' he continued, casting about for something that would turn the conversation away from promises and cordial altogether – 'the best thing ever he said was: "England's difficulty is Ireland's opportunity"', exclaimed Phil Lahy, as the happy apothegm suddenly flashed into his mind at the very moment that he was about taking refuge in a severe fit of sneezing. 'And you'll see Ireland yet …' Here Phil stopped short, as if he had lost the thread of his discourse – but after a good pull at the tumbler, he seemed to find it again, and added, 'when a redcoat will be as great a curiosity as a white blackbird. There's a storm brewin',' he continued, with a portentous scowl. 'And the day will come when we can drive the invader out of Ireland – wud square-bottles, as Mat the Thrasher said the other day.'

'But I don't like to hear you running down the farmers,' observed Father Hannigan.

'I don't run down the farmers – except when they deserve it.'

'Manufacturers are good,' continued Father Hannigan; 'and we'll have enough of them when our fine harbours are crowded with the shipping of America – and of the whole world. But for all that I'd be sorry to see the homes of the peasantry disappearing from our hills and our plains, and the people crowded into factories.'

[†] *Old Dan*: Daniel O'Connell.

225

'You're right,' exclaimed Phil Lahy, almost with a shout. 'Princes or lords may flourish or may fade. Mat has a new song that touches upon that.'

'Come, Mat, give us the new song,' said Father Hannigan.

'I'm afeard I haven't it be heart right yet, sir,' replied Mat.

'Oh, we'll excuse you; we'll excuse all mistakes,' rejoined the priest. 'Come, Mr Hanly,' he called out to Lory – who with a dozen others was battering the floor to the tune of 'O'Connell's Trip to Parliament' – 'We're going to get a song. Give the poor pipers and fiddlers a rest. Come, Mat, up with it!'

There was a general movement towards the table, and all waited anxiously for Mat the Thrasher's new song, of which many of the company had heard.

Mat leant back in his chair, and with a huge hand resting on the table, and clutching one of the gilt buttons on the front of the blue body-coat with the other, he turned his eyes to the roof beams, and sang in a fine mellow voice:

THE PEASANT-FARMER'S SONG
FOR THE TIME TO COME

I've a pound for to lend, and a pound for to spend –
And *céad mile fáilte* my word for a friend;
No mortal I envy, no master I own –
Nor lord in his castle, nor king on his throne.
Come, fill up your glasses, the first cup we'll drain
To the comrades we lost on the red battle plain!
Oh, we'll cherish their fame, boys, who died long ago –
And what's that to any man whether or no?

The spinning-wheels stop, and my girls grow pale,
While their mother is telling some sorrowful tale,
Of old cabins levelled, and coffinless graves,
And ships swallowed up in the salt ocean waves.

But, girls, that's over – for each of you now
I'll have twenty-five pounds and a three-year-old cow;
And we'll have *lán na mhála* at your weddings I trow –*
And what's that to any man whether or no?

Come here, *bhean na tighe*, sit beside me a while,†
And the pride of your heart let me read in your smile.
Would you give your old home for the lordliest hall?
Ha! – you glance at my rifle that hangs on the wall.
And your two gallant boys on parade-day are seen
In the ranks of the brave 'neath the banner of green;
Oh! I've taught them to guard it 'gainst traitor and foe –
And what's that to any man whether or no?

But the youngest of all is the 'white-headed boy' –
The pulse of your heart, and our pride and our joy:
From the dance and the hurling he'll steal off to pray,
And will wander alone by the river all day.
He's as good as the priest at his Latin I hear,
And to college, please God, we'll send him next year.
Oh, he'll offer the Mass for our souls when we go –
And what's that to any man whether or no?

Your hands, then, old neighbours! one more glass we'll drain;
And *céad mile fáilte* again and again!
May discord and treason keep far from our shore,
And freedom and peace light our homes evermore.
He's the king of good fellows, the poor, honest man;
So we'll live and be merry as long as we can,
And we'll cling to old Ireland through weal and through woe –
And what's that to any man whether or no?

---

* *Lán na mhála:* a full bag, i.e. plenty.
† *Bhean na tighe:* woman of the house.

There was a shout of applause at the conclusion of Mat's song; and some of the women were seen to wipe the tears from their cheeks with their aprons. Bessy Morris raised her eyes to his; and as she laid her hand upon his arm while turning away her head to reply to a question of Hugh Kearney's, Mat pressed his hand over his eyes, and caught his breath, as if he had been shot through the body.

'That's a right good song, Mat,' said Father Hannigan.

'The chorus,' observed Phil Lahy, who seemed in a mood for contradiction, 'is as ould as the hills.'

'So much the better,' replied the priest. 'Are we going to get a song from anyone else?'

'Billy Heffernan has another new wan,' said a voice from the crowd.

'Don't mind it!' exclaimed Phil Lahy, contemptuously, ''Tis a "come-all-ye".' By which Phil meant that Billy Heffernan's new song belonged to that class of ballads which invariably commence: 'come all ye tender Christians, I hope you will draw near'.

''Tis a come-all-ye,' repeated Phil Lahy. 'Don't bother us wud it.'

The twang of the fiddles, followed by the sound of drone and chanter, however, showed that the dancers were becoming impatient, and had urged the musicians to strike up.

YEATS THE DISCIPLE[*]

W. B. Yeats, correctly described by historian T. W. Moody as O'Leary's most distinguished disciple, said that John O'Leary was the 'handsomest old man' that he had ever seen, and that, 'from O'Leary's conversation and from the Irish books he lent or gave me, has come all I have set my mind to since'.

[*] Joe Ambrose.

Yeats admired O'Leary's learning and vision of Ireland but felt that, 'His once passionate mind, in the isolation of prison and banishment, had as it were dried and hardened into certain constantly repeated formulas, unwieldy as pieces of lava.'

He didn't attend O'Leary's funeral when the old man died in 1907, saying that: 'I shrank from seeing about his grave many whose Nationalism was different from anything that he had taught or that I could share. He belonged, as did his friend John F. Taylor, to the romantic conception of Irish Nationality on which Lionel Johnston and myself founded, so far as it was founded on anything but literature, our Art and our Irish criticism. Perhaps his spirit, if it can care for or see old friends now, will accept this apology for an absence which has troubled me.'

Was it for this the wild geese spread
The grey wing upon every tide;
For this that all that blood was shed,
For this Edward Fitzgerald died,
And Robert Emmet and Wolfe Tone,
All that delirium of the brave?
Romantic Ireland's dead and gone,
It's with O'Leary in the grave.

1916

A 1913 Letter from Tom Clarke
to Joe McGarrity[*]

Joe,

It is worth living in Ireland these times – there is an awakening – the slow, silent prodding and the open preaching is at last showing results ... we are breathing air that compels one to fling up his head and stand more erect ... It [the Manchester Martyrs commemoration] was a magnificent demonstration – the finest thing of its kind I ever witnessed in Dublin or anywhere else – and let me tell you, no other party in Ireland today could have brought the people together – so many different and opposing sections for any purpose – except ourselves.

Speech at the Grave of O'Donovan Rossa[†]

It has been thought right, before we turn away from this place in which we have laid the mortal remains of O'Donovan Rossa that one among us should, in the name of all, speak the praise of that valiant man, and endeavour to formulate the thought and the hope that are in us as we stand around his grave. And if there is anything that makes it fitting that I rather than another, I rather than one of the grey-haired men who were young with him and shared in his labour and in his suffering, should speak here, it is perhaps that I may be taken as speaking on behalf of a new generation that has been re-baptised in the Fenian

---

[*] 'God save Ireland': Manchester Martyr demonstrations in Dublin, 1867–1916', by Owen McGee, *Eire-Ireland* 2001.
[†] Patrick Pearse. Original handwritten manuscript in the Pearse Museum, Dublin. Speech delivered 1 August 1915.

faith and that has accepted the responsibility of carrying out the Fenian programme.

I propose to you then that, here by the grave of this unrepentant Fenian, we renew our baptismal vows; that, here by the grave of this unconquered and unconquerable man, we ask of God, each one for himself, such unshakable purpose, such high and gallant courage, such unbreakable strength of soul as belonged to O'Donovan Rossa.

Deliberately here we avow ourselves, as he avowed himself in the dock, Irishmen of one allegiance only. We of the Irish volunteers and you others who are associated with us in today's task and duty are bound together and must stand together henceforth in brotherly union for the achievement of the freedom of Ireland. And we know only one definition of freedom: it is Tone's definition, it is Mitchel's definition, it is Rossa's definition. Let no man blaspheme the cause that the dead generations of Ireland served by giving it any other name or definition than their name and their definition.

We stand at Rossa's grave not in sadness but rather in exaltation of spirit that it has been given to us to come thus into so close a communion with that brave and splendid Gael. Splendid and holy causes are served by men who are themselves splendid and holy. O'Donovan Rossa was splendid in the proud manhood of him, splendid in the heroic grace of him, splendid in the Gaelic strength and clarity and truth of him. All that splendour and pride and strength was compatible with a humility and a simplicity of devotion to Ireland, to all that was olden and beautiful and Gaelic in Ireland, the holiness and simplicity of patriotism of a Michael O'Cleary or of an Eoghan O'Growney.* The clear true eyes of this man almost alone in his day visioned Ireland as we of today would surely have her: not free merely, but Gaelic as well; not Gaelic merely, but free and noble as well.

* Gaelic scholars.

In a closer spiritual communion with him now than ever before or perhaps ever again, in spiritual communion with those of his day, living and dead, who suffered with him in English prisons, in communion of spirit too with our own dear comrades who suffer in English prisons today, and speaking on their behalf as well as on our own, we pledge to Ireland our love, and we pledge to English rule in Ireland our hate. This is a place of peace, sacred to the dead, where men should speak with all charity and with all restraint but I hold it a Christian thing, as O'Donovan Rossa held it, to hate evil, to hate untruth, to hate oppression; and, hating them, to strive to overthrow them. Our foes are strong and wise and wary; but, strong and wise and wary as they are, they cannot undo the miracles of God who ripens in the hearts of young men the seeds sown by the young men of a former generation. And the seed sown by the young men of '65 and '67 are coming to their miraculous ripening today.

Rulers and Defenders of Realms had need to be wary if they would guard against such processes. Life springs from death: and from the graves of patriot men and women spring living nations. The Defenders of this Realm have worked well in secret and in the open. They think that they have purchased half of us and intimidated the other half. They think that they have foreseen everything, think that they have provided against everything; but the fools, the fools, the fools! – they have left us our Fenian dead, and, while Ireland holds these graves, Ireland unfree shall never be at peace.

PHYSICAL FORCE IN IRISH POLITICS[*]

Ireland occupies a position among the nations of the earth unique in a great variety of its aspects, but in no one particular is this singularity more marked than in the possession of what is known as a 'physical force party' – a party, that is to say, whose members are united upon no one point, and agree upon no single principle, except upon the use of physical force as the sole means of settling the dispute between the people of this country and the governing power of Great Britain.

Other countries and other peoples have, from time to time, appealed to what the first French Revolutionists picturesquely described as the 'sacred right of insurrection', but in so appealing they acted under the inspiration of, and combated for, some great governing principle of political or social life upon which they, to a man, were in absolute agreement. The latter-day high falutin' 'hillside' man, on the other hand, exalts into a principle that which the revolutionists of other countries have looked upon as a weapon, and in his gatherings prohibits all discussion of those principles which formed the main strength of his prototypes elsewhere and made the successful use of that weapon possible. Our people have glided at different periods of the past century from moral force agitation, so-called, into physical force rebellion, from constitutionalism into insurrectionism, meeting in each the same failure and the same disaster and yet seem as far as ever from learning the great truth that neither method is ever likely to be successful until they first insist that a perfect agreement upon the end to be attained should be arrived at as a starting-point of all our efforts.

To the reader unfamiliar with Irish political history such a remark seems to savour almost of foolishness, its truth is so ap-

* James Connolly. First published in *Irish Worker*, 25 October 1913.

parent; but to the reader acquainted with the inner workings of the political movements of this country the remark is pregnant with the deepest meaning. Every revolutionary effort in Ireland has drawn the bulk of its adherents from the ranks of the disappointed followers of defeated constitutional movements. After having exhausted their constitutional efforts in striving to secure such a modicum of political power as would justify them to their own consciences in taking a place as loyal subjects of the British Empire, they, in despair, turned to thoughts of physical force as a means of attaining their ends. Their conception of what constitutes freedom was, in no sense changed or revolutionised; they still believed in the political form of freedom which had been their ideal in their constitutional days; but no longer hoping for it from the acts of the British Parliament, they swung over into the ranks of the 'physical force' men as the only means of attaining it.

The so-called physical force movement of today in like manner bases its hopes upon the disgust of the people over the failure of the Home Rule movement; it seeks to enlist the people under its banners, not so much by pointing out the base ideals of the constitutionalists or the total inadequacy of their pet measures to remedy the evils under which the people suffer, as by emphasising the greater efficacy of physical force as a national weapon. Thus, the one test of an advanced Nationalist is, in their opinion, one who believes in physical force. It may be that the persons so professing to believe are Republicans; it may be that they are believers in monarchy; it may be that Home Rule would satisfy them; it may be that they despise Home Rule. No matter what their political faith may be, if only they are prepared to express belief in the saving grace of physical force, they are acclaimed as advanced Nationalists – worthy descendants of 'the men of '98'. The '98 Executive, organised in the commencement by professed believers in the physical force doctrine, started by proclaiming its adherence to the principle of national independence 'as understood by Wolfe Tone and the United Irishmen', and in less than twelve months from doing so, deliberately rejected a similar resolution and elected on its governing body men notorious for their Royalist proclivities. As the '98 Executive represents the advanced Nationalists of Ireland, this repudiation of the Republican faith of the United Irishmen is an interesting corroboration of the truth of our statement that the advanced Nationalists of our day are utterly regardless of principle and only attach importance to methods – an instance of putting the cart before the horse, absolutely unique in its imbecility and unparalleled in the history of the world.

It may be interesting, then, to place before our readers the Socialist Republican conception of the functions and uses of physical force in a popular movement. We neither exalt it into a principle nor repudiate it as something not to be thought of.

To my mind an agitation to attain a political or economic end must rest upon an implied willingness and ability to use force. Without that it is mere wind and attitudinising. The only force available to the worker is economic force; the capture of political power when it does come will come as a result of the previous conquest of economic power, although that conquest can be and should be assisted by the continual exercise of political action by those who have grasped the full meaning and purpose of the working class fight.

THE 1916 PROCLAMATION
POBLACHT NA HÉIREANN

THE PROVISIONAL GOVERNMENT OF THE IRISH REPUBLIC

TO THE PEOPLE OF IRELAND

IRISHMEN AND IRISHWOMEN: In the name of God and of the dead generations from which she receives her old tradition of nationhood, Ireland, through us, summons her children to her flag and strikes for her freedom.

Having organised and trained her manhood through her secret revolutionary organisation, the Irish Republican Brotherhood, and through her open military organisations, the Irish Volunteers and the Irish Citizen Army, having patiently perfected her discipline, having resolutely waited for the right moment to reveal itself, she now seizes that moment, and, supported by her exiled children in America and by gallant allies in Europe, but relying in the first on her own strength, she strikes in full confidence of victory.

We declare the right of the people of Ireland to the ownership of Ireland, and to the unfettered control of Irish destinies, to be sovereign and indefeasible. The long usurpation of that right by a foreign people and government has not extinguished the right, nor can it ever be extinguished except by the destruction of the Irish people. In every generation the Irish people have asserted their right to national freedom and sovereignty; six times during the last three hundred years they have asserted it to arms. Standing on that fundamental right and again asserting it in arms in the face of the world, we hereby proclaim the Irish Republic as a Sovereign Independent State, and we pledge our lives and the lives of our comrades-in-arms to the cause of its freedom, of its welfare, and of its exaltation among the nations.

The Irish Republic is entitled to, and hereby claims, the allegiance of every Irishman and Irishwoman. The Republic guarantees religious and civil liberty, equal rights and equal opportunities to all its citizens, and declares its resolve to pursue the happiness and prosperity of the whole nation and all of its parts, cherishing all of the children of the nation equally and oblivious of the differences carefully fostered by an alien government, which have divided a minority from the majority in the past.

Until our arms have brought the opportune moment for the establishment of a permanent National, representative of the whole people of Ireland and elected by the suffrages of all her men and women, the Provisional Government, hereby constituted, will administer the civil and military affairs of the Republic in trust for the people.

We place the cause of the Irish Republic under the protection of the Most High God. Whose blessing we invoke upon our arms, and we pray that no one who serves that cause will dishonour it by cowardice, inhumanity, or rapine. In this supreme hour the Irish nation must, by its valour and discipline and by the readiness of its children to sacrifice themselves for the common good, prove itself worthy of the august destiny to which it is called.

Signed on Behalf of the Provisional Government.

Thomas J. Clarke, Seán Mac Diarmada, Thomas MacDonagh, P. H. Pearse, Eamonn Ceannt, James Connolly, Joseph Plunkett

A Song of a Fighting Race?[*]

Peadar Kearney, a Dublin working-class house painter and songwriter, is generally credited with having written *The Soldier's Song*, the Irish national anthem. What Kearney, a member of the Supreme Council of the IRB according to his famous nephew Brendan Behan, certainly did write was the original English-language lyrics for the song. It is those words which contain allegedly divisive lyrics concerning 'children of a fighting race' who are 'impatient for the coming fight'.

Kearney did not write the Irish language lyrics most commonly sung to the tune these days. Neither did he write the music for a melody normally attended to in an instrumental orchestral version. Kearney is really the instigator of the anthem, rather than the author of anything that one ever hears on football terraces or at elegant state soirées.

There is little ambiguity about the song's political and revolutionary origin. It was initially a rebel song written by IRB members Kearney and Paddy Heaney with a view to encouraging militant sentiment and action. Kearney and Heaney were both members of the Oliver Bond 1798 Club and it was for that activist grouping that they wrote the anthem in 1907. Bulmer Hobson first published Kearney's lyrics in the IRB's mouthpiece, *Irish Freedom*, in 1912.

Kearney (1883–1942) joined the Gaelic League in 1901, the IRB in 1903 and the Irish Volunteers in 1913. He fought during the Easter Rising alongside Thomas MacDonagh at Jacob's Biscuit Factory but avoided capture afterwards. He subsequently wrote a whimsical song about the Rising, *A Row in the Town*:

I'll sing you a song of a row in the town,
When the green flag went up and the crown rag came down,

'Twas the neatest and sweetest thing ever you saw,
And they played the best game played in Erin go Bragh.

He was active in the Tan War until interned in Ballykinler Camp in 1920. Writing about those times, he put some context on his song-writing motivations: 'We lived as revolutionaries in a period of revolution. We had no thoughts for the morrow. As far as we were concerned we were simply units in a movement.' His best-known song, other than the national anthem, is *The Bold Fenian Men*, but he wrote a batch of patriotic and pro-worker odes.

Paddy Heaney, who worked out the stirring air to *The Soldier's Song* on his accordion, died in poverty when he was 29 and was buried in an unmarked grave in Drumcondra Cemetery.

After 1916, the song became tremendously popular amongst the Irish Volunteers, eventually emerging as the marching tune of the IRA. Other patriotic ditties, such as *God Save Ireland* and *A Nation Once Again*, had previously been the country's unofficial anthems, but they'd been effectively hijacked by the post-Parnell Parliamentary Party which was good at wrapping the green flag around itself for theatrical effect.

When the Civil War broke out Kearney, swayed by his friendship with Michael Collins and by his loyalty to the IRB, took the Free State side. Like many members of his family, he leaned towards the left and eventually drifted back into the Republican fold.

The Soldier's Song was translated into Irish as *Amhrán na bhFiann* by Liam Ó Rinn (1888–1950), who drafted the Irish language versions of the 1922 Free State Constitution and De Valera's 1937 Constitution. He was, in his day, a noted Hellenist, litterateur and writer of talent. Ó Rinn's lyrics were first published in *An tÓglach* in 1923. It was adopted as the national anthem by the Free State in 1926.

Kearney died in relative poverty, never terribly happy about the paltry sums he had been paid for *The Soldier's Song* copyright. His two nephews, Brendan and Dominic Behan, carried on his various cultural and political interests. Both were notable songwriters. Brendan wrote *The Old Triangle* (popularly recorded by The Pogues and The Dubliners) while Dominic was responsible for *The Patriot Game* which was 'adapted' by Bob Dylan and turned into *With God on Our Side*.

By 2006, *The Soldier's Song* was being much debated. A vocal unionist minority toiling in the media would occasionally suggest, for mischief's sake, that the anthem was no longer an appropriate part of the nation's creation myth – that it should be replaced by something more calming. At the same time, conversely, two major auctioneering houses organised sales at which manuscript copies of *The Soldier's Song* were expected to go for six- and seven-figure sums. The 'Irish History Sale' and the 'Independence' auction offered up between them, a cornucopia of patriotic heritage relics such as the Official Peadar Kearney Archive and signed letters from Daniel O'Connell, Parnell, Pearse, de Valera, Yeats, Joyce and Shaw, not to mention 1798 Rebellion weapons. There was media chatter concerning whether or not Ireland's birthright was going under the hammer or being made available to the highest bidder.

The Soldier's Song

We'll sing a song, a soldier's song,
With cheering rousing chorus,
As round our blazing fires we throng,
The starry heavens o'er us;
Impatient for the coming fight,
And as we wait the morning's light,
Here in the silence of the night,
We'll chant a soldier's song.

Chorus:
Soldiers are we
whose lives are pledged to Ireland;
Some have come
from a land beyond the wave.
Sworn to be free,
No more our ancient sire land
Shall shelter the despot or the slave.
Tonight we man the gap of danger
In Erin's cause, come woe or weal
'Mid cannons' roar and rifles peal,
We'll chant a soldier's song.

In valley green, on towering crag,
Our fathers fought before us,
And conquered 'neath the same old flag
That's proudly floating o'er us.
We're children of a fighting race,
That never yet has known disgrace,
And as we march, the foe to face,
We'll chant a soldier's song.

Chorus

Sons of the Gael! Men of the Pale!
The long watched day is breaking;
The serried ranks of Inisfail
Shall set the Tyrant quaking.
Our camp fires now are burning low;
See in the east a silv'ry glow,
Out yonder waits the Saxon foe,
So chant a soldier's song.

Chorus

Amhrán na bhFiann

Seo dhibh a cháirde duan Óglaigh,
Cathréimeach briomhar ceolmhar,
Ár dtinte cnámh go buacach táid,
'S an spéir go min réaltogach
Is fonnmhar faobhrach sinn chun gleo
'S go tiúnmhar glé roimh thíocht do'n ló
Fé chiúnas chaomh na hoiche ar seol:
Seo libh canaídh Amhrán na bhFiann.

Curfá:
Sinne Fianna Fáil
A tá fé gheall ag Éirinn,
buion dár slua
Thar toinn do ráinig chugainn,
Fé mhóid bheith saor.
Sean tír ár sinsir feasta
Ní fhagfar fé'n tiorán ná fé'n tráil
Anocht a théam sa bhearna bhaoil,
Le gean ar Ghaeil chun báis nó saoil
Le guna screach fé lámhach na bpiléar
Seo libh canaídh Amhrán na bhFiann.

Cois bánta réidhe, ar árdaibh sléibhe,
Ba bhuachach ár sinsir romhainn,
Ag lámhach go tréan fé'n sár-bhrat séin
Tá thuas sa ghaoith go seolta
Ba dhúchas riamh d'ár gcine cháidh
Gan iompáil siar ó imirt áir,
'S ag siúl mar iad i gcoinne námhad
Seo libh, canaídh Amhrán na bhFiann.

Curfá

245

A bhuíon nách fann d'fhuil Ghaeil is Gall,
Sin breacadh lae na saoirse,
Tá scéimhle 's scanradh i gcroíthe namhad,
Roimh ranna laochra ár dtire.
Ár dtinte is tréith gan spréach anois,
Sin luisne ghlé san spéir anoir,
'S an bíobha i raon na bpiléar agaibh:
Seo libh, canaídh Amhrán na bhFiann.

Curfá

Tan War and Civil War

The Fenian Path to Freedom[*]

Today in Ireland, although through improved economic conditions, which have been worldwide and in which it was not possible altogether to prevent us sharing, helped by a better living on the land, bought very dearly by the purchase back again of a great part of our country from those who had never any right to it, we have been lifted out of the worst slough of destitution; although we have been turning our eyes towards the light of liberty and learning to lift our heads again as Irish men and Irish women with a land of our own, and with traditions and hopes of which no nation need feel ashamed, yet still from east to west, from north to south, we are soaked, saturated, and stupefied with the English outlook.

Only slowly, laboriously, do we turn in our chains and struggle to free ourselves from the degrading lie that what is English is necessarily respectable, and what is Irish, low and mean. Even at this moment when our daily papers and our weekly papers are writing of our newly-won freedom and rejoicing over our national hopes, they continue to announce in their leading columns the movements of English society and the births and marriages of upper-class English nonentities.

But by the completeness with which England converted us into hewers of wood and drawers of water, she in the end defeated her own purpose.

Feebly resisting at the moments when we were less completely crushed, when a brief interval came between the long periods of starvation, when we had a moment in which we could reflect upon our condition, we gradually awoke to the cause of our miseries, and we grew to learn if we would be economically

---

[*] *The Path to Freedom* (1922), Michael Collins.

free we must be nationally free, and if we would be spiritually free we must be nationally free.

The coming and the presence of the English had deprived us of life and liberty. Their ways were not our ways. Their interests and their purposes meant our destruction. We must turn back again the wheels of that infamous machine which was destroying us. We must get the English out of Ireland.

Our efforts at first were naturally timid, and they were often futile because we were too much concerned with the political side – confused in this by the example of England where nationality was always expressed that way, and was principally a matter of political organisation.

Repeal of the Union was little more than a cry gaining what real strength it had from the more vigorous hostility of the Young Ireland movement, which revived our old literature, which recovered Irish history, and spread a new spirit. That spirit was not wholly martial, but what Irishman will say today that it was not beneficial, even so?

The Fenians came and once and for all raised the banner of Ireland's freedom, with a definite military policy which, though unsuccessful at the time, had its full effect in bringing before men's minds the real road to Irish salvation.

The Fenian idea left a torch behind it with which Tom Clarke and Seán MacDermott kindled the fires of Easter Week, and, though seemingly quenched, these were soon blazing brightly again at Solohead, at Clonfin, at Macroom, at Dublin, at many a place in Clare, in Mayo, and Monaghan, and Donegal during the recent struggle.

After the Fenians, years of death again, while famine raged over the land, till Parnell emerged to struggle for independence under the name of Home Rule which, though accompanied by the social and economic revolt of Davitt's national land policy, was bringing us back again to the dangerous idea of seeking freedom by means of some form of political weapon.

The weakness inherent in Parnell's policy was obviated by his intense personal hostility to the English.

He never forgot the end in the means. But it lost that saving protection when it fell into the hands of those who succeeded him and who, in the lotus-like atmosphere of the Westminster Parliament, forgot the national spirit and lost touch with the minds and feelings of their countrymen.

The collapse came when in the hands of weaker men the national effort became concentrated at the foreign parliament on English political lines. The methods adopted by the parliamentarians, the forum they had chosen, made their crumbling an easy matter, and from the English point of view it greatly helped division in their ranks, and with division came the inevitable dissipation of energy.

We would have an identical situation today had we chosen the same methods and fought on the same battlefield for the last five years. In that parliamentary period, however, the people at home were growing in national consciousness and in strength and courage. The Gaelic revival and the learning of our national tongue were teaching a new national self-respect. We recalled the immortal tales of our ancient heroes, and we began to look to a future in which we could have a proud, free, distinct nation worthy of the past.

We learned that what we wanted was not a political form of Home Rule or any other kind or form of Home Rule, but a revival of Gaelic life and ways. Economic thought and study showed us that the poverty which afflicted us came from the presence of the English and their control over us; had come from landlordism and the drain of English taxation, the neglect of Irish resources, and the obstruction to Irish industries by the domination of the English Parliament. And we saw that we must manage these things for ourselves.

And, besides the hope of material emancipation, we grew to think of love of our land, and all that it had given us and had still to give us, and what we could make of it when it was our own once more. And we became filled with a patriotic fervour before which, when the time came, force would prove impotent. The expression of this new hope and new courage manifested itself in the Easter Week Rising.

The leaven of the old Fenianism had been at work in our midst. Tom Clarke, a member of the old Fenian Brotherhood, came out from jail after sixteen years' penal servitude to take up the work where he had left it off.

Seán MacDermott, tramping through Ireland, preached the Fenian gospel of a freedom which must be fought for, enrolled recruits, and, by his pure patriotism and lovable unselfish character, inspired all with whom he came in contact to emulate him and to be worthy of his teaching.

Our army was in existence again. It was not brought into being, as is wrongfully supposed, by the example of Carson's recruiting in North-East Ulster. It needed no such example. It was already in being – the old Irish Republican Brotherhood in fuller force.

JOINING THE IRB[*]

The IRB Circle to which we belonged was centred at Doon. There were very few people around our part of the country that could be relied upon and so we had to cycle eight or nine miles to attend those circle meetings. Packy Ryan of Doon was the Centre of the Circle and it was at Ryan's that I first met Seán McDermott who, I believe, was on some kind of an organising mission around Munster. It may have been at Kilmallock because Packy Ryan also had a place there … We were only ordinary members and, being little more than boys, we were just

[*] Dan Breen, witness statement.

looked upon as handy messengers and suchlike, so that we did not know about what was going on except what we could see for ourselves.

Treaty Debates[†]

Countess Markievicz: I repeat what I said before, they went over there and had powers to sign but they could not sign away the liberties of the Irish people unless we have been meeting here in Dáil Éireann, the Parliament of the Irish Republic, as a fraud. From whom do we derive our powers? Do we not derive them from the people? As a Republican it is nothing new to me. Like Seán T. O'Kelly I have been many years a Republican. You all know how I was raised at the Lee by my uncle who was a '67 man and from him I got my inspiration. I believe with him and have a firm faith in the Fenian tradition. I have evidence of it that the old Fenian tradition, unwavering and uncompromising, is buried in the graves where lie the bodies of Tom Clarke, Pádraig Pearse, Seán MacDermott, John MacBride, Tom MacDonagh, Plunkett and others. Is there anyone here who would tell me that Tom Clarke lifted his hand for that thing? Is there anyone here who would tell me that any of the young men who fought and fell in 1916 would have lifted their hands for it? (Voices, Yes).

Richard Hayes:[‡] To me it seems that the signing of this Treaty was the final result, the culmination of a whole series of compromises, during the past four or five months – all necessary compromises. One of the very first acts in the negotiations was a compromise.

† Dáil Éireann debates.
‡ *Richard Hayes*: pro-Treaty TD for Limerick. He retired from politics in 1924 and was eventually the Irish film censor.

Our army was not defeated, it had not surrendered, and yet the enemy capital was selected as the meeting place for the two delegations. As a political proposition in relation to an immediate settlement with England it seems to me that the Republic ceased to exist four or five months ago. I agree with Deputy Mellows that the real Republic, the Republican ideal, still exists, and is still cherished in the hearts even of those people who support this Treaty. I think that it has been unfair and unjust, the criticism that has been levelled at the Delegation over these negotiations. They were selected by this assembly and by the Cabinet of this assembly to make a bargain, not on the Republican basis, but on the basis of association with Britain's Commonwealth. They made that bargain and they have brought back the bargain, and I think, considering the governing circumstances, that it is a pretty good bargain. I am firmly convinced of one thing regarding this Treaty, and it is this: but for the oath contained in it, ninety-nine per cent of this Dáil would accept it, as a compromise at least. I say that the oath is just as unpalatable to those who are voting for the Treaty as it is to those who are voting against it. Some Deputies referred to the clash of the oath, the incompatibility of the oath with the Fenian tradition. A night or two before the adjournment I happened to be reading the recollections of a Fenian leader, and I came across in it his opinion of the oaths to English monarchs. As a personal explanation I may say here that I wrote out that opinion and showed it to a friend out here in the lobby, and next day it appeared in leaded type in one of the Dublin newspapers, surrounded with a frame. I want to make it clear that I had nothing to do with getting it into the paper. The Fenian leader I refer to was John O'Leary. I think every member of this assembly will agree that John O'Leary, up to the day of his death was a consistent and unrepentant Fenian. I have here this opinion. It is not taken out of its context. 'Let England cease to govern Ireland, and then I shall swear to be true to Ireland, and to the Queen or King of Ireland, even though the Queen or King also so happen to be Queen or

King of England. It has never been with me, and never shall be, any question of forms of government, but simply freedom from foreign control.' If I may say so, while reading the book, memory carried back to me the first occasion in my life on which I saw the Fenian leader, John O'Leary, and the first occasion on which I saw the Chairman of the Delegation, Arthur Griffith; they were chatting together in a Dublin street. I think if John O'Leary were in this assembly he would see eye to eye with Arthur Griffith on this question. I do not intend to delay the House any longer. I shall finish up by saying this: If I were convinced this Treaty meant the final reconciliation of Ireland with England I would have very little hesitation in deciding upon which way my vote should go. But it is not the end (hear, hear). The adoption of this Treaty will enable us, as the Chairman of the Delegation said in his opening address, to rebuild here in this country, the old Gaelic civilisation that went down at the Battle of Kinsale (hear, hear). Its adoption will mean the revival and spread of Gaelic culture. It will mean the leavening into every body's Irish life the old traditional, and the old heroic memories. These things are not mentioned in the Treaty clauses, but they are implied there, and any one of them is just as important as, say, fiscal autonomy. I support this Treaty because it places in the hands of the Irish nation powerful weapons, material weapons and spiritual weapons that will enable it to achieve its full destiny. (Applause).

John O'Mahony: Some of our friends on the other side who are voting for this so-called Treaty seem to have blinded themselves into the belief that they can be Free Staters and remain good Republicans as well. They may so blind themselves but they cannot blind us, and they cannot blind the country or the world. No one knows better than the plenipotentiaries that as far as those who voluntarily accepted are concerned, this Georgian State is a final abandonment of the claim to independence; and those who support this Treaty will very soon find also that, on an issue of national principle like this there can be no such thing as running with the hare and hunting with the hounds (applause and counter-cheers). The two oaths are too fiercely conflicting to admit of either reconciliation or approachment. Any attempts to compose them must fail now as it failed before.

Kevin O'Higgins: What two oaths?

John O'Mahony: This oath and the oath to the Irish Republic. We had, as far as the oath is concerned, the same situation in the days of the New Departure.* No matter who may talk about free Irish Constitutions there is no difference between this oath that is before us now and the Westminster oath then, except this: the Westminster oath was only a single-springed trap for unwary Irishmen, while this new one that the plenipotentiaries want us to accept secures us forever with a treble spring. When the policy of the New Departure was proposed the Irish Republican Brotherhood, which Mr P. S. O'Hegarty described a couple of weeks ago as the sheet anchor of Irish nationalism, promptly and absolutely turned it down. Thus foiled in Ireland, Davitt and his friends sought to win the support of the Clan-na-Gael; and the Supreme Council of the IRB immediately sent the veteran, John O'Leary, to America to counteract their efforts. Addressing the Clan-na-Gael in New York, O'Leary denounced the proposal as immoral and impolitic. 'There is,' he said, 'to be a pretence of loyalty, but in reality treason all along the line. I do not believe in a policy of dust throwing and lying, but that is the policy of the New Departure. The Fenian Movement is purely a national movement. Though I were to stand absolutely alone I would resist this dishonest and unholy alliance. I believe in righteous means as well as righteous ends.' What John O'Leary said of the New Departure Republicans in 1878 can, with even more

---

* New Departure: the alliance between Parnell's Parliamentary Party and, amongst others, the Fenians.

force, be said of the self-deluded Free State Republicans in the Dáil today (applause). In spite of all this, Davitt, O'Connor Power, J. F. X. O'Brien, John O'Connor, and other members of the Fenian organisation persisted in their policy and took the Oath of Allegiance. When John O'Leary learned what they had done his only comment was: 'I wish the British Sovereign joy of the British oaths of turncoats who have already taken and broken the Republican oath.' Would not the unconquerable old Fenian leader, if he were here to-day, use the same words? Would he not employ even stronger language of those Dáil Deputies who are tumbling over each other in their eagerness to break the Republican oath that they took in August last to take this Oath of Allegiance to the British monarch and thereby to help the British Government to enforce this, its latest Coercion Act in Ireland? Whatever the result of the vote on this question, we who are against the surrender of our national independence can face ourselves, face the people, and face the country with the consciousness that we have done our duty to the Republic that we swore to maintain and uphold.

THE MODERN WORLD

On Language and the Irish Nation[*]

The Ireland which we desire would be the home of a people who valued material wealth only as the basis of right living, of a people who were satisfied with frugal comfort and devoted their leisure to the things of the soul; a land whose countryside would be bright with cosy homesteads, whose fields and villages would be joyous with the sounds of industry, with the romping of sturdy children, the contests of athletic youth and the laughter of happy maidens; whose firesides would be forums for the wisdom of old age. It would, in a word, be the home of a people living the life that God desires that men should live ....

For many the pursuit of the material is a necessity. Man, to express himself fully and to make the best use of the talents God has given him, needs a certain minimum of comfort and leisure. A section of our people have not yet this minimum. They rightly strive to secure it and it must be our aim and the aim of all who are just and wise to assist in that effort. But many have got more than is required and are free, if they choose, to devote themselves more completely to cultivating the things of the mind and, in particular, those that mark us out as a distinct nation.

The first of these latter is the national language. It is for us what no other language can be. It is our very own. It is more than a symbol, it is an essential part of our nationhood. It has been moulded by the thought of a hundred generations of our forebears. In it is stored the accumulated experience of a people, our people who, even before Christianity was brought to them, were already cultured and living in a well-ordered society.

The Irish language spoken in Ireland today is the direct descendant without break of the language our ancestors spoke in those far off days. As a vehicle for three thousand years of

* Éamon de Valera. Broadcast on Radio Éireann, 17 March 1943.

our history, the language is for us precious beyond measure. As the bearer to us of a philosophy, of an outlook on life deeply Christian and rich in practical wisdom, the language today is worth far too much to dream of letting it go. To part with it would be to abandon a great part of ourselves, to lose the key to our past, to cut away the roots from the tree. With the language gone we could never again aspire to being more than half a nation.

For my part, I believe that this outstanding mark of our nationhood can be preserved and made forever safe by this generation. I am indeed certain of it, but I know that it cannot be saved without understanding and co-operation and effort and sacrifice. It would be wrong to minimise the difficulties. They are not light. The task of restoring the language as the everyday speech of our people is a task as great as any nation ever undertook. But it is a noble task. Other nations have succeeded in it, though in their case when the effort was begun, their national language was probably more widely spoken among their people than is ours with us. As long as the language lives, however, on the lips of the people as their natural speech in any substantial part of this land we are assured of success if – *if* we are in earnest.

It is a task in which the attitude of the people is what counts most. It is upon the individual citizen, upon you who are listening to me, that the restoration of the language finally depends. The state and public institutions can do much to assist, but if the individual has not the inclination or the will power to make the serious efforts initially required, or to persevere till reasonable fluency is attained, outside aids will be of little use ….

The restoration of the unity of the national territory and the restoration of the language are the greatest of our uncompleted national tasks. Let us devote this year especially to the restoration of the language; let the year be one in which the need for this restoration will be constantly in our thoughts and the language itself as much as possible on our lips.

The physical dangers that threaten, and the need for unceasing vigilance in the matters of defence as well as unremitting attention to the serious day-to-day problems that the war has brought upon us should not cause us to neglect our duty to the language.* Time is running against us in this matter of the language. We cannot afford to postpone our effort ....

Bail ó Dhia oraibh, agus bail go gcuire Sé ar an obair atá romhainn. Go gcumhdaí Dia sinn agus gur fiú sinn choíche, mar náisiún, na tíolacaí a thug Pádraig chugainn. Go dtuga an tUile-chumhachtach, A thug slán sinn go dtí seo ón anachain is ón mí-adh atá ar oiread sín náisiún eile de bharr an chogaidh seo, scáth, agus dídean dúinn go dtí an deireadh, agus go ndeonaí Sé gur fiú sinn cion uasal a dhéanamh sa saol nua atá romhainn.

DESMOND GREAVES
HOLDING A HAND IN THE FLAME†

I first met Desmond Greaves in England through my husband, Cathal MacLiam. Cathal was living in one of the rooms in the house where Desmond lived at Cockpit Chambers, Northington Street, Holborn, around the corner from Bloomsbury and a few hundred yards from the Connolly Association office where he worked each day.

Desmond's flat was very much a bachelor quarters, extremely untidy and dusty, lined with bookshelves and with masses of books and papers piled all over the place. I remember that a pile of old telephone directories held up one of the chairs, so that one had to clear a space around the table when having a meal. Cathal lived in another flat downstairs.

* Second World War.
† Helga MacLiam, A Contribution to the 17th Desmond Graves Summer School, 2005.

I had come from post-War Germany to work as a nurse in Harrogate, Yorkshire, in 1949 and had met Cathal. When I came down to London, Cathal, who was very active in the Connolly Association and had become a kind of protégé of Desmond's, who was of course the older man, brought me to meet him at the flat.

I can still see him in his shorts – for it was summer – and his string vest, for he didn't make many concessions to appearances, at least at that time. He became somewhat more conservative later when he got older.

And Desmond's flat was something else again. I saw a mound of old bed linen piled in the bath; for instead of washing it he would go out and buy new linen all the time, to save time and trouble.

As I was soon engaged to Cathal, Desmond allowed me to get rid of the mound of bed linen by washing it, for he had kept several other offers of help from various females at bay. And later he actually allowed us to wall-paper and thoroughly spring-clean his flat.

That first evening he introduced me to Indian curry. I had never had a curry before. Desmond had also gone down to Soho to buy German pumpernickel in my honour. But the curry was so hot! 'I was warned that the chillies were unexpectedly sharp', he said, and indeed they were. They were much too hot even for him, so that we all had to resort to yoghurt to cool ourselves afterwards.

Desmond of course was a first-class cook – he used say cooking was applied chemistry, and he was by profession a research chemist and I had many meals with him afterwards. He told me once that he planned to write a cookery book, but it was one of several unfinished projects.

All the active Connolly Association would go selling the *Irish Democrat* around the Irish pubs at weekends in the 1950s and 1960s. And Desmond himself would regularly sell the paper that he edited and wrote much of. They were using it to try to draw the attention of the Irish community in Britain, and through it the British labour and trade union movement, to the misdeeds of prime minister Lord Brookeborough's Unionist regime in the six counties.

This was a peak period of Irish emigration and there were thousands of men in the Irish pubs in Kilburn, Camden Town, Paddington, Shepherd's Bush and Hammersmith – most of them working in Britain's building trade. I remember the story of the Irishman who told the *Irish Democrat* paper-seller, 'Be off with you. I would not wipe my behind with that paper' ... And the reply, 'You should be careful doing that, for there are sharp points in it!'

Cathal and I got married in 1955 and Desmond Greaves was the best man at our wedding. After the wedding we went to Schmidt's German restaurant in Charlotte Street for the wedding breakfast, but found it closed. So we went into the lounge of a pub where I remember we breakfasted on crisps and Babycham. Then we went on to Schmidt's for lunch, while Desmond, I remember, had to go to Birmingham in connection with the *Irish Democrat*.

In January 1957 Cathal and I moved to Dublin as Cathal was threatened with being called up under Britain's conscription laws, which were still in force.

In the late 1950s, 1960s and for two decades after, Desmond Greaves used to come regularly to Dublin every couple of months or so, especially while he was doing his researches and interviews for his biographies of James Connolly, Liam Mellows and Seán O'Casey. And for much of that time he used to stay with us, initially in our house in Finglas and from 1968 at our house in Belgrave Road Rathmines.

He would land from the Holyhead boat at Dun Laoghaire, where Cathal and sometimes I would meet him. They would then buy a few bottles of wine and spend the evening talking at our place – often into the early and middle hours of the morning. As Desmond lived most of the time on his own in London and later at his family house in Birkenhead, Merseyside, which he inherited after his sister's death, and as he was an intensely sociable person, I think that he used 'let his hair down' when he came to Ireland, having people to talk to for hours and hours into the night. It was as if he was making up for lost time.

He was a brilliant conversationalist, very lively and vivacious and with a vast range of knowledge, as he was both a scientist and a historian and literary person. He could talk with authority on such a wide range of subjects that being with him on those occasions was always interesting. He was great company, and we had lots of fun and many good laughs.

He never married himself. I think he felt that doing the political work he was so committed to, on a tiny wage in the conditions of the 1950s, when he went full-time on the *Irish Democrat*, was not compatible with the responsibilities of a wife and family. I sometimes think that we provided a kind of alternative family for him, where he could share in the family life that he did not have himself. He was very good with children, had a natural understanding for them and their ways, and from the early days he never arrived at our place without bringing with him several bars of chocolate. We used to call him 'Onkel Desmond' to the children, but he soon became known as 'Onkel Coco-lade' to them!

One incident in particular stands out in my memory from our years in Finglas. One day this big polished limousine stopped outside our front door and a man in military uniform stepped out and knocked: 'Was Mr Greaves at home?' It happened that he was in town at the time, but he would be back later.

This was President de Valera's aide-de-camp and the car was the presidential limousine itself. Seemingly Desmond had written to President De Valera seeking an interview with him about the time he had spent with Liam Mellows in America in 1919 and he had sent the President a copy of his biography of

James Connolly with the request. He had said in his letter that he would be staying at our place in Finglas on his next visit to Dublin.

De Valera had expressed an interest in giving his views on Mellows to the man who had written the Connolly book, so when Desmond returned home he got in touch with Áras an Uachtaráin and the next day the presidential limousine came down again and brought him up to the Park to meet de Valera, with whom he spent a couple of hours chatting.

De Valera told Desmond, according to what he told us himself afterwards, that he had learned many new things about Connolly and understood his life and period better from reading the Connolly biography. He showed Desmond around some of the rooms in the Áras and pointed out the big tree in the garden which he said Queen Victoria had planted, as if this were highly significant.

I remember Desmond saying that he had got the impression from de Valera's words that the fact that he was now living in the place where Queen Victoria had once planted a tree, summed up for him the significance of the Irish Revolution, and the advances it had achieved!

He used also reminisce sometimes about de Valera discussing Mary MacSwiney and the hardline members of Sinn Féin from which de Valera had broken away when he founded Fianna Fáil in 1926. De Valera had remarked to him about Mary MacSwiney, 'She would have held her hand in that flame, pointing to the fire ... But I was not made of that metal'.

'And the more fool she was', Desmond used to comment afterwards. 'De Valera had far too much sense than to be holding his hand in a flame!'

Of course our neighbours in Finglas were greatly impressed by the presidential car arriving at our front door and whisking our house-guest up to see the president. It greatly raised our standing and reputation with some of them!

It was while we were in Finglas in the middle 1960s that Cathal Goulding, Seán Garland and some other leading Republicans came to see Desmond for the first time. My husband Cathal was Cathal Goulding's first cousin, although they had never met before, or at least not for years.

This meeting may have been suggested by Roy Johnston, who had joined the Republican Movement at that time, although I am not sure.* But in any case a group of them came one evening, a veritable delegation, it seemed. Cathal met his first cousin for the first time and they stayed talking about politics as usual until the early hours, when it became too much for me and I went to bed.

I remember Desmond Greaves as a quite extraordinary person . . . Full of life and good humour. Full of interesting things to say and point out. Great company and always considerate and polite in personal relations. He was one of the really significant people that I have met in the course of my life and I am glad to be able to contribute these modest reminiscences about him.

The Republican Congress
and the Spanish Civil War[†]

The Republican Congress, founded in 1934, came about when left wing republican intellectuals like Peadar O'Donnell and George Gilmore left the IRA which, with the emergence of Fianna Fáil, was being consigned to the fringes of political life. The IRA was also, like many 1930s organisations, divided along left/right lines. The principal right-wing IRA leader, the divisive Seán Russell, steered the organisation into political irrelevance

---

* Controversial radical scientist active in the Connolly Association and various republican left organisations; latterly associated with green politics.
† Joe Ambrose.

in the face of Fianna Fáil's remorseless rise and hegemony of the conservative republican high ground.

The Congress, a reaction against IRA intellectual inertia and a bleak economic environment, believed that a united Ireland could only be achieved through a struggle which uprooted capitalism. At the IRA's 1934 Bodenstown rally, clashes occurred between Congress supporters and the IRA. Protestant Congress members from West Belfast, carrying a banner which proclaimed 'Unite Protestant, Catholic and Dissenter to break the connection with Capitalism', were attacked by certain IRA factions.

The Congress split at its first annual conference held in Rathmines Town Hall on 8 and 9 September 1934. One group felt that a united front of leftist republicans could challenge the dominance of the mainstream political parties. Their Congress opponents believed that they should form a conventional political party which would seek a worker's republic. This stance was supported by Peadar O'Donnell and the Communist Party of Ireland. The Republican Congress soon petered out, with its leading lights making their way to Spain where, as part of the Connolly Column, they fought against Franco's fascist-supported Nationalist forces.

Patrick Byrne was, along with IRA left winger Frank Ryan and Frank Edwards, joint secretary of the Republican Congress.[‡]

Frank Ryan joined the East Limerick Brigade of the IRA in 1922. He fought on the Republican side in the Irish Civil War, and was wounded and interned. A UCD graduate, he became editor of *An Phoblacht* in 1929 and was appointed to the IRA Army Council.

In 1936, Ryan went to Spain to fight with the International Brigades. He was eventually captured and, in mysterious circumstances, fell into the hands of the Nazi government in Berlin. He died in the German capital. The circumstances surrounding his

---

‡ *Frank Edwards*: a Waterford-based Communist who rose to prominence during the Spanish Civil War,

final years have lead to ongoing, and somewhat outlandish, efforts to portray Ryan as a fascist sympathiser. Given his consistent public and private opposition to fascism, his central role in the development of Irish socialism, his progressive position within Irish republicanism, and the recollections of comrades such as Tom Jones, claims that he had fascist inclinations have the whiff of blackguardism and fanatical revisionism about them.

He is immortalised in one of Shane McGowan's best songs, *The Sickbed of Cuchullainn.*

MEMORIES OF THE REPUBLICAN CONGRESS 1934–84[*]

On four occasions in the past year I have been asked to speak to Irish and Socialist groups on the subject of the Republican Congress. When I spoke at a meeting in Manchester, under the auspices of the Labour Committee on Ireland, a member of the audience, a Professor of History, told me that it was my 'duty' to commit to writing the events I had tried to describe, as a permanent record. He pointed out that very little is known from the standpoint of the rank and file of great radical movements of the past, for the same reason that working people were not always literate, and those who were, had not the time or the means of recording the struggles in which they were engaged. So that too often what we know of the Levellers, the Luddites, the Chartists and the Fenians, has been absorbed from the unsympathetic writings of middle class hacks, and hostile bourgeois historians.

Of the Republican Congress movement in Ireland in the 1930s little has been recorded. There are two pamphlets by George Gilmore, and the splendid serial, also from his pen, that has appeared in recent issues of the *Irish Democrat*. The subject

* Patrick Byrne, *Irish Democrat*, May 1984.

is also mentioned in *Frank Ryan* by Seán Cronin and in *Peadar O'Donnell – Irish Social Rebel* by Michael McInerney. Of course, the files of the *Republican Congress* and the other papers published by the Congress, *The Irish People*, and *The Irish Democrat* will provide a mine of information for the student of revolutionary movements of the period. Writing in London, without reference to these sources, I must rely mainly on my memory of those exciting events, and the wonderful people I had the honour and privilege of working with in the fight against Fascism and for a Socialist Ireland.

My earliest memories are of the Easter Rebellion in Dublin in 1916. I was rising four years of age at the time and vividly recall the panic and prayers within our home, and the gun fire and red skies without. Growing up in such a revolutionary era, I naturally gravitated in time to membership of Sinn Féin and its 'military wing', the IRA. The organisation then (1929) bore little, if any, resemblance to the present 'Provos'. The IRA was still a powerful, well-organised and well-disciplined organisation. It was only three years since the leadership had included Éamon de Valera, Seán Lemass, Frank Aiken, and other civil war leaders who, deciding upon a new approach, had taken their seats in the Dáil, and only failed by the Speaker's casting vote to bring the Free State government down. In the general election in 1932 they were victorious.

Fianna Fáil had received considerable support from the IRA in the election campaign. Two days after taking office talks were resumed between De Valera and the Army Council (IRA) about the possibility of fusing the two movements. They both drew their support from the urban and rural working class and the small farming community and their aims were almost identical. The outcome, however, was inconclusive.

This was a time of great depression in Western Europe in general, and in Ireland, north and south, in particular. There was a quarter of a million unemployed in the island out of a population of about four millions. Conditions in the North were, if anything, worse than in the Free State. The shipyards were almost at a standstill. 20,000 workers in the linen industry were idle. In the slums of Belfast 8,000 children were declared by the Belfast Executive Committee to be suffering from malnutrition.

The South was also enduring severe economic depression There was mass unemployment, poverty and starvation in the crowded slums of Dublin, Waterford, Cork and elsewhere; stagnation in the countryside. Evictions from smallholdings, and mass emigration were on a scale unequalled since the 1880s.

The gathering storm of frustration and anger broke in Belfast. The *Irish Press* of 4 October 1932 reported '10,000 unemployed marched in protest against the scale of relief paid in certain distress schemes. Eight shillings a week for a man to support his wife and family.' On 12 October the *Press* reported: 'Cordon around Belfast. Street fighting in widely separated areas. Revolver and rifle firing by police on huge crowd of unemployed, especially in the Falls and Shankill area. John Greggan of Millfield shot dead. Samuel Baxter of Regent Street died of wounds received in an attack made on an armoured car that had become trapped in a trench'. The *Belfast Telegraph* confessed that 'There was an exchange of mischief-makers all over the city. It was significant that for once the religious question did not enter into the trouble. Youths from Protestant areas were to be found in Catholic districts and vice versa.'

In this situation, while the revolution was being served up on a plate in Belfast, what was the IRA leadership doing? Organising a 'Boycott Bass' Campaign. Because of some disparaging remarks the Bass boss, Colonel Grettin, was reported to have made about the Irish, some IRA leaders took umbrage and sent units out onto the streets of Dublin and elsewhere to raid pubs, terrify the customers, and destroy perfectly good stocks of bottled Bass, an activity in which I regret to say I was engaged.

The Fianna Fáil Party under the leadership of De Valera was now in government and endeavouring to implement the old Sinn Féin policy of 'self-reliance'. At that time agriculture was largely based on cattle ranching. Fianna Fáil would speed the plough, break up the large under-utilised estates, and make the soil of Ireland available for the people of Ireland. To a great extent this policy succeeded. One spin-off was that when war came in 1939, the country was largely self-sufficient in food and as the ports had been returned in a position to remain neutral.*

The battle for the Land Annuities commenced in 1933. The Land Annuities were payments made twice yearly by the farmers to meet the capital cost that had been involved in buying out the landlords at the time of the Treaty. The new Free State government had agreed to take over the collection of the tribute through the Land Commission and the sum involved some £5 millions being duly transferred to London. The payment of these annuities had been bitterly resented, and when an agitation to have them abolished commenced in County Donegal, instigated by the redoubtable Socialist-Republican leader, Peadar O'Donnell, the movement spread nationwide. The Fianna Fáil government with the utmost reluctance were sucked into the campaign and legislation to withhold the annuities was passed in the Dáil. The National Government in Westminster, led by the Labour traitors, Ramsey MacDonald and J. H. Thomas, over-reacted to this measure and imposed crippling taxes on all Irish goods entering Britain.

This cold, or economic, war lasted for six years. Irish industrialists were hard hit, but the farming community, especially the big cattle ranchers, sustained heavy losses.

Nevertheless, despite the hardship caused by these punitive measures, the people in general remained loyal to Fianna Fáil, but not all. The opposition party then known as Cumann na nGaedheal developed a 'military wing' called the Blueshirts. This was a Fascist organisation composed mainly of disgruntled Free

---

* Britain initially held on to three strategic Irish ports, known as the 'Treaty Ports', when they withdrew from the territory which became the Free State. The most important of these was Queenstown/Cobh. The Fianna Fáil government regained these ports in 1938.

State officers, political opportunists, seasoned with lumpen-proletarian elements and led by a former police commissioner Eoin O'Duffy, who declared at a meeting in west Limerick in 1933 that 'What the Blackshirts did for Italy and the Brownshirts did for Germany, the Blueshirts will do for Ireland.' O'Duffy's 'March on Dublin' was planned for 13 August and there was a general mobilisation of Blueshirts to coverage on Leinster House. At the last moment the march was prohibited by the government, but already the city was swarming with Blueshirt bands. The IRA leadership had remained withdrawn from this crisis, except to exhort their followers to avoid 'party Politics', but large numbers of republicans and socialists were on the street to counter Blueshirt demonstrations. In February 1934, the Army Council (IRA) issued an order that volunteers were 'not to take part in any action against Fascist-imperialist organisations as this was not the policy in the Army.'

This policy of isolation from the developing class struggle and non-resistance was causing great discontent in the rank and file of the Republican movement. The crisis came at the IRA Annual Convention on 17 March 1934 in Dublin. Michael Price called for a declaration of a 'workers republic' as the aim of the army. The Right leadership was shocked. Seán Russell said that they 'were not interested in party politics'. Peadar O'Donnell called for a Republican Congress that would rally all shades of anti-fascist and republican opinion. This was opposed by the executive committee who won by one point. Thereupon Peadar O'Donnell, Michael Price, George Gilmore and Frank Ryan left the convention and the IRA.

This procedure was to be repeated at similar conventions all over the country. At the Dublin Brigade convention, at which I was a delegate, a motion calling for the adoption of a socialist policy was opposed by Seán MacBride, who carried the meeting by a small majority. The dissidents, including myself, immediately withdrew.

A special conference convened at Athlone on 7–8 April 1934 was attended by over 200 former IRA leaders and prominent republicans and socialists and the call was issued for a Republican Congress: 'We believe that a Republic of a United Ireland will never be achieved except through a struggle which uproots capitalism on its way. We cannot conceive a Free Ireland and a subject working class.'

A supporting call was received from a special conference of Trade Unionists in Belfast:

> We are convinced that the horrors of the capitalist economic system, the menace of Fascism … the question of Irish National unity are inter-related problems, the solution of which can only be found in the solidarity of the workers, small farmers and peasants North and South.'

The statement called for a Republican Congress and was signed by William McMullen, Chairman, Belfast Trades Council; William Craig (AEU); Murtagh Morgan (President IT&GWU, Belfast); J. Swindenbank (ETU); John Campbell, Daniel Loughran and P. Hadden (Northern Ireland socialist party). (All Protestants)

The organisation of Congress branches now proceeded throughout the country. A headquarters was established at 112 Marlborough Street, Dublin and a weekly paper, *The Republican Congress*, was launched. There was a new and wonderful spirit abroad, attracting especially the young. In fact some of our youthful helpers were so eager, I recall, especially Miriam Gogarty, Oliver Norton and Miriam James, whom I feared were taking time off from school for Congress work.

Nora Connolly in her last book wrote of the period: 'Then the Republican Congress came along, when there was a vacuum for political movement in Ireland. It was purely socialist as well. We wanted to start a new party and we wanted the Republican Congress to be the next government. We had so many people that it could have been. Everything was socialism at the time. The Republican Congress was very strong. It was a grand time. Often I would travel up and down the country with Mick Price organising branches.'

In Dublin where I was actively involved, five branches were established, soon to be joined by a sixth branch composed of British ex-service men with Captain Jack White as Chairman. This branch was a direct result of a new approach I had advocated to ex-soldiers in an article 'A message to ex-servicemen' which was published in *The Republican Congress* in November 1934. On Armistice Day a contingent of British ex-servicemen, proudly displaying their medals, marched with Republican Congress branches through cheering crowds of Dubliners in a demonstration against war and poverty. I had urged this new approach because of the disgust I felt when I saw some ex-servicemen being set upon for wearing their medals and poppies on their ragged coats.

Our past involvement with the IRA weighed heavily for a time on the new organisation. An attempt was made to create a 'military wing' by resurrecting the Irish Citizen Army. We still had stocks of arms. There was more drilling in the hills and on one occasion when entering Congress headquarters in Marlborough Street, I saw through an open basement window, a class of workers engaged in small arms (revolver) drill.

This addiction to the traditional 'physical force' side of the Republican Movement had limited advantages in that our members were used to discipline and quick mobilisation, but it was disastrous in that the struggle was not in a military stage and amongst other things it provided an escape route for opportunist Trade Union Leaders who were quite happy to see terrorism used as a substitute for industrial action.

For example, on one occasion when there was trouble on a public works project in a certain area of Dublin, it was decided to take action against a contractor who was behaving badly towards the workforce, by putting out of action a fleet of vehicles on the site. I was entrusted with this task; so with five men, all armed, we approached the scene of action. Bill Scott (later to serve in the

International Brigade) seemed to appear from nowhere. 'Get to hell out of it, Pat. The place is swarming with the Special Branch.' I immediately 'dismissed' the squad telling them to separate and make their way quickly out of danger. I learned afterwards that the proposed sabotage had been discussed at an open trade union branch meeting. Other more ambitious militaristic adventures, including a raid on a barracks for arms, were rejected overwhelmingly in Committee.

Eventually, realistic political activity took over from militarism and it was agreed to give the IRA their guns back (or most of them) provided they were ceremoniously received!

Congress branches everywhere took part in trade union activity, employing for the first time in Ireland the techniques of the mass picket. On one occasion 200 of our members were arrested for picketing a large store in Dublin where some employees were receiving a weekly wage of 12 shillings. The 200 served a term in Mountjoy Jail.

Tenant Leagues were formed in the cities. In Dublin and Waterford especially shocking slum conditions were revealed. In both cities some clerical involvement (as slum landlords) was uncovered. Every week *The Republican Congress* carried new horror stories of the Dublin slums. Thirty thousand families were living in single rooms. Forty-nine per cent of the city's housing was unfit for habitation. At this time I was Chairman of the Dublin United Tenant Leagues. I have only space to give three typical examples of life in the Dublin slums. I quote from reports in our paper:

> Climbing a rickety stairs I entered a small room over a vegetable store, or more properly speaking, a stable in the vicinity of Parnell Square. There was no fire (in April). There was one bed on which lay a married girl of 19, who was expecting a baby. The bedclothes were old coats. The husband, who was unemployed, was receiving 9 shillings a week outdoor assistance, of this sum six shillings went on rent, leaving three shillings for food and other necessities. On the day of my visit they had been living on rice for two days, but this was now exhausted.

In the front 'parlour' of a house in Coleraine Street live the Keogh family. The room is eight feet square. It contains two beds, a table, and some chairs. At night 11 human beings pack into this den. On one bed seven of the children sleep. On the other the parents and two children rest.

Families of 12 are frequently found living in single rooms. In one house in Holles Street, 49 people are living.

The Tenant Leagues, run by Republican Congress personnel, organised rent strikes for better conditions. On one occasion the Third Dublin District Committee carried on a rent strike for two months affecting five streets in the vicinity of Westland Row, and finally won a 25% reduction in rent. At the same time the Fourth District Committee won rehousing by the Dublin Corporation for the tenants of Magee Court, a collection of filthy cottages fit only for the vermin abounding therein.

The rent strikes were most alarming. We told the tenants to withhold the rent, but not to spend it, a difficult injunction for people on the borderline of starvation to comply with. We held street meetings in alleyways and courts, using borrowed chairs for a platform, and arranged to fight off any eviction fight.

Similar activity was taking place in Waterford where Frank Edwards ran foul of a local church dignitary. Frank was at that time a teacher in Mount Zion Christian Brothers School. He was asked by the Bishop of Waterford and Lismore to sign an undertaking that he would not remain a member in any organisation of which the Catholic Church disapproved. He refused, and was promptly sacked from his teaching post.

Frank, in an article published in the book, *Survivors*, recalled an issue of *The Republican Congress* which displayed prominently on the front page a beautiful Red Flag with the words of Jim O'Connell's 'Red Flag' underneath.* Frank wrote: 'This caused nervous readers to protest that they were already under sufficient pressure from certain quarters without going out to seek it.' He wondered why Frank Ryan had taken this step.

* The lyrics of a song, *The Red Flag*.

278

I was in the Congress headquarters in Marlborough Street with Frank Ryan when the issue arrived, bearing the red flag. I asked Frank why he had come out so strong. He told me that at the time of the Truce in July 1921, he was commanded to take his unit of the East Limerick Battalion to a local creamery that had been taken over by the workers who were flying the red flag, and to eject them. Frank carried out his orders and hauled down the red flag. This had since weighed heavily on his conscience, and he was now making amends.

The Congress branches did not confine their activities to tenant league agitation. They were engaged in assisting miners on strike at Castlecomer, taking part in hunger marches, and in rallies and demonstrations of all kinds. I was frequently in Belfast at this time and spoke at meetings deep in Shankill territory.

The movement now had to bear the full weight of reaction, lay and clerical. Connolly House, the headquarters of the Communist Party, was attacked by a mob and burned. Earlier, the Workers' College in Madame Despard's house in Eccles Street, had been their target. I was present in both places when under siege.[†]

In Connolly House on the night of the attack I was in a room on the ground floor setting some leaflets from an antique printing press that had once been used for Connolly's *Workers Republic* in 1913. I was not a member of the CP, but they allowed me this facility.[‡] There were books and papers on display in the front window. Suddenly this was shattered by flying stones. There was a mob gathering outside. I dashed out to bolt the street door. There was a meeting in progress upstairs. Paddy Flanagan of the National Union of Railwaymen was lecturing to about 80 people. Our first consideration was to get the 'civilians' out which we did by a back door, before the mob completed the encirclement of the building. We then went through the drill for a siege. Brian O'Neill was going about with a woodman's axe (I don't know

† *Charlotte Despard:* an English radical pacifist, close to Maud Gonne.
‡ Communist Party.

where he got it). Johnnie Nolan and Jim Prendergast were barricading the stairs using benches from the lecture room.

I was on the first floor with Seán Murray and others. The lights were extinguished and we opened the windows to lessen the dangers of flying glass. We could see the mob outside. In between singing hymns and hurling abuse at us, they were chucking books and papers on a fire they had going in the middle of the street in Nazi fashion. Then bricks and all kinds of missiles came crashing into the darkened room, which we promptly hurled back. The mob was so dense we caused a number of injuries – 27, I learned, were hospital cases. Some were beaten up on the stretchers before entering the ambulance by the mob who thought they were our people. Meanwhile, a hayloft had been discovered – they were still stables for horses in the area – and its contents were piled against the door and set alight. At this stage, around midnight, Seán Murray gave the order to retire, which we did across the road to safety. Connolly House, a large building four stories high was burned to the ground. The police did nothing during all the commotion, except look on, obviously sympathetic to the rioters.

I was a student in the Workers College when the mob attacked. With other students, about 80, I was taking a course in political economy (Marx). European history, and Revolution in Theory and Practice. Madame Despard, then an old frail woman with a heart of a lion, awarded a gold watch at the end of the term to the best student, which I regret to say I wasn't. The mob attack followed the usual pattern, hymn singing, swearing, and brick throwing. Leslie Daiken was in charge of the defence. At the time, structural repairs were being undertaken inside the house, so we had plenty of 'ammunition' to hurl at the crowd in the street. We were saved this time by the intervention of some IRA stalwarts, principally Mick Kelly, O/C Dublin Brigade, who masquerading as police officers ordered the mob to disperse at gunpoint.

The College had been receiving the full treatment from the capitalist press, and the pulpit. A story was current that inside the door at Eccles Street was placed a 'Sacred Heart' mat for the students to wipe their boots on. This was a barefaced lie.

In June 1934, for the first time, a contingent of workers numbering about 500 travelled from the Shankill and Bally-macarret areas of Belfast in a fleet of coaches to take part in the annual Wolfe Tone commemoration in Bodenstown, Co. Kildare. On arrival in Dublin they went to Arbour Hill to lay wreaths on Connolly's grave, and then travelled to Bodenstown to take part in the parade, behind their banners reading 'Wolfe Tone Commemoration 1934 – Shankill Road branch – Break the Connection with Capitalism' and 'James Connolly Club, Belfast – United Irishmen of 1934'. One of the men who carried the latter banner, Jim Straney, died crossing the Ebro, the last major offensive of the Republican forces in Spain. The Congress branches left the assembly field at Sallins as part of the huge parade, but when our Belfast friends tried to follow us, their path was barred by a cordon of the IRA with orders to prevent them from leaving unless they agreed to keep their banners furled. This the Belfast men refused to do, but charged the cordon and fought their way through to join the Republican Congress contingent numbering several thousand and march with them through Sallins village behind the Workers Union of Ireland band playing 'The Red Flag'.

The cemetery, however, was well guarded by the Tipperary Brigade.* To avoid an unseemly outcome, the wreaths were laid on the roadside, and we withdrew to Sallins. The *Irish Times* commented next day on the irony of Ulster Protestants being prevented by Tipperary Catholics from honouring Wolfe Tone.

Meanwhile preparations were going ahead for the holding of the Congress. There was strong trade union support. The Workers' Union of Ireland, the second largest in the South of Ireland, had affiliated. Their leader, the great Jim Larkin, was a

* The Tipperary Brigade of the IRA.

staunch supporter and frequently spoke on Congress platforms. Other Unions giving support were the Miners, the Printers, the Seamen, the Woodworkers, the Garment workers, Plasterers, Women Workers' Union, tram and busmen, and many others. The ITGWU in the North gave us their full support, but in the South the leaders were holding off to see how matters would turn out. Within the Congress branches a new, young team was emerging. The greatest was Cora Hughes, a beautiful, brave and eloquent girl. Other young leaders in Dublin, where I was mainly engaged, were Charlie Donnelly (killed in Spain), Bobby Walsh, Nora McGinley, Joe Leonard, Kay Fitzpatrick, Rosie Burke, Flann Campbell and Maggie Doyle. Amongst the still youthful 'veterans' were Kit Conway, Jack Nalty (both killed in Spain), Larry O'Connor, Peter Ledwith, Joe Doyle, Billy Kelly, Robert Emmet, Lorcan Leonard, Dinny Coady (killed in Spain), and many others, all in Dublin. In Castlecomer there was Mick Brennan; in the west Brian Corrigan and Tony Lavelle, and in the North Victor Halley and Jack McGougan.

The Republican Congress was held on 29–30 September 1934 in Rathmines Town Hall. When I arrived on the morning of the 29th I saw a mob taking shape in a street facing the Town Hall, numbering about 200, behind a banner reading 'God bless our Pope'. There was some apprehension inside the Town Hall, Frank Ryan asked me whether I had 'any stuff' (guns) but I hadn't. He felt that we should take this precaution: mobs can swell very fast and can be very dangerous. So, with Larry O'Connor, Chairman of the Dublin Congress, we went to Christy 'Sniper' Clark's house in Dominick Street, Christy was a quartermaster in the born-again Irish Citizens' Army. We returned to Rathmines with some 'stuff' – just to be on the safe side. As things turned out, the mob failed to attract the numbers they expected, and faded away.

In my view this was the first truly Socialist Conference to be held in Ireland since Connolly's death. There was a strong representation from the North. William McMullen, Chairman of the Belfast Trades Council presided. One hundred and eighty-three delegates were present from all parts of Ireland, from the Shankill Road to Achill Sound. Workers from the western seaboard expressed their grievances and their hopes in Irish (the only language some of them knew). There were a large number of fraternal delegates from Britain and the United States. All the resolutions were practical, dealing with employment, housing, fuel, transport, the youth, the unemployed, and the need for a Socialist way forward. There was a refreshing absence of chauvinist jargon.

On the central issue, however, the Congress was split down the middle. This was whether the Congress should resolve itself into a new revolutionary Socialist Party, or remain as a united front of all progressive forces against Fascism.

Peadar O'Donnell, Chairman of the Republican Congress, in a recent letter to me has provided a definition of our aims:

> The central idea of the Republican Congress was that an identifiable working class vanguard should mobilise all the independent forces. The other view was that we declare for a Workers' Republic. The details of the Congress you probably know better than me, but the essential feature of it was that it saw itself mobilising all the independence forces behind a clearly recognisable workers' vanguard. You will remember the depth of working class support.

The voting was 99 for a United Front, and 84 for a Socialist Party. O'Donnell, Ryan, Gilmore and Murray led for a united front. Against were Roddy Connolly, Michael Price, Nora Connolly, and others. Personally I favoured the idea of a new Socialist Party, but loyalty to Peadar, Frank Ryan and Murray determined my vote. Looking back I think it was a great mistake that we did not go for a Worker's Party. Michael Price said to me after the vote: 'You have put the revolution back 100 years.'

From then on the movement lost momentum. Trade Union support melted away, the Connollys and others retreated into the oblivion of the Labour Party. Roddy Connolly was distressed, as indeed most of us were. Nora took it very hard. In her last book she had written: 'The Communists did not want a Republican Congress. They were out for a United Front, but this was something Russia wanted, not what we wanted.'

Although the Republican Congress had received a shattering blow, it did not succumb as some writers would have us believe. A depleted Congress organisation carried on, and was to receive a new infusion of life when the Spanish Civil War commenced in 1936. Before that, in April 1936, the Republican Congress contingent taking part in the annual Easter parade to Glasnevin Cemetery were subjected to attacks by organised Fascists all along the route. The *Irish Press* reported:

> Shrieking the most obscene abuse … hurling stones and railings torn from graves, the gangsters did not shrink from pursuing the processionists into the cemetery itself and transforming it into a bedlam of hatred.

The main target of the mob was Captain Jack White. He had been injured with a blow of an iron cross wrenched from a grave. It was necessary to get him away quickly. Fortunately, the Rosary had started and this caused a lull during which Tom O'Brien and myself got him away. Captain White wrote afterwards: 'By the aid of two Republican Congress comrades, who knew the geography, we left by an inconspicuous back door. Slipping under a barbed wire fence, the Congress comrades and I dropped on to the railway and soon emerged into safety and a Glasnevin tram.'

On the following day, Easter Monday, Willie Gallagher, Communist MP for West Fife, was listed as one of the speakers at a Congress Rally in College Green. There was a very large crowd, mostly hostile, but no platform for the speakers (the owner of the lorry had been intimidated). Peadar O'Donnell mounted a street lamp standard and commenced speaking. This was the signal for a volley of stones, bricks and bottles which crashed against the wall of the Bank of Ireland behind us. At this stage the police stopped the meting. Peadar O'Donnell, Gene Downey and myself were taken into 'protective' custody and removed to College Street police station. We could hear the mob roaring for our blood outside in between singing hymns, 'Faith of our Fathers' was top of the charts.

Amongst other activities, the Congress continued to fight slum tenants' battles. On the night after the College Green affair, a meeting of the Dublin Tenant's League were due to meet in the new Congress headquarters in Middle Abbey Street. I expected that after the events of the weekend, which had been well covered in all the papers (with appropriate editorial comment) that few tenants would turn up. To my great surprise, there was a full attendance, and a vote of complete confidence in us was enthusiastically passed.

In Spain in July 1936, Franco commenced his revolt against the Spanish Government. The Congress became the rallying ground for all who supported the legally elected democratic government. The general election of February 1936 brought the Popular Front to power. In a Cortes (Parliament) of 475 seats, the Popular Front held 278 seats, made up of 146 Republicans, 98 Socialists, 21 Communists and 13 other Radicals. Although the Communists had only 21 seats, the press in general hailed the result as a victory for 'the Reds'.

The *New York Herald-Tribune* of 6 September 1936 (not a radical paper) summarised the election results as follows:

> The February elections were contested on the issue which is still the issue in Spain. Shall the Spanish Republic be retained on the lines of social and agrarian reforms laid down in its founding and its constitution? Or shall it be discarded in all its fundamental elements? Seventy-five percent of 13 million Spanish voters cast their ballots for the preservation and continuance of the Republic.

On our side, an Irish battalion, to be led by Frank Ryan, was raised to serve with the International Brigade. I was not directly concerned in this, and I hope some comrade who was involved and fought in Spain will write this story. Perhaps Joe Monks, ('Spanish Joe', not to be confused with another Joe Monks, an active Congress worker in Dublin) or Alec Digges, or Mick Brennan, who served in the Republican Air Force, will undertake this task, before its too late.

A new Congress paper, *The Irish Democrat*, was founded at a meeting in Dublin in March 1937. The speakers included Dr Owen Sheehy Skeffington, Sam Haslett, Chairman of the Northern Ireland Socialist Party, Seán Murray of the Communist Party, and myself for the Republican Congress of which I was now Joint Secretary with Frank Ryan. Ernie O'Malley sent a message of support. The editor was Frank Ryan. He had returned wounded from Spain in March 1937, and went back a year later.

While he was at home, I went with him, Joe Doyle, Robert Emmet, Lorcan Leonard and some others to a meeting in the Mansion House, Dublin, to introduce a new printing of James Connolly's works. Some clown behind us kept interrupting the speakers with the cry 'What about the works of St Patrick?' Frank soon turned around, grabbed the offender by the lapels, shook a massive fist under his nose and advised him to keep his bloody mouth shut, or he'd 'get the works of Frank Ryan'.

At this time, all over Britain, committees were being set up to send food to hard pressed Republican Spain. In Dublin the 'Irish Foodship for Spain Committee' was established, under the presidency of Fr Michael O'Flanagan, a republican priest who had been chaplain to the first Dáil in 1919, and acting President of the Republic while De Valera was in the United States in 1920. The Vice-Presidents were the Earl of Listowel, Professor Rudmos Browne, Lennox Robinson, Maud Gonne MacBride, Dorothy McArdle, Frank Edwards and Peadar O'Donnell. I was appointed full time Organising Secretary.

Our headquarters was at 14 Sackville Street, off O'Connell Street. The premises, which were quite large, had not been used for some time, and were in need of an infusion of fresh paint. The office telephone was connected, but there were no directories. How long would we have to wait for them? In the event, ten minutes. Dinny Coady, who was present during the inspection, had disappeared for that length of time, now re-appeared with a complete set. Naturally, I did not ask him where he got them. In the office next morning, a boy about 16 years of age presented himself. He said that he had heard that I was looking for a decorator, and if so my search was over. He was a painter by trade, and with the help of another 'man' would do the job for me. He said his name was Brendan Behan. Before long, he and his mate (another boy about the same age) had transformed the place. I paid them £50 and they were delighted. Brendan, years later, told me that this was the first wage he had ever earned, and it was his first job. The Committee got down to the task of raising money fast. Our speakers addressed meetings all over Ireland, including Belfast where an active supporting Committee was in existence. Appeals were printed and widely distributed. I recall one slogan read '6d will buy a bar of soap, a tin of milk, and a bandage'. It was difficult and, at times, dangerous work. Some of our collectors were beaten up. However, there was considerable sympathy for the Spanish people, holding out in Madrid, and elsewhere, and the indiscriminate bombing of Guernica and other towns caused widespread condemnation. The open intervention by Italian Fascists and the German Nazis on the side of Franco, and the reports of refugees arriving in Dublin from Berlin and Vienna, brought into our funds generous donations from Jewish firms and the Jewish community, as well as from liberals, trade unionists and Republicans. By the time our ship was due to sail, a considerable amount had been subscribed in goods of all kinds, food, clothing, medical supplies, soap and cash, which was used in bulk buying of food on a large scale.

Early one morning in March 1938 a convoy of lorries left Sackville Place for Belfast. We flew Irish tricolours until we came to the border and then changed them for Spanish Republican tricolours. Despite an assurance that the convoy would be cleared through Customs, we were stopped by the RUC and 'impounded' in Newry barracks. Our arrest (I had 20 men with me) caused a storm in Belfast, and the local Foodship Committee (President, Lord Antrim) speedily obtained our release. The convoy of trucks was intact except for some bags of floor which had been bayoneted by the RUC, presumably looking for arms. On the dockside in Belfast next morning, we saw our ship being loaded. The dockers were friendly and made a collection for our funds. The ship beat the blockade off the Spanish coast by German and Franco's warships, and arrived safely at Almeria ...

Early in 1939 it was clear that the fall of the Republic in Spain was imminent. Frank Ryan had been captured on 31 March 1938, by Italian troops. He escaped the death sentence imposed by court martial due largely to the intercession of de Valera, then head of the Irish Government. After the outbreak of war in September 1939, he was taken by the Germans to Berlin in the expectation that he would engage in anti-British propaganda. He never did so. He was well treated, however, and acted for a time as a kind of unofficial Irish envoy until his health failed. He died in Dresden in June 1944.

With the fall of the Spanish Republic, and the outbreak five months later of the Second World War, the Republican Congress movement that had shown such promise, disintegrated.

Out of the entire Republican movement in Ireland, the Congress alone had opposed the march of fascism and supported the Spanish Republic. The Congress alone had made inroads into sectarianism in the North and had won a measure of Protestant support unknown since 1798. It had tried to extend the Irish revolution beyond the bourgeois limits set for it by consecutive Irish capitalist governments and political parties and organisations masquerading as Republican, and to achieve by the united action of all progressive forces of the left in Ireland the Socialist Republic envisaged by James Connolly and for which he gave his life.

FIANNA FÁIL AND THE REPUBLICAN CONGRESS[*]

Peadar O'Donnell, the socialist republican writer, had long been a close friend of Dan Breen's. O'Donnell's wife was one of the women who'd nursed him back to good health after one of his Tan War scrapes. In 1934–5 O'Donnell was at the centre of the Republican Congress, an umbrella organisation which sought to unite Republicans and socialists. O'Donnell persuaded Breen, by then a prominent Fianna Fáil backbencher, to lend his considerable weight to the new movement.

Republican Congress activists included members of Saor Eire and former IRA left-wingers like George Gilmore and Frank Ryan. It sought the destruction of ranchers and the establishment of a worker's republic.

On 22 September 1935, Breen chaired a convention where Republican and left-wing activists passed a resolution proclaiming the Congress's, 'oneness with the people of North-East Ulster against whom conscription has been already threatened, and appeal with special urgency to the workers of Belfast to take over their section of the front against Imperialism, firm in the conviction that the well-being of the whole Irish working class cannot be safe-guarded in an Ireland still held within the British Empire and in the grip of Imperial banking interests. There cannot be a free working class within a subject Ireland.'

The meeting gave rise to much speculation that a new political party was about to be formed. Such a party could, in 1935,

---

[*] *Dan Breen and the IRA,* Joe Ambrose.

have had a devastating effect on Fianna Fáil. The party had only just gotten into its stride, and was anxious to be a broad church within which all manner of nationalists could coalesce. Breen was the most prominent Fianna Fáiler supporting the Congress, but there were indications that a number of the party's councillors and local organisers were sympathetic.

The *Irish Press*, de Valera's paper, reported that, 'since the last convention moves have been made for the formation of an "Independent Republican Party". A number of leading members of the IRA have expressed themselves in favour of the establishment of such an organisation. Some advocate a policy of entering the Dáil and others stand for an abstention policy.'

That was enough for de Valera – huge pressure was brought to bear on the likes of Breen. They disengaged from the Congress. George Gilmore wrote in *The Irish Republican Congress*: 'The pressure brought to bear by the Fianna Fáil Party leaders upon their too-Republican branch officers forced them off the platform … and many of the trade union leaders, when left without that shelter, withdrew also.'

Even the Olives are Bleeding[*]

Charlie Donnelly (1914–1937) grew up in Dundalk and Dublin where he befriended radical political activists from the IRA, the Communist Party and Saor Eire. At UCD he studied English, history and Irish. He wrote for a variety of student publications but failed his first year examinations, probably because he was swiftly becoming a full time political activist. Quitting UCD in 1934, he joined the Republican Congress, where he was associated with political heavy hitters like Frank Ryan and George Gilmore. Arrested and briefly imprisoned for picketing a Dub-

---

[*] Joe Ambrose.

lin bakery, his vigorously anti-republican father expelled him from the family home and, for a while, he was homeless, sleeping rough in parks around Dublin. Donnelly was a gifted poet who would have been a considerable voice in Irish literature had he lived and matured.

When the Republican Congress split in 1934 Donnelly, at the age of 20, was elected to the National Executive. In 1935 he was arrested for assaulting a Guard at a demonstration and locked up for a month. In 1935 he moved to London where he agitated on behalf of the Republican Congress, working as a dishwasher in pubs and cafes while writing journalism for an international news agency.

In July 1936, on the outbreak of the Spanish Civil War, he urged the Republican Congress to send fighters to the International Brigades. He reached Spain in January 1937 and at Albacete, an insignificant town near Valencia which acted as the International Brigade's training headquarters, he met up with Frank Ryan and the Connolly Column, attached to the American Abraham Lincoln Battalion.

On 15 February, having received some basic military training, the Lincoln Battalion pitched themselves into the famed battle of Jarama near Madrid. Donnelly reached the front on 23 February and was promoted to the status of field commander. On 27 February, his unit engaged in a frontal assault on the Nationalist pro-Franco forces. They were pinned down by machine gun fire all day. In the evening the Nationalists launched a counter-attack. One veteran later recalled, 'Charlie Donnelly, the commander of an Irish company, is crouched behind an olive tree. He has picked up a bunch of olives from the ground and is squeezing them. I hear him say something quietly between a lull in machine gun fire: "Even the olives are bleeding".'

A few minutes later, as his men retreated, Donnelly was shot three times, in his right arm, his right side and his head. He collapsed and died instantly.

The Rise of Fianna Fáil,
the Decline of the Republican Congress[*]

The 1932 election proved to the farsighted republicans that in practice the theory of abstention from politics confined the effectiveness of the IRA machine to an influence from the left on the policy on Mr de Valera's party. They urged that the IRA should act as an independent force and held that with its influence, it could, if it tried, convene a united front of all shades of republicans big enough to raise the republic as a practical political goal, clear of what they described as de Valera's 'judicial formulae'. This was the view of a small majority of the organisation, and a minority of the leadership. After the vote of the leadership had succeeded in defeating the proposal for a republican conference, members of the IRA supporting the idea formed a separate political organisation, the Republican Congress, to organise a united front. They were attacked as 'tired revolutionaries', supporters of the Free State, Communists and enemies of religion, among other things, and expelled from the IRA. That was the first stage of the decline.

In the long run the Republican Congress Movement, opposed both from the government side and the IRA side and supported only by a small number of trade unions and the Communist Party, proved unable to accomplish the task it had set itself.

The government attacks on the IRA launched shortly afterwards, raised a new crisis inside that organisation. The IRA leaders debated whether they should support the Labour Party, resuscitate the practically defunct Sinn Féin abstentionist party – or form a new party. Eventually they did what, before, they had wrongly accused the Congress republicans of doing – formed a political party, Cumann Phoblacht na h-Éireann.

[*] 'Eleventh Hour for the Irish Republican Army', Charles Donnelly, *International Press Correspondence*, 4 July 1936.

Its formation consummated the process of disintegration. What was left of the Dublin IRA organisation, once a powerful contingent, revolted against this entry into 'politics'. Throughout the country the strength of the army rapidly weakened.

A Free State general election will be held next summer. It will be contested, on an abstractionist basis, by the new republican party. The leaders of the new party claim that the present determined attack on republicanism is directed to disorganising the new party in view of the election.

The fact remains, however, that, on the eve of an election, de Valera feels able, with safety, to operate the Coercion Act, enforce the ban on the IRA, repeatedly suppress its organ, arrest its leaders and sentence them to long periods of imprisonment.

The explanation of this, in the long run, is the failure of the IRA over the last three years to win an independent mass backing and to free its politics from the limitations of a fanatical militarism which has isolated it from a population essentially in sympathy with its objects. A more immediate cause is the political terrorism, recent instances of which are the ostensible reasons for the arrests and other actions against the IRA. The IRA have on several occasions emphasised that the arrests have no connection with the shootings, and at all events, it is certain that IRA headquarters had no connection with the shootings. These unfortunate occurrences, outbursts of political neurosis due to the abuse of real healthy political activity, have, however, done much to make possible the attack on the organisation.

The banning of the Bodenstown commemoration ceremony indicates a really bad position. Bodenstown cemetery, in County Kildare, is the burial place of Wolfe Tone who planned with the French Revolutionary Directorates for the establishment of an Irish republic, and whose efforts were finally defeated in 1798. Wolfe Tone is recognised by all sections as the founder of the national movement, and Mr de Valera's own party holds a commemoration at Bodenstown on the Sunday succeeding the IRA ceremony. The banning of the demonstration indicates the determination of the government to stand by the letter of the law making the IRA illegal; in other words, a determination to smash the IRA once and for all. We must conclude that de Valera believes he can do so without seriously endangering his prospects at the coming election.

This calculation will almost certainly prove correct if the form of opposition taken at the election is that of a republican abstentionist party. It is the nemesis of the purely militaristic policy so long and stubbornly pursued by the IRA leadership, that even its own members, not to mention casual supporters, are far from clear as to the differences of policy between that organisation and the government party. It is doubtful, indeed, whether many of the leaders themselves have any clear conceptions, except as to methods.

De Valera is at present elaborating a proposed new constitution for the Free State, on which he will take his stand in the election. The new party intends to fight on a republican ticket; members returned will not enter the Free State Dáil, but will meet as a separate Assembly. Under no shape or form, and in none of its ramifications, must the Free State be 'recognised'. It is possible, though not very likely at a time when important social issues are forcing themselves on the people, that after a long period a greater number of candidates would be returned 'outside' than 'inside' the Free State assembly, republicans in the meantime enjoying the advantages of government completely free from their control. Long before such an event, however, the IRA would have ceased to exist.

It remains to be seen whether, at this eleventh hour, the leaders of the IRA will put their hands to the work of creating a labour republican people's front making effective the opposition to coercion which otherwise will reach no further than small-town grumbles. One thing is certain, that if those who are backing the abstentionist party venture, made the attempt, many of the government party branches and labour parties could be brought behind a republican programme, linked with popular economic reforms. Coupled with the numerous republican sections, these would form a serious challenge to the government.

CHARLIE DONNELLY: AN APPRECIATION[*]

I am enclosing copies of two poems by Charlie Donnelly. His death, just a year ago when men just had to fling themselves across the path of the fascist advances, is one of the tragedies of those breathless days. Today we are in a better position to utilise men of Charlie's calibre in their proper sphere. It's not the death of the poet I lament – for I never thought of him in that role: modern poetry is something I generally prefer to see written as prose. It is the revolutionary thinker I mourn. With a few more years experience, for he was still too much of the student, Charlie would have been invaluable to us. I always wanted to pull him out of the Battalion but, as you may recall the circumstances in January, I didn't get my chance. Charlie and I used to be on opposing wings when he first came into the movement in Ireland. He was all theory then and had little use for my stance, as he called it. He went to work in London – dishwashing for a while – for a year and then wrote me to agree that there was a lot in my point of view. In fact he made the mistake of swinging temporarily too much away from internationalism. But, after that year, what an asset he would have been to the Irish revolutionary movement.

* Frank Ryan, *The Workers' Republic*, July 1938. Appreciation of Charles Donnelly by Frank Ryan, written to Paul Burns of the Lincoln Battalion, International Brigade.

Wrap the Green, Red, and Black Flags Around Me[*]

One of O'Duffy's officers on his return told a *Connacht Tribune* reporter that one day on the Madrid front 'some of our men reported that they saw the Irish Tricolour flying on a hill in the "Red" lines'.

That was the nearest O'Duffy's men evidently got to the front, where the Irish Unit, under Frank Ryan, has seen service since last December.

Below, Patrick Murray, an Irish exile, who joined the Irish Unit, tells, in the New York *Sunday Worker*, how the traditional Irish shout of 'Up the Republic', echoed in the foothills around Madrid as the boys from the four provinces charged for freedom and democracy:

The trench line along the Sierra Almaden was busy with activity as the men of the International Brigade worked to improve their position. Far below them they could see minute dots on the landscape working their way slowly forward amid little puffs of smoke from bursting six-inch shells. In another hour the advance guard of Italian Fascism would be within long rifle range of their hastily constructed trenches. The decisive battle for possession of the rich Almaden mercury mines would be fought on the morrow.

Somewhere along the trenches a rich Irish brogue was heard singing: 'Wrap the green flag around me'. Almost immediately, the song echoed back from the mountain peaks behind them as men from Mayo, Kildare, Dublin, Belfast, Limerick and almost every other Irish county joined in the air. The Irish Unit, vanguard of Irish democracy, held the key position covering the pass to the lowlands towards which the Fascist thrust was directed.

---

[*] Patrick Murray, *Irish Democrat*, 24 July 1937.

Suddenly the rumour spread: 'The O'Duffy's are below'. The song stopped immediately as the men gathered together in little clusters to discuss this news. They had fought on the Guadarramas, in University City, at Guadalajara and on the Jarama front. But nowhere had they been in contact with the men under General O'Duffy who had come to Spain 'to defend the faith.'

Many an Irish Republican Army veteran slept that night with his rifle butt for a pillow and a grim smile on his lips. Half of them had served under O'Duffy's warders and had entered the inhuman regime of Mountjoy Prison in Dublin, for the crime of advocating complete independence for Ireland.[†]

At dawn, when the order came to go over the top, the Irish moved forward. Let Frank Ryan, commandant of the Irish Unit, tell of it:

When the order came to go over you should have seen our lads charge shouting the old war cry 'Up the Republic!' But we found ne'er an Irishman in the opposite trenches. Mostly they were Italians, who broke and ran as soon as our lad's cries reached their ears. We found out later that O'Duffy's men are mostly doing police work back in Salamanca.

Ryan and O'Duffy are the two Irishmen who have taken leading positions in their homeland on the Spanish issue. Early, Ryan organised a group of Irish Republican Army veterans in extreme secrecy and sailed for Spain against the overwhelming opposition of the Irish press. Sometime later O'Duffy announced the formation of the 'Irish Brigade' for the 'defence of the Faith' in Spain. The entire reactionary Press, Lombard Murphy's *Independent* leading, was open to O'Duffy. Funds came pouring in. His well-equipped detachment sailed for Spain and landed in the north. While Ryan's men were fighting on all fronts, O'Duffy's band contented itself with policing Salamanca and fighting intermittent skirmishes with their Moorish, Italian

---

† O'Duffy had a prominent role in the Irish Civil War and subsequently ran the Free State police force.

and Spanish allies in Salamanca bar-rooms. Ryan was invalided home in April to recuperate from a wound received on the Jarama front. He has since returned to Spain where he again assumed command of the Irish Unit. O'Duffy and his men recently reached Dublin without having endured more than a series of bar-room brawls.

Frank Ryan is today a symbol of the Ireland of the future. He is in his middle thirties and has fought since his late teens in the ranks of the Irish Republican Army. He is the one IRA veteran whom Scotland Yard compliments with a shadow on his infrequent trips though England. For many years he was editor of *An Phoblacht*, which has been suppressed by the Free State Government. His leading role in the fight for Irish independence brought him many prison terms, the latest of which ended in 1932 with the accession of the de Valera government to office and the proclamation of a general amnesty for political prisoners.

Ryan's militant nationalism has not stopped there, as was the sad fate of many another Irish leader. Today, he has realised the intimate connection between the Irish struggle for complete independence and the world struggle against fascism as carried on by Father Michael O'Flanagan, among others. Writing from Albacete on March 20, he expressed it as follows:

We have got to let the world know that the lives of Conroy, Conway, Boyle and all the other Irish lads now buried in Spain have not been wasted, that their deaths are not tragedies. Honour for those who died for the freedom of all humanity. They could have remained at home and been regarded as 'soldiers of Ireland'. Instead they came here because they believed it was their duty to do so. They came here asking neither pay nor preferment, coming to participate in this decisive fight against fascism. And for my part, while it would be wrong to accuse me of bringing them here, I would never regret having done so. Our 50,000 who died in the World War were sacrificed uselessly. No life given here is given in vain. Look at it from a purely selfish viewpoint – which is better – that some of us should die here, or that thousands should die at home? For if Fascism triumphs here, Ireland's trial will soon be at hand.

His word pictures of the fighting along the Jarama front are among the best to come from the trenches. Writing to a friend in America from his hospital bed, he said:

'Yes, I am still alive here in a military hospital after a bad shaking up a fortnight ago. The Irish contingent had just returned from the trenches and were resting in a small village called Chincon, when the order came to go up the line again.

'From then on, for three days, we were in action on the Jarama front (that's where Franco had driven a wedge in, south of Madrid, menacing the only road out of Valencia.) We had been previously in the University City, in Caso de Campo, and Guadarramas trenches. We were also with the division attacking Cordoba, but Jarama was the toughest fighting I ever saw.

'Artillery, while pretty accurate on both sides, is not intensive in Spain – 3 or 4 field pieces to a battalion is the custom. The machine-gun fire was terrific, and then there were mortars, tanks, and aeroplanes. Old Great War veterans with us tell me the machine-gun fire was more intensive than in 1914–18. We were fighting German and Italian regulars. They were dressed in corduroy uniforms.

'They made many mistakes, particularly by attacking us in mass formation. In one machine-gun nest of five men I saw five German passports taken from the pockets of the dead men.

'I saw letters in Italian taken from Fascist infantry the same day. I must admit those Fascists fighting at Jarama were good fighters and were well officered. They were obviously picked troops, for the section is the key to Madrid.

'If the Fascists succeeded there, Madrid is isolated. Need I tell you our casualties were terrific? The 1st Company of the Unit led the attack. After the first day's fighting it was reduced from 143 to 58 men.

'My Company O/C, Kit Conway, of Dublin, my right-hand man, was killed in this battle.* Our Unit O/C was wounded, and it looked like I was the only officer that would be left. At dawn of the second day, this machine-gun fire drove us back, so I let the men retreat a mile. They were decided on another attack, and went forward again, and meeting desperate fire, we reoccupied our positions.

'On the fourth day of the fighting (which was continuous – there were occasions when there were only 300 of us in one long line between the Fascists and the Madrid Road); I got a flesh wound in the left arm from a bullet that went through the head of a chap beside me. Again a shell exploded beside our temporary trench, something hit me in the left hip. It must have been a stone, because it made me lame and bruised my leg but made no cut.

'I felt OK and we decided to dash ahead of the barrage to better our position. Shortly after we gained this position, I received a bullet in the left shoulder which, I am told, hurt a muscle and wrenched a tendon. A French doctor has just told me that I will have to rest for quite a while. I expect to be back in the trenches by the end of May.'

While Ryan was fighting in the front line trenches he did not forget that there were other battlefronts where the war against Fascism was being carried on. Home in Dublin, he undertook to aid the Republican struggle through the establishment of a weekly publication, the *Irish Democrat*. He recently broadcast the following appeal to Americans on behalf of the *Democrat*.

'At home in Ireland during my brief stay I found that the greatest need is an organ which will voice the thoughts of the plain people and organise all anti-Imperialist elements into one united Republican movement, North and South. To fill that need we founded the *Irish Democrat*. I appeal to America to help it.

* Conway actually came from Burncourt, County Tipperary. Active in the Third Tipperary Brigade of the IRA during the War of Independence, he was a member of Seán Hogan's Flying Column.

'It deserves the support of all lovers of liberty both in Ireland and throughout the world. The cause it fights is the same old cause that has made the name of Ireland great. As a bulwark against world Fascism, the *Democrat* should become one of the most important organs of liberal thought.

'Returning to my duty in Spain, I express the hope that later on I may come to America to thank your great people, personally, on behalf of the Irish Unit, and to work there in the great cause of the freedom of the human race.'

CATHAL GOULDING, THE FLAXEN FOE[†]

Cathal Goulding (1922–1998) was a painter/decorator who was involved, as a teenager, in Fianna Éireann, the youth wing of the IRA. He signed up to that organisation along with his close friend and fellow painter/decorator, the writer Brendan Behan. When he was 17 he joined the IRA. He rose through the ranks to become, in 1962, an extremely divisive IRA chief of staff. Goulding's grandfather was a Fenian and his father fought in the 1916 Rising.

In 1953 Goulding, along with co-conspirators such as future Provisional IRA chief of staff Seán MacStíofáin, was involved in a plot to capture British weaponry. This escapade resulted in him serving six years in prison. MacStíofáin subsequently recalled their trial: 'Without retiring, the jury found us guilty in a record 90 seconds by the simple procedure of turning to each other and nodding their heads.' As a result of his incarceration he missed out on the IRA's unsuccessful Border Campaign.

He became the IRA's quartermaster-general and in the 1960s he was pivotal to that organisation's shift towards a pseudo-revolutionary Marxist position which favoured social campaigning rather than military action. He came to believe that

† Joe Ambrose.

the British had purposely divided the Irish working class along sectarian lines to keep them from uniting and overthrowing their oppressors. Eventually he favoured class, as opposed to armed, struggle. This interpretation caused a fundamental split within the IRA, the nastiest and most deep-seated since the Civil War. In 1969 the organisation split into the wholeheartedly militarist Provisional IRA and the Official IRA which had Goulding at its helm. The Officials adopted a pseudo-ceasefire in 1972.

David McKittrick's obituary to Goulding, published in the London *Independent*, claimed that, 'In 1969 Goulding was often to be found in the fashionable bars around St Stephen's Green, drinking with writers, musicians and painters, a recognised feature of Dublin bohemia. His revolutionary style at that time was closer to Berkeley campus and the Rive Gauche than to the bogs and back streets where the IRA tradition was rooted. Critics of his leadership invariably portrayed him as a good but easily influenced man fallen among Marxist highbrows. The pubs of Dublin were a world away from the grim sectarian realities of Belfast, where August 1969 brought hand-to-hand fighting in the back streets and the first deaths of the Troubles. Northern Republicans claimed that Goulding had fiddled while Belfast burned, and that what they needed was guns and not quixotic dreams of uniting Catholic and Protestant workers in a new utopia.'

Despite a reputation for Stalinist radicalism, Goulding lived for many years in splendour on Dublin's Ailesbury Road with Dr Moira Woods. Their 20-year relationship began in 1971.

A dashingly handsome man, Goulding had children with, amongst others, Dr Woods and Beatrice Behan, Brendan's widow. Their son, Paudge Behan, is a successful actor who inherited his father's good looks and charm.

By the end of his life he was a somewhat lonely political figure, a Napoleon on Elba. The Official IRA never ceased to exist but, over the years, declined into gangsterism and, ironically, property management.

THE PROVO TRAINING MANUAL[*]

Sometimes crudely printed and roughly bound at anonymous printing works, *The Green Book*, the Provisional IRA's training manual, was allegedly given to every fully trained volunteer. Only two editions of the work have made their way into the public domain.

One appeared in 1956 when the IRA, engaged in what is known as the Border Campaign, was a comprehensively side-lined and largely irrelevant organisation. The other – featured here – dates from 1977 when the Provisional IRA were at the height of their powers, internationally acknowledged leaders of the global armed resistance movement, allied to various Pales-tinian factions, to maverick governments such as the Ghadaffi regime in Libya and to the Sandinista leadership in Nicaragua.

In 1977, chief of staff Seamus Twomey, an IRA leader of the old school, was arrested with a copy of *The Green Book* in his possession. In the years which intervened between the end of the border campaign and the arrest of Twomey, the IRA had split into two murderously hostile factions. The Official IRA became a socialist-orientated and Soviet-aligned body popularly known as the Stickies while the Provisional IRA or Provos tended to-wards seeing themselves as part of an international anti-colonial movement.

The Provos' self-image as a body of men and women in the mould of Che Guevara or Mao Tse Tung is much in evidence in *The Green Book*, a tome anxious to disassociate itself from the na-tionalistic jingoism or chauvinism popularly associated with the IRA in the public imagination. Clearly based on lecture notes, it is sometimes repetitive and occasionally contradictory. Approved by a committee of senior IRA leaders, then polished off by a sin-

[*] Joe Ambrose.

303

gle author, the quality of the writing varies from the crude and the unsophisticated through to the witty and worldly wise.

The 1977 *Green Book* advocated the Provos' 'Long War' strategy. The thinking behind this was quite simply that, given a variety of factors (such as majority support for the British connection within Northern Ireland's territory) the struggle was going to be a long one. Would-be IRA Volunteers could expect the British – and the unionists – to put up stiff resistance to their plans for a British withdrawal and a united Ireland. The Provos were focused on a long war of attrition.

The Green Book made heavy personal demands on recruits: 'The Army [IRA] as an organisation claims and expects your total allegiance without reservation. It enters into every aspect of your life. It invades the privacy of your home life. It fragments your family and friends, in other words claims your total allegiance. All potential Volunteers must realise that the threat of capture and of long jail sentences are a very real danger and a shadow which hangs over every Volunteer.'

The book gave IRA members information on the political thinking of the IRA, a potted history of the struggle between Britain and Ireland, the military objectives of the IRA, guerrilla warfare tactics, the role of propaganda in revolutionary politics, and how to deal with and overcome British interrogation techniques. The section dealing with interrogation techniques is excerpted here.

In 2003, giving testimony to the Saville Inquiry into Bloody Sunday, onetime IRA leader Martin McGuinness denied that he had ever read *The Green Book*. 'When I was in the IRA there was no such book,' McGuinness said. 'I don't know when it came into existence.' When asked what the phrase 'Green Book' meant, he said: 'I think it means the book was green.'

The Green Book gives many valuable insights into Provo thinking and experience. Written by a group of senior and experienced officers, it is an incongruous mixture of pop psychology (hugely popular in the late 1970s), pop history, hardcore learned-the-hard-way advice, and the cold-blooded analysis of its own game-plan by one of the most competent and focused guerrilla armies operating in the world at that time.

It seems likely that the advice concerning what might happen to an IRA member immediately after capture is based on personal experience and wholly accurate. The suggestion that would-be interrogators are closet homosexuals seems somewhat risible today, but the suggestion that the captured revolutionary might expect to be sexually humiliated is probably all too accurate. The book seemed to assume that IRA members would be male, although there were many women active in the paramilitary movement at that time.

The Green Book doles out advice concerning the dark arts of guerrilla warfare with the same enthusiasm as Machiavelli's *The Prince* or Mario Puzo's *The Godfather* doled out similar advice on politics and capitalism. Freedom fighters or terrorists all over the world are no doubt avidly digesting it, or something much like it.

THE GREEN BOOK[*]

ANTI-INTERROGATION

Arrest

Most Volunteers are arrested on or as a result of a military operation. This causes an initial shock resulting in tension and anxiety. All Volunteers feel that they have failed, resulting in a deep sense of disappointment. The police are aware of this feeling of disappointment and act upon this weakness by insults such as 'You did not do very well: you are only an amateur: you are

[*] Published secretly in 1977.

only second-class or worse'. While being arrested the police use heavy-handed 'shock' tactics in order to frighten the prisoner and break down his resistance. The prisoner is usually dragged along the road to the waiting police wagon, flung into it, followed by the arresting personnel, e.g., police or Army. On the journey to the detention centre the prisoner is kicked, punched and the insults start. On arrival he is dragged from the police wagon through a gauntlet of kicks, punches and insults and flung into a cell.

What a Volunteer Should Do When Arrested

1. The most important thing to bear in mind when arrested is that you are a Volunteer of a revolutionary Army, that you have been captured by an enemy force, that your cause is a just one, that you are right and that the enemy is wrong and that as a soldier you have taken the chance expected of a soldier and that there is nothing to be ashamed of in being captured.

2. You must bear in mind that the treatment meted out to you is designed to break you and so bleed you of all the information you may have with regard to the organisation to which you belong.

3. They will attempt to intimidate you by sheer numbers and by brutality. Volunteers who may feel disappointed are entering the first dangerous threshold because the police will act upon this disappointment to the detriment of the Volunteer and to the benefit of their own ends. Volunteers must condition themselves so that they can be arrested and if and when arrested they should expect the worst and be prepared for it.

Interrogation

After the prisoner has been placed in a cell, he may be left for some time alone. During this lull, police officers, 'The Interrogators', will crowd around the outside of the cell door from time to time, shouting threats and insults, telling the prisoner what they will do to him when they go into the cell.

After some time the interrogators will enter the cell and ask the prisoner to make a confession. During this period he may be subjected to assaults and abusive language, depending on the circumstances surrounding the charge. At this stage he will be fingerprinted and other questions will be put to him, related to the specific charge or other charges. Usually his name and address will be taken, place of employment, occupation, educational standard and so forth. After this he will be again isolated in his cell while his 'interrogators' check his identity, usually with local police, his home and place of employment. In this period of time the police will attempt to establish his political beliefs, if any, his associates, his police record, if any, and in this way build up a file on him.

Most probably 'his associates' and general pattern of movement will give a pretty good idea to the police if the person is involved in or is sympathetic to a political organisation. Armed with this body of information the police will re-enter the cell and accuse the prisoner of all sorts of activity. If the evidence does not indicate a degree of guilt on the specific charge, he will be accused of all kinds of vague activity.

The purpose of these vague accusations is to implant a feeling of guilt in the prisoner. If, however, the police have some evidence or strong beliefs, linking him with a specific charge, pressure will be applied immediately. This pressure will take the form of physical and psychological torture; most probably he will be punched and kicked around the cell while they scream at him to make a confession, indicating to him that they know all. One or more of the interrogating officers will act in a particular and brutal manner, if they fail to get a confession or on admission of guilt they will leave the cell, telling the prisoner they will be back and threatening him with the most barbaric forms of torture, implying that they extracted confessions from better men than he.

Another set of interrogators will enter the cell, possibly carrying a file with the prisoner's name written on it. They will act quite friendly and sympathetic towards him, telling him that they do not condone the activity of the previous interrogators, that they were mad, crazy and possibly they will kill him when they come in later, they will go to extremes to impress the prisoner of their own sympathy towards him, and ask him to make a confession to them indicating that they do not want the previous interrogators 'to get at him again'.

They will probably guarantee him that if he makes the confession they will not allow the former interrogators to re-enter the cell, this will be coupled with a warning that otherwise they cannot guarantee him safety. When the prisoner refuses to confess they will pretend to become very annoyed and disappointed at his lack of co-operation. They may strike him across the face or in the stomach while telling him that he ought to be thankful to them, that they saved him from the previous interrogators and indicating that his behaviour and attitude is a thankless way to repay their kindness.

The interrogators will then open up a file and pretend to read extracts from it, related to the prisoner's past life and activities, even the most intimate and private aspects of his life will be read to him, and possibly a general account of his movements and associates. Most of this information may have been supplied by his friends, employer, school, family, or girlfriend, it may also be 'Pub Talk', local gossip, information supplied by touts or information extracted from other prisoners. This detailed information is designed to frighten the prisoner and to shatter his confidence in his associates and organisation. If, however, they get no confession, they will leave the cell, but before doing so they will give the prisoner their names and tell him to ask for them at any time he wishes to, again indicating that the next set of interrogators are crazy, drunk, and will do him severe damage, then they leave the cell.

After a period of time another set of interrogators will enter the cell, again these interrogators will be particularly brutal and nasty towards him. They will attack him immediately in a most hostile and vicious manner, suggesting to him that if he did not confess to the former interrogators he will confess to them, they will let him know that they have a reputation for getting confessions from people like him, implying that everyone they met confessed before they were finished with them.

The torture used will now take on a three-fold purpose:

1. Physical Torture.
2. Subtle Psychological Torture.
3. Humiliation.

1. Physical Torture
The physical torture will be in the form of beatings, kicking, punching and twisting of limbs, it may even be burning from cigarette ends.
2. Psychological Torture
This will be in the form of threats to his family, his friends and himself, e.g. threats of assassination and threats to castrate him
3. Humiliation
This takes the form of stripping the prisoner of his clothes and remarks passed about his sexual organs.

This period of interrogation may last for as long as two hours or more and at the end of that period they may produce a factual or faked confession from an associate. Failing to get their confession they leave the cell, telling him they will be back and when they do come back they will break every bone in his body.

This process can continue for seven days without a break, the minimum of sleep is allowed and if they deem it necessary, no sleep will be allowed. Lack of sleep causes the prisoner to become confused.

Because of the existing laws which authorise the police to detain a person for seven days, it means in effect that the process of interrogation can continue to disorientate their victim, due in the main to lack of sleep.

Interrogation can have many different phases, depending on the evidence or information which the police have gathered. It is obvious that a Volunteer captured carrying out an operation is already seen to be guilty, especially if captured with a weapon, bomb etc., in this case the police have all the evidence needed to obtain a conviction and interrogation becomes unnecessary. Most likely the Volunteer will be beaten up in the police stations for what he has done, not for what he knows. If interrogated under these circumstances it will be to get information on the organisation to which he belongs and on his comrades. Another shady aspect directly related to interrogation is blackmail and bribe. When the police cannot obtain a confession they may attempt to blackmail the Volunteer. This may be in the form of threats to spread scandalous stories about the Volunteer. Stories or threats may be designed to hit at the character of the Volunteer such as a threat to tell his comrades or his organisation that he told everything or that he had been working for them for years. The other phase of this shady interrogation is bribe. A Volunteer may be promised money, a passport and a safe passage to any country he so desires if he co-operates.

The Interrogation – analysis

The best defence in anti-interrogation techniques is to understand the techniques as practised by police forces. The purpose of interrogation is to get a confession. If the interrogators knew what they were searching for there would be no need for interrogation, therefore interrogation is necessary only when the police are unaware of information, which would lead to a conviction. The best anti-interrogation is to SAY NOTHING. All police forces work from a story, suspicion or clue, therefore when a Volunteer is arrested they strive to build on that clue, on that suspicion and the only way that can be done is to obtain information from their victim. They usually start by questioning their victim, writing down a recording of what he says, comparing this information with information already in their possession, looking for differences which contradict the information previously gained, going back to their victim, pointing out these differences, resulting in the victim changing his alibi in order to suit this difference. The police will again check this new story with other information and again look for a difference or mistake narrowing the prisoner's alibi down until finally it breaks. All of these changes in his statements will be recorded and used as evidence against him, evidence which will without doubt be accepted by the court and so lead to his conviction. This cannot be over stressed: when arrested SAY NOTHING. Ask to see your solicitor and doctor immediately and keep on doing so.

Do not indulge in conversation with the police
After the prisoner had been placed in his cell, we have seen earlier in the lecture how the police had crowded outside the cell door shouting insults and banging on the door. The purpose of this exercise is to frighten the prisoner and so arouse anxiety in their victim. When anxiety has been aroused all natural, rational defence barriers break down or weaken. When this happens the prisoner becomes irrational and becomes more prone to interrogation. In other words an anxious man is easier to intimidate by interrogation than a cool, calculating person. During the time the prisoner is left alone in the cell he should, in as far is as possible, ignore the police, the threats and the insults and he should marshal all facts surrounding his arrest. He should bear in mind that he can be detained for no more than seven days if he remains silent or possibly years in prison if he speaks. Most Volunteers speak from a sense of fear thinking mistakenly that if they speak, torture or ill treatment will not be used. It is a recorded fact that interrogators are guided by a simple rule of thumb: If a prisoner won't speak he may be innocent and inter-

rogation may be a waste of time, if he speaks a little there is always more and so interrogation is necessary, therefore the prisoner who speaks a little in order to avoid abuse is in effect inviting more abuse from his interrogators who will always assume there is something more. Therefore the best defence is to remain COOL, COLLECTED, CALM, and SAY NOTHING.

We have seen earlier in the lecture how the first batch of interrogators will enter the cell usually insulting, shouting and beating the prisoner. Volunteers should understand that this first batch of interrogators usually fingerprint, ask name, address etc. At this stage a little is known about the prisoner and therefore the task of the interrogator is to identify him positively. Again the prisoner must bear in mind that everything he says will be recorded and compared with existing information in the possession of the police. The purpose of abusing the prisoner at this stage is called the 'softening up period', usually one or more will act in a particularly nasty manner. This interrogation may last not more than one hour and is only a preliminary investigation. The purpose of using heavy-handed techniques and sheer hostility is an opening for the following batch of interrogators, whom we have seen act in a particularly sympathetic manner.

This set of interrogators, we have seen, acted in a friendly and sympathetic manner towards the prisoner, offering him cigarettes and friendship. Volunteers should be well aware and on guard against this feigned friendship. These interrogators pretend to be sympathetic towards the aims and objects of the movement, going to lengths to impress the Volunteer, pretending that they too believe in a united Ireland. They will, no doubt, tell the Volunteer that their father or grandfather was in the same organisation and that they were forced by economic circumstances to join the police force and they are now merely passing the time until they are pensioned off. They will try to convince the Volunteer it is in his interest to make a confession to them in order to escape from the previous interrogators who, they claim, are anti-Republican and are not interested in getting a confession but are only interested in beating the prisoner up. The Volunteer should understand that these seemingly kind police officers may be acting the tough cop with his comrades who had been or are arrested.

Finally we have seen how these interrogators, pretending to become upset, had stretched forward and beat the Volunteer about the face and body, declaring that their advice and friendship was being returned or repaid with a stubborn attitude and a refusal to make EVEN A PART OF A CONFESSION. This technique is as old as police forces, they attempt to win over the friendship and trust of the prisoner, hoping that if their prisoner falls into that trap he will become upset, not so much at the punching about the face which he received from them but at his own refusal to co-operate: this perhaps is the most dangerous type of interrogation and one which leaves the prisoner in a psychological vulnerable position.

Another technique is called TOP SECRET FILE TECHNIQUE; this involves the interrogators bringing into the cell a file with the prisoner's name printed on it. The police will open this file in the presence of the prisoner as we have seen earlier in the lecture. They proceed to read from this file parts of the prisoner's past life, even to the most intimate details and a general account of his movement and friends, especially those associated or known to have contacts or sympathies with a political organisation, e.g., Sinn Féin. They also have information gathered from various sources such as employer, neighbours, PUB TALK OR LOCAL GOSSIP. Very often the PUB TALK and gossip is factual, this arises from the Volunteer or Volunteers in general speaking in pubs under the influence of alcohol, telling close friends and girlfriends and boasting in a bravado manner about their exploits and the exploits of others. This type of bravado is POSITIVELY DANGEROUS, not only to the Volunteer and his associates but to the Movement in general. Another dangerous aspect of interrogation is 'an associate's confession', this involves an interrogator approaching the Volunteer with a signed or unsigned, factual or unfactual confession of an associate. Volunteers must understand, (in the first place) this confession may be a hoax and in the second, even if it is a factual confession of his associate, this confession is not an indication of guilt and will not be accepted in court unless his associate who made the confession is prepared to turn State or Crown witness and is prepared to swear its truth in the witness box. Very often a Volunteer may break under severe physical and psychological torture and make a confession, but rarely is prepared to turn Crown or State witness and swear against his comrades. If this technique is employed by the police DON'T FALL FOR IT, it is a trick to weaken the Volunteer and so get him to make and sign a statement.

Another dangerous technique employed is bringing the prisoner who made a statement into the same room as the Volunteer who refuses to co-operate, usually they are left on their own and the prisoner who made a statement may try to entice his comrade to do likewise. If this happens to you always bear in mind that you are not alone because the room is always bugged and any talk is recorded. Another important point to bear in mind is when the prisoner who confessed and perhaps implicated you approaches, don't launch a verbal attack on him because this verbal attack on him would be an implication of your guilt. Always speak friendly to him and suggest he must be mistaken, that he is ill and advise him to seek medical attention.

Another important point to be remembered and one which is extremely important: DON'T GET INVOLVED IN A POLITICAL CONVERSATION. This technique is a universal tactic and one which recurs repeatedly. When Volunteers refuse to make a confession and when all other tactics of interrogation have failed, the police usually, if not always, attempt to get the Volunteer to speak on political matters. This is a technique

314

which many Volunteers fail to recognise. Its purpose is to fling the Volunteer off balance, to sound out his political thinking, to break his silence and so make it easier for him to speak freely. This tactic has been used against Volunteers and very often to their own detriment. When a Volunteer has been arrested and the usual terror tactics used against him, this display of friendship has a weakening effect upon him and can be explained in psychological terms.

As we have seen earlier in this lecture, these seemingly friendly interrogators will give their names to the prisoner before they leave the cell, telling him that the next set of interrogators are crazy, anti-Republicans who are out to do him harm. They will tell him to call upon them at any time he so wishes and they will do their best to save him from brutal treatment. All Volunteers must understand and understand in the clearest possible way that no interrogator is his friend, that they are the enemy, the instruments of coercion, the tools of suppression and a more dangerous enemy than the interrogators who will beat him up. These people act a part in a well-rehearsed play, and are using subtle psychological techniques in order to undermine the morale of the Volunteer. All Volunteers are well versed in brutal treatment as practised by police and the Army. They understand what physical torture means, but now you will have to understand the meaning and application of psychological torture. Perhaps the term is an uncommon one, but its effects are far reaching.

We have seen earlier in the lecture how the 'heavy squad' now enters the scene and proceeds to attack the Volunteer in a most vicious and brutal manner. This shock treatment is well rehearsed and is meant to push the Volunteer into a physical and mental corner, in other words they hope that their shock treatment will knock the Volunteer off balance, and off guard in the hope that he will confess. They will shout statements to the effect that they have a reputation for extracting confessions, that they have never yet failed and that he will not fool them.

Now we must analyse this approach. The first thing of importance we note is the shouting in conjunction with the physical torture. The shouting as we shall see is a more important interrogation technique than the physical torture. Again, why shout? Why boast? Why tell the Volunteer that they are experts at extracting information? This shouting and boasting is merely an assurance to the police that they can get a confession, it is the first obvious sign of their own weakness, a compensation for their own shortcomings and all Volunteers should and ought to look upon this display as a modern war dance. Just as primitive people held war dances, and built totem poles in order to compensate themselves for their own known weaknesses, so two frustrated interrogators will shout and boast in front of the prisoner to compensate themselves for their own weakness. The best anti-interrogation technique when a Volunteer finds himself in this situation is to look upon the police officers as he would look upon primitive people, wearing the head of a dead animal, hoping that by doing this they gain the strength or cunning of the animal whose head they wear. All Volunteers should look upon shouting, boasting policemen as they would look upon primitive people doing a war dance.

Psychological torture

We have seen that this type of torture is widespread and usually in the form of threats to the Volunteer in question, to his friends and family, threats to assassinate him, to blacken his character, to castrate him; loss of sleep, poor quality of food and continuous noise. This in conjunction with the physical torture and fear of physical torture builds up anxiety that borders on hysteria. All of this is designed to smash down the Volunteer's natural defence mechanism, usually a person held for a period of time, perhaps seven days, living in an environment of fear and indecision, constantly being threatened, cut off from all natural contacts, deprived of his usual social surroundings, lack of sleep etc. This can and does form disorientation and disillusionment:

during this period the Volunteer will get no sleep or very little sleep. Living this type of vague existence for a number of days can leave its mark and deserves an independent lecture.

Humiliation

We have seen that this type of interrogation technique invariably is stripping the prisoner of all his clothes and remarks passed about his sexual organs. Volunteers should be aware of the proven fact that clothes are an important aspect of the individual's character or make up. By removing his clothes the interrogators hope to remove the Volunteer's character and make up. Psychologically this is symbolic and by doing this the police like to humiliate the Volunteer and so lift away the barriers, just as they find barriers preventing them from getting a confession. A person's clothes become symbolic of this barrier and by removing them they hope to remove the natural defence mechanism of the Volunteer.

The second part of the humiliation is to pass derogatory remarks about the Volunteer's sexual organs. This is quite common in all police stations, north, south, and in England. Volunteers should attempt to understand the mentality which underlies this act and so be better prepared to meet this angle if and when it happens to them. Just as they removed the Volunteer's clothes, which symbolised a defence mechanism or natural barrier, so too by passing derogatory remarks about the Volunteer's sexual organs they attempt to humiliate the Volunteer and by so doing to weaken his will to resist. The mere act of doing this has deeper undertones than one would guess. Volunteers should understand that from a psychological point of view this act is called a penis complex.* This complex is inherent in the homosexual and although the interrogators themselves may be married men with a family it indicates suppressed homosexual tendencies.

* *Penis complex:* this is presumably a reference to penis envy, a term from Freudian psychoanalysis which is often, as in this case, mistakenly thought to refer to anxieties between men about the size of their genitals.

317

When the Volunteer realises and understands this proven fact he should not have great difficulty in triumphing over his interrogators. He should look upon them as homosexuals with the immunity of the establishment, as people who become sadistic from the homosexual tendencies which underlie them.

SEAMUS COSTELLO[*]

Seamus Costello was born in Bray, County Wicklow in 1939 and was executed by his political enemies in 1977. His story encapsulates the fragmentation of covert republican life in the decades after the Tan War. During the IRA's 1956–62 campaign he commanded an active service unit in South Derry. He was one of the leading lights within the IRA challenging their strategy in the aftermath of that campaign, suggesting that the movement needed to move in a leftwards direction.

By 1966, he was entrusted with the task of delivering the oration at the IRA's Wolfe Tone commemoration at Bodenstown. This speech heralded the shift to the left which was then stirring the IRA. 'We believe,' he declared, 'that the large estates of absentee landlords should be acquired by compulsory acquisition and worked on a co-operative basis with the financial and technical assistance of the State. Our policy is to nationalise the key industries with the eventual aim of co-operative ownership by the workers, nationalisation of all banks, insurance companies, and loan and investment companies.'

Costello pushed Sinn Féin to contest the 1967 local elections in selected areas, standing successfully himself in Bray. In 1968, he stood in a Wicklow by-election, garnering more than 2000 votes. His constituency was subsequently dismantled to ensure that his political power base evaporated. A great lover of Wicklow, he

[*] Joe Ambrose.

regarded it as being Ireland in a microcosm. 'It has,' he said on RTÉ during the 1968 election campaign, 'within its borders all the problems common to a nation – small farmers trying to eke out a living on poor mountain farms; inadequate housing, and industrial workers with a depressed standard of living.'

When the IRA divided into the mutually hostile Provisional IRA and Official IRA in 1969–70, Costello sided with the Officials. The Officials, known to their detractors as the Stickies, swiftly turned their backs on armed struggle and active opposition to the British presence in Northern Ireland in favour of community politics and entryism into the media and the trade unions. The Official IRA publicly adopted a ceasefire stance in 1972, but this particular ceasefire applied mainly to the British army. For many years thereafter the Official IRA remained in business, waging internecine battles on the republican socialist fringe while maintaining exceptionally active bank robbing units, drug peddling networks and late night drinking dens.

Costello rejected this line and in 1974 formed the breakaway Irish Republican Socialist Party (IRSP) and the Irish National Liberation Army (INLA). An avowedly Marxist organisation in the Connolly tradition, at the IRSP's inaugural convention it expressed its support for the legalisation of abortion and for equal rights for gays and lesbians. 'Any revolutionary movement that cannot defend its own membership,' Costello said a few months later, 'and cannot demonstrate its capability of defending its own membership, goes out of business anyway. We are in business as a serious revolutionary organisation and we are not going to be put out of business by anybody. The IRSP is organised and it is here to stay.'

The Stickies, amongst many others, set about crushing the IRSP. The murderous internecine wars which ensued stymied the party's growth despite the curiously pragmatic Costello's personal popularity in Bray, his obvious talent, personal charm and charisma.

In the late 1970s, the INLA/IRSP enjoyed pockets of popularity and influence in parts of Belfast and south Dublin.

In 1977, Costello was shot and killed in murky circumstances by a member of the Official IRA as he sat in his car on Dublin's North Strand. By the time of his death, his hopes and aspirations lay shattered around him and sections of his organisation were degenerating into nihilistic or narcoterrorist gangs at each other's throats. It could fairly be said of Costello that he played a dangerous game and lost.

He was at various times chief of staff and director of operations in the Official IRA, vice-president of Official Sinn Féin, leader of the IRSP and *de facto* leader of the INLA.

Civil rights activist Bernadette McAliskey wrote about Costello after his death:

> There is no doubt that the struggle continues and its victory or defeat is not measured solely by the number or quality of our fallen comrades individually. Yet it is equally true that in every generation of struggle the combination of circumstances, history and the nature of the struggle itself, produces from the ranks of its rebels a few, and a very few individuals who, notwithstanding the fundamental principles of organisation, political correctness and practical ability, common to many, rise head and shoulders above the rest, with a potential for leadership, far beyond the ranks of the already committed. Such a comrade was Seamus Costello.

BOBBY SANDS[*]

Bobby Sands (1954–1981) was an IRA member, community activist, and part time writer whose death on hunger strike in Belfast's Maze Prison, commonly known as the Long Kesh H Blocks, altered the course of the Northern Ireland conflict which had been smouldering or blazing since 1968. Sands' death, and the deaths of the other IRA/INLA hunger strikers, brought the southern Republic to a grinding halt and, for a while, it looked as if that state, was going to be dragged kicking and screaming into the war.

The hunger strikes caused a huge surge in support and sympathy for the republican position. It is generally believed that Sinn Féin manipulated the tumultuous situation and built a political power base on top of the graves of the dead hunger strikers.

Sands is thought to have joined the IRA in 1972. He was jailed when found in possession of firearms. Released in 1976, he became a community leader in West Belfast's Twinbrook. In 1977, he was charged with possession of firearms and sentenced to 14 years. Sent to Long Kesh, a high security purpose-built facility, he wrote a variety of articles for *An Phoblacht*. In 1980, he was appointed officer commanding the IRA prisoners in Long Kesh.

A genial longhaired appearance, characteristic of young men during the 1970s, was partially responsible for a certain Che-like luminosity which eventually came to surround Sands. It is, however, worth noting that he was, at heart, a party line republican, politically radical but socially somewhat conservative. He was answerable to, and obedient to, the republican movement's shadowy high command. He emerges from his diaries as a man of mild religious faith who writes about having a good relation-

---

[*] Joe Ambrose.

ship with his God, a man who understood and accepted military authority.

The Long Kesh blanket protest began in 1976, with republican prisoners refusing to wear prison uniforms, wearing blankets instead. They demanded that they should be treated like political prisoners fighting for a political cause, as opposed to being regarded as ordinary criminals guilty of offences against society who had been convicted under different legislation administered by different, more democratically accountable, legal arrangements.

This did not work out and the agitation escalated by 1978 into the strange dirty protest which horrified sections of the people. Prisoners smeared their excrement onto their cell walls. English pop artist Richard Hamilton created some of the most memorable images of the dirty protest. Films and photographs of bedraggled handsome long-haired young men were flashed all over the world's media. The journalist Tim Pat Coogan wrote a book, *On the Blanket*, which became a bestseller in the Republic.

On 1 March 1981, under Sands' command and leadership, a policy of hunger striking until death in pursuit of political status was instigated. Hunger strikes had been widely used throughout the history of Irish republicanism and the strike led by Sands was the second within a short period of time. He was the first to go on strike and the first to die. He, and the young men who subsequently died, sought – amongst other things – the right not to wear prison uniforms or to do prison work.

When a parliamentary vacancy arose in the Fermanagh/South Tyrone constituency, Sands was put forward as the republican candidate and elected to the House of Commons. This caused a global sensation and the entire subject of the British presence in Northern Ireland was successfully hoisted onto the international agenda. 'The North', became a red hot potato south of the border.

Sands, by now known internationally, died after 66 days on hunger strike. Over 100,000 people lined the route of his funeral. Substantial protests, reminiscent of the Manchester Martyrs marches, took place all over Europe. Sands was name-checked in various songs, streets in France and Iran were called after him, films were made about his life.

Sands' hunger strike diary was leaked to the media in the days leading up to his death and was subsequently published, with some impact, in pamphlet form. Sands wrote it on sheets of toilet paper which were rolled up into little balls and smuggled out of prison. This diaries were subsequently included in *Writings from Prison*, published by Mercier Press.

He remains an iconic force to be reckoned with. Tom Morello from popular punk rock group 'Rage Against the Machine', whose best-known album came emblazoned with a cover image of Che Guevara, told MTV in 2000 that Sands was one of his adolescent heroes:

> When I was sixteen, twelve or so IRA hunger strikers died, including Bobby Sands. I had a little Irish Catholic in me, but I didn't know much about the Troubles. But I knew these were kids who were about my age who were literally dying for a political cause that they believed in. I was looking around me, and we had some kids who were trying to lose weight to make the wrestling team and others who were focused on the homecoming stuff. That was the time I thought beyond the walls of my high school and the culture that gets drilled into you.

In the long term, Sands' death, and the mandate which came in its trail, brought about the politicisation of the movement to which he belonged. Within six months of his death, graffiti began to appear around Dublin which promised, 'We'll never forget you Jimmy Sands'.

Bobby Sands' Diary[*]

Sunday March 1st, 1981

I am standing on the threshold of another trembling world. May God have mercy on my soul.

My heart is very sore because I know that I have broken my poor mother's heart, and my home is struck with unbearable anxiety. But I have considered all the arguments and tried every means to avoid what has become the unavoidable: it has been forced upon me and my comrades by four-and-a-half years of stark inhumanity.

I am a political prisoner. I am a political prisoner because I am a casualty of a perennial war that is being fought between the oppressed Irish people and an alien, oppressive, unwanted regime that refuses to withdraw from our land.

I believe and stand by the God-given right of the Irish nation to sovereign independence, and the right of any Irishman or woman to assert this right in armed revolution. That is why I am incarcerated, naked and tortured.

Foremost in my tortured mind is the thought that there can never be peace in Ireland until the foreign, oppressive British presence is removed, leaving all the Irish people as a unit to control their own affairs and determine their own destinies as a sovereign people, free in mind and body, separate and distinct physically, culturally and economically.

I believe I am but another of those wretched Irishmen born of a risen generation with a deeply rooted and unquenchable desire for freedom. I am dying not just to attempt to end the barbarity of H-Block, or to gain the rightful recognition of a political prisoner, but primarily because what is lost in here is lost for the Republic and those wretched oppressed whom I am deeply proud to know as the 'risen people'.

* *Writings from Prison* by Bobby Sands.

There is no sensation today, no novelty that October 27th brought. A reference to the earlier hunger strike. The usual Screws were not working. The slobbers and would-be despots no doubt will be back again tomorrow, bright and early.

I wrote some more notes to the girls in Armagh today. There is so much I would like to say about them, about their courage, determination and unquenchable spirit of resistance. They are to be what Countess Markievicz, Anne Devlin, Mary Ann Mc-Cracken, Marie MacSwiney, Betsy Gray, and those other Irish heroines are to us all. And, of course, I think of Ann Parker, Laura Crawford, Rosemary Bleakeley, and I'm ashamed to say I cannot remember all their sacred names.[†]

Mass was solemn, the lads as ever brilliant. I ate the statutory weekly bit of fruit last night. As fate had it, it was an orange, and the final irony, it was bitter. The food is being left at the door. My portions, as expected, are quite larger than usual, or those which my cell-mate Malachy is getting.

Monday 2nd

Much to the distaste of the Screws we ended the no-wash protest this morning. We moved to 'B' wing, which was allegedly clean.

We have shown considerable tolerance today. Men are being searched coming back from the toilet. At one point men were waiting three hours to get out to the toilet, and only four or five got washed, which typifies the eagerness of the Screws to have us off the no-wash. There is a lot of petty vindictiveness from them. I saw the doctor and I'm 64 kgs. I've no problems.

The priest, Fr John Murphy, was in tonight. We had a short talk. I heard that my mother spoke at a parade in Belfast yesterday and that Marcella cried.[‡] It gave me heart. I'm not worried about the numbers of the crowds. I was very annoyed last night

[†] *Ann Parker, Laura Crawford, Rosemary Bleakeley:* three members of Cumann na mBan, the women's wing of the IRA. Parker was killed in 1972, Crawford in 1975, and Bleakeley in 1976.
[‡] Sand's sister.

when I heard Bishop Daly's statement.* Again he is applying his double set of moral standards. He seems to forget that the people who murdered those innocent Irishmen on Derry's Bloody Sunday are still as ever among us; and he knows perhaps better than anyone what has and is taking place in H-Block. He understands why men are being tortured here – the reason for criminalisation. What makes it so disgusting, I believe, is that he agrees with that underlying reason. Only once has he spoken out of the beatings and inhumanity that are commonplace in H-Block.

I once read an editorial, in late '78, following the then Archbishop Ó Fiaich's 'sewer pipes of Calcutta' statement. It said it was to the everlasting shame of the Irish people that the archbishop had to, and I paraphrase, stir the moral conscience of the people on the H-Block issue. A lot of time has passed since then, a lot of torture, in fact the following year was the worst we experienced.

Now I wonder who will stir the Cardinal's moral conscience ...

Bear witness to both right and wrong, stand up and speak out. But don't we know that what has to be said is 'political', and it's not that these people don't want to become involved in politics, it's simply that their politics are different, that is, British.

My dear friend Tomboy's father died today. I was terribly annoyed, and it has upset me.

I received several notes from my family and friends. I have only read the one from my mother – it was what I needed. She has regained her fighting spirit – I am happy now.

My old friend Seanna has also written.

I have an idea for a poem; perhaps tomorrow I will try to put it together.

Every time I feel down I think of Armagh, and James Connolly. They can never take those thoughts away from me.

---

* Cahal Daly was heavily involved in the discourse surrounding the IRA, and was a great opponent of theirs.

Tuesday 3rd

I'm feeling exceptionally well today. (It's only the third day, I know, but all the same I'm feeling great.) I had a visit this morning with two reporters, David Beresford of *The Guardian* and Brendan Ó Cathaoir of the *Irish Times*. Couldn't quite get my flow of thoughts together. I could have said more in a better fashion. 63 kgs today, so what?

A priest was in. Feel he's weighing me up psychologically for a later date. If I'm wrong I'm sorry – but I think he is. So I tried to defuse any notion of that tonight. I think he may have taken the point. But whether he accepts it, will be seen. He could not defend my onslaught on Bishop Daly – or at least he did not try.

I wrote some notes to my mother and to Mary Doyle in Armagh; and will write more tomorrow. The boys are now all washed. But I didn't get washed today. They were still trying to get men their first wash.

I smoked some 'bog-rolled blows' today, the luxury of the Block!

They put a table in my cell and are now placing my food on it in front of my eyes. I honestly couldn't give a damn if they placed it on my knee. They still keep asking me silly questions like, 'Are you still not eating?'

I never got started on my poem today, but I'll maybe do it tomorrow. The trouble is I now have more ideas.

Ag rá an phaidrín faoi dhó achan lá atá na buachaillí anois. Níl aon rud eile agam anocht. Sin sin.†

Wednesday 4th

Fr Murphy was in tonight. I have not felt too bad today, although I notice the energy beginning to drain. But it is quite early yet. I got showered today and had my hair cut, which made

† The boys are now saying the rosary twice every day. I have nothing else tonight. That's all.

me feel quite good. Ten years younger, the boys joke, but I feel twenty years older, the inevitable consequence of eight years of torture and imprisonment.

I am abreast with the news and view with utter disgust and anger the Reagan/Thatcher plot. It seems quite clear that they intend to counteract Russian expansionism with imperialist expansionism, to protect their vital interests they say.

What they mean is they covet other nations' resources. They want to steal what they haven't got and to do so (as the future may unfortunately prove) they will murder oppressed people and deny them their sovereignty as nations. No doubt Mr Haughey will toe the line in Ireland when Thatcher so demands.

Noticed a rarity today: jam with the tea, and, by the way the Screws are glaring at the food, they seem more in need of it than my good self.

Thursday 5th

The Welfare sent for me today to inform me of my father being taken ill to hospital. Tried to get me to crawl for a special visit with my family. I was distressed about my father's illness but relieved that he has been released from hospital. No matter what, I must continue.

I had a threatening toothache today which worried me, but it is gone now.

I've read Atkins' statement in the Commons.* Mar dheá.† He pledged that the British government would not budge an inch on the political status issue. It does not annoy me because my mind was prepared for such things and I know I can expect more of such, right to the bitter end.

I'm saying prayers – crawler! (And a last minute one, some would say). But I believe in God, and I'll be presumptuous and say he and I are getting on well this weather.

---

* Humphrey Atkins was the Northern Ireland Secretary 1979–81.
† *Mar dheá:* nonsense, like fun.

I can ignore the presence of food staring me straight in the face all the time. But I have this desire for brown wholemeal bread, butter, Dutch cheese and honey. Ha!! It is not damaging me, because, I think, 'Well, human food can never keep a man alive forever', and I console myself with the fact that I'll get a great feed up above (if I'm worthy).

But then I'm struck by this awful thought that they don't eat food up there. But if there's something better than brown wholemeal bread, cheese and honey, etcetera, then it can't be bad.

Friday 6th

There was no priest in last night or tonight. They stopped me from seeing my solicitor tonight, as another part of the isolation process, which, as time goes by, they will ruthlessly implement. I expect they may move me sooner than expected to an empty wing. I will be sorry to leave the boys, but I know the road is a hard one and everything must be conquered.

I have felt the loss of energy twice today, and I am feeling slightly weak.

They (the Screws) are unembarrassed by the enormous amount of food they are putting into the cell and I know they have every bean and chip counted or weighed. The damned fools don't realise that the doctor does tests for traces of any food eaten. Regardless, I have no intention of sampling their tempting morsels.

I am sleeping well at night so far, as I avoid sleeping during the day. I am even having pleasant dreams and so far no headaches. Is that a tribute to my psychological frame of mind or will I pay for that tomorrow or later! I wonder how long I will be able to keep these scribbles going.

My friend Jennifer got twenty years. I am greatly distressed.[‡] I have no doubts or regrets about what I am doing for I know what I have faced for eight years, and in particular for the last

---

‡ Jennifer McCann was sentenced to twenty years for shooting at a member of the RUC.

four-and-a-half years, others will face, young lads and girls still at school, or young Gerard or Kevin and thousands of others.*

They will not criminalise us, rob us of our true identity, steal our individualism, depoliticise us, churn us out as systemised, institutionalised, decent law-abiding robots. Never will they label our liberation struggle as criminal.

I am (even after all the torture) amazed at British logic. Never in eight centuries have they succeeded in breaking the spirit of one man who refused to be broken. They have not dispirited, conquered, or demoralised my people, nor will they ever.

I may be a sinner, but I stand – and if it so be, will die – happy knowing that I do not have to answer for what these people have done to our ancient nation. Thomas Clarke is in my thoughts, and MacSwiney, Stagg, Gaughan, Thomas Ashe, McCaughey. Dear God, we have so many that another one to those knaves means nothing, or so they say, for some day they'll pay.

When I am thinking of Clarke, I thought of the time I spent in 'B' wing in Crumlin Road jail in September and October '77. I realised just what was facing me then. I've no need to record it all, some of my comrades experienced it too, so they know I have been thinking that some people (maybe many people) blame me for this hunger-strike, but I have tried everything possible to avert it short of surrender.

I pity those who say that, because they do not know the British and I feel more the pity for them because they don't even know their poor selves. But didn't we have people like that who sought to accuse Tone, Emmet, Pearse, Connolly, Mellows: that unfortunate attitude is perennial also …

I can hear the curlew passing overhead. Such a lonely cell, such a lonely struggle. But, my friend, this road is well trod and he, whoever he was, who first passed this way, deserves the salute of the nation. I am but a mere follower and I must say Oíche Mhaith.†

* Sands' son and nephew, respectively.
† Goodnight.

Tuesday 10th

It has been a fairly normal day in my present circumstances. My weight is 59.3 kgs. and I have no medical problems. I have seen some birthday greetings from relatives and friends in yesterday's paper which I got today. Also I received a bag of toiletries today.

There is no priest in tonight, but the chief medical officer dropped in, took my pulse, and left. I suppose that makes him feel pretty important.

From what I have read in the newspapers I am becoming increasingly worried and wary of the fact that there could quite well be an attempt at a later date to pull the carpet from under our feet and undermine us – if not defeat this hunger strike – with the concession bid in the form of 'our own clothes as a right'.

This, of course, would solve nothing. But if allowed birth could, with the voice of the Catholic hierarchy, seriously damage our position. It is my opinion that under no circumstances do they wish to see the prisoners gain political status, or facilities that resemble, or afford us with the contents of, political status. The reasons for this are many and varied, primarily motivated by the wish to see the revolutionary struggle of the people brought to an end. The criminalisation of Republican prisoners would help to furnish this end.

It is the declared wish of these people to see humane and better conditions in these Blocks. But the issue at stake is not 'humanitarian', nor about better or improved living conditions. It is purely political and only a political solution will solve it. This in no way makes us prisoners elite nor do we (nor have we at any time) purport to be elite.

We wish to be treated 'not as ordinary prisoners' for we are not criminals. We admit no crime unless, that is, the love of one's people and country is a crime. Would Englishmen allow Germans to occupy their nation or Frenchmen allow Dutchmen to do likewise? We Republican prisoners understand better than anyone the plight of all prisoners who are deprived of

331

their liberty. We do not deny ordinary prisoners the benefit of anything that we gain that may improve and make easier their plight. Indeed, in the past, all prisoners have gained from the resistance of Republican jail struggles.

I recall the Fenians and Tom Clarke, who indeed were most instrumental in highlighting by their unflinching resistance the 'terrible silent system' in the Victorian period in English prisons. In every decade there has been ample evidence of such gains to all prisoners due to Republican prisoners' resistance.

Unfortunately, the years, the decades, and centuries, have not seen an end to Republican resistance in English hell-holes, because the struggle in the prisons goes hand-in-hand with the continuous freedom struggle in Ireland. Many Irishmen have given their lives in pursuit of this freedom and I know that more will, myself included, until such times as that freedom is achieved.

I am still awaiting some sort of move from my cell to an empty wing and total isolation. The last strikers were ten days in the wings with the boys, before they were moved. But then they were on the no-wash protest and in filthy cells. My cell is far from clean but tolerable. The water is always cold. I can't risk the chance of cold or 'flu. It is six days since I've had a bath, perhaps longer. No matter.

Tomorrow is the eleventh day and there is a long way to go. Someone should write a poem of the tribulations of a hunger-striker. I would like to, but how could I finish it. *Caithfidh mé a dul mar tá tuirseach ag eirí ormsa.*[*]

---

[*] Must go as I'm getting tired.

Young Ireland – 150 Years Later[†]

In July 150 years ago this part of Tipperary was at the centre of our nation's history. These events represented Ireland's participation in a European-wide series of risings. 1848 was the Year of Revolutions. The monarchy was overthrown for the last time in France. An all-German parliament sat for the first time in Frankfurt. In Ireland, the rebellion that broke out here was a protest at the appalling degradation of the Famine, which was decimating a population of 8 million people in 1848 through starvation and emigration against a background of much official neglect and indifference, and where the goodwill that existed was simply not enough.

The 1848 Rebellion in Ballingarry was as rich in symbolism, as it was deficient in military organisation and prowess. William Smith O'Brien was never cut out to be a general. 1848 was the year that the tricolour, approved for the first time, symbolising peace between the traditions of the Orange and the Green, was brought home from Paris. After the United Irishmen, Young Ireland was an important and a noble attempt to unite the two traditions in support of national independence.

The revolt was an attempt by the leaders of Young Ireland to assert national dignity and rights. The 1840s was the decade when the Union was finally discredited in most of Ireland, and when all the promises made at the time of the Act of Union about Ireland being treated equally within the United Kingdom were shown to be hollow and empty. It was a period of huge social crisis and human tragedy and upheaval.

The names of the men of 1848 shine through the pages of history: Thomas Francis Meagher, 'Meagher of the Sword', John

† Speech (abridged) given by Bertie Ahern [as Taoiseach] on the 150th Anniversary of the 1848 Rebellion, delivered at Ballingarry, Co Tipperary, 30 July 1998.

Mitchel, Michael Doheny, Charles Gavan Duffy, John Blake Dillon, Thomas d'Arcy McGee, James Fintan Lalor and Fr John Kenyon. The next generation of leaders, the Fenians were present as young men, like James Stephens, Charles Kickham, and John O'Leary. All these names live on. Sharing in their honour are all the people who lived in this district at that time who followed them....

This was a poor but heavily populated part of the country 150 years ago. The hopes of participation in the industrial revolution built around the mines, as revealed by names such as New Bermingham, were never realised. A generation earlier, this part of Tipperary witnessed the battle of Slievenamon in the 1798 rebellion....

For ever associated with the fray is the image of this house,* where the police were put under siege. While O'Brien parleyed, wanting no violence, shots rang out and two died....

This house is an important historic monument, and is part of our national heritage. Accordingly, in this the 150th anniversary of the 1848 Rising, the state seeks to purchase the house and a small amount of the surrounding land. It would be our wish that the house would be refurbished and made the site of a permanent exhibition commemorating Young Ireland and the events of the Famine Rebellion of 1848 in this area....

The government are convinced that in addition to material progress we have a duty to look after our cultural patrimony, especially where it is of such historic significance. It is further testimony to the proud role that the people of Tipperary played in history.

The leaders of the rebellion were tried and convicted, and subsequently transported. Many of them left diaries and letters, making this one of the best documented events in Irish history. A good many of them achieved high office in other English-speaking countries that their talents deserved at home.

---

* The Ballingarry 'Warhouse' around which the Young Irelanders made their stand.

In the year of the historic Good Friday Agreement, it is right that we remember earlier noble attempts to bring peace with justice and true democracy to our island. The men of 1848 wanted nothing better than to see the two traditions working together for the common good of their country and for the relief of so much suffering and hardship. Two hundred years after 1798 and one hundred and fifty years after 1848, we in this generation have a unique opportunity to see if we can succeed, where so many hopes failed in the past, in making a better shared future for all the people of this island.

CONCLUSION

This book has charted the twists and turns of the body of thinking which relates to the covert Fenian ideal as it played out in Irish history. Only during the years of the Tan War did the forces informed by that viewpoint coalesce, agree to disagree, and act in anything like unison. Beforehand there were endless factional organisations and incessant splits which had their roots in personality clashes, ideological differences, venal mind-sets and the contrary nature of humanity. From the day that the Dáil started debating the Treaty which led to the Civil War, up until the present day, the splits and factionalism have returned to haunt 'the cause'. Perhaps this is as it should be, because revolutionary politics must always be the business of the most opinionated amongst us, the most passionate, the most idiosyncratic of our sisters and brothers.

After the Good Friday Agreement Fianna Fáil and Sinn Féin entered into a battle for the Fenian mantle. In Wicklow, those two organisations organise mutually hostile commemorations of Liam Mellows, a man of the left unlikely to have had much sympathy for either party. In the north of Ireland, Fianna Fáil is in the process of intruding into electoral territory which Sinn Féin has come to think of as its own. Down south, the process is happening in reverse. During his time in office, as Taoiseach, Bertie Ahern threw himself eagerly into the reopening of the Ballingarry Warhouse where the Young Irelanders staged their doomed rebellion. He also reinstated the state-sanctioned remembrance of the 1916 Rising. It remains to be seen if the Republic's new leader, Irish language enthusiast Brian Cowen, will be equally enthusiastic about other aspects of Fenianism. Fine Gael, somewhat ironically the lineal inheritor of the IRB mantle (for the IRB, by and large, supported the Free State side in the Civil War), seems to have washed its hands entirely of that tradition.

Modern Ireland, in the main, declares itself proud of its 'Gaelic' past, of its history of successful insurgency, of its plucky independent status. But it is a strangely apolitical place where all ideology and intellectual life has been subsumed into one great big tourist attraction.

This was precisely the self-contented atmosphere which the IRB men of 1916 rebelled against and tried to destroyed.

Acknowledgements

Thanks to Tommy Hannon, Brother Patrick, Dermot Moroney, R. Dudley Edwards, Denis Bethall, Donal McCartney, Margaret McCurtain, Fergus Darcy, Michael Laffan, Fouad Elasri, Fraser Clark, Hein Vink, Paul Hawkins, Seb Tennant, Tav Falco, David Kerekes, Shane Cullen, Bianca, Mattia Zaparello, Hotel Muniria Tangier, Lars Movin, Peter Playdon, Brendan Maher at *Start* magazine, Daniel Figgis, Kid Congo Powers, Richard Morgan, Anne Foley for the Marx on Ireland book, Stewart Home, Tony White, Tiago Almeida, Deirdre Behan, Paul Lamont at outsideleft.com, Dan Stuart, Jocelyn Bradell, Danny Morrison for information of the evolution of *The Green Book*, Val Needham, Eamonn O'Meara, Martin Mansergh, Gerardine Ambrose O'Meara, Pat and Claire Keegan, Caroline Ambrose, James Needham, Pat and Rena Norris, Josie Heffernan, Jimmy Norris, Ann Ambrose, Gerry Ambrose, Nuala Walker, Mary McAuliffe, Lucy Bradell, Thelma Blitz, Spencer Kansa, all the people who showed up for my readings at Waterstones, the Old Shoe Store, and the Chelsea, Nathan Penlington, Mary Feehan, Eoin Purcell, Patrick Crowley, Catherine Twibill, Tipp FM, Tipp Mid West, *Nenagh Guardian, Tipperary Star, Clonmel Nationalist*, Chris Stein, Marabet, Ulick O'Connor, Aiden Gillen, John Foley, Malcolm Kelly, Ottman, Laki Vazakas, Anne Marie Brophy and her staff at Thurles Library, Newstalk FM, www.fethard.com, Victor Bockris, Hannan Internet on Bab Aganau Marrakesh, the British Library, Tony Jennings, Ed on 45, John Sinclair.

Two sections of this book – *The Felon's Track* by Michael Doheny and *The Wearing of the Green – The Manchester Martyrs* by A. M. Sullivan have been substantially edited. Doheny's reminiscence was cut because most contemporary readers will find the author's remorseless evocation of nature in all its splendour exhausting. Sullivan's account has been shortened because he clearly thought that repetition was the better part of valour and many of the stirring scenes which he so graphically described were then described all over again. In both cases the full text can be easily accessed online. In some of the older texts I have made more minor cuts for reasons of clarity.

I would like to thank Manus O'Riordan, Ann O'Sullivan, Department of the Taoiseach, Government Press Office, David Granville, Rena Dardis and Des Geraghty for their kind help in tracing copyright owners. Thanks to *The Irish Democrat* for permission to reproduce 'Wrap The Green, Red, and Black Flags Around Me', 'Desmond Greaves – Holding A Hand in the Flame' and 'Memories of the Republican Congress'. Thanks to Helga MacLiam for 'Desmond Greaves – 'Holding A Hand in the Flame'. *The Irish Democrat* is the newspaper of the Connolly Association – *www.irishdemocrat.co.uk*. Thanks to the Ireland and the Spanish Civil War site http://www.geocities.com/irelandscw/ – an outstanding resource – for 'The Rise of Fianna Fáil, The Decline of the Republican Congress', and for 'Charlie Donnelly: An Appreciation'.

Ambrose, Joe, *Dan Breen and the IRA* (Cork, 2006)

— *Seán Treacy and the Tan War* (Cork, 2007)

— 'Brotherhood', *Headpress Journal* No. 28, John Sinclair (ed.), (London, 2008)

Bourke, Marcus, *John O'Leary; A Study in Irish Separatism* (Georgia, 1967)

Brown, Malcolm, *The Politics of Irish Literature: from Thomas Davis to W.B. Yeats* (London, 1973)

Callanan, Frank, *T.M. Healy* (Cork, 1996)

Campbell, Christy, *Fenian Fire: The British Government Plot to Assassinate Queen Victoria* (London, 2002)

Comerford, R. V., *Charles J. Kickham; A Study of Irish nationalism and literature* (Dublin, 1979)

— *The Fenians in Context: Irish Politics and Society, 1848-82* (Dublin, 1985)

Connolly, James, *Labour in Ireland* (Dublin, 1910)

— *The Re-Conquest of Ireland* (Dublin, 1915)

Cronin, Seán, *The McGarrity Papers* (Tralee, 1972)

Curran, Joseph M., 'The Decline and Fall of the IRB', *Eire-Ireland* (Dublin, 1975)

Doheny, Michael, *The Felon's Track or History of the Attempted Outbreak in Ireland* (Dublin, 1920)

Doherty, G. & Keogh, D., *1916 – The Long Revolution* (Cork 2007)

Elliott, Marianne, *Wolfe Tone: Prophet of Irish Independence* (New Haven, 1989).

— *Robert Emmet, The Making of a Legend* (London 2003)

English, Richard, *Armed Struggle: The History of the IRA* (London, 2003)

— *Irish Freedom: The History of Nationalism in Ireland* (London, 2006)

Garvin, Tom, *Nationalist Revolutionaries in Ireland 1858–1928* (Oxford, 1987)

Geoghegan, Patrick M., *Contesting Ireland: Irish Voices Against England in the Eighteenth Century* (Dublin, 2000)

— *Robert Emmet: a life* (Dublin, 2004)

Griffith, Arthur, *Thomas Davis, The Thinker and Teacher* (Dublin, 1922)

Hardiman, Adrian, 'The (Show?) Trial of Robert Emmet', *History Ireland* (Dublin, August 2005)

Kenny, Michael, *The Fenians* (Dublin, 1994)

Lecky, W. E. H., *History of Ireland in the Eighteenth Century* (London, 1892)

MacDonncha, Mícheál, 'Centenary of Amhrán na bhFiann – The Soldier's Song', *An Phoblacht* (Dublin, 2007)

MacManus, M. J. (ed.), *Thomas Davis and Young Ireland* (Dublin, 1945)

Mansergh, Martin, *Legacy of History* (Cork, 2003)

Martin, F. X. (ed.), *Leaders and Men of the Easter Rising: Dublin, 1916* (Dublin, 1967)

McGee, Owen, '"God save Ireland": Manchester Martyr demonstrations in Dublin, 1867–1916', *Eire-Ireland* (Dublin, 2001)

— *The IRB: The Irish Republican Brotherhood from The Land League to Sinn Féin* (Dublin, 2005)

Meagher, Thomas Francis, *Meagher of The Sword*, Arthur Griffith (ed.) (Dublin, 1916)

Mitchel, John, *Jail Journal* (Dublin, 1914)

Moody, T. W. (ed.), *The Fenian Movement* (Dublin and Cork, 1968)

Moody, T. W. & Martin, F. X. (eds), *Course of Irish History* (Cork 2001)

Ó Broin, Leon, *Fenian Fever: An Anglo-American Dilemma* (London, 1971)

— *Revolutionary Underground: The Story of the Irish Republican Brotherhood, 1858–1924* (Dublin, 1976)

O'Connor, Ulick, *A Terrible Beauty is Born: The Irish troubles, 1912–1922* (London, 1975)

O'Leary, John, *Recollections of Fenians and Fenianism* (London, 1896)

Ó Luing, Sean, *Fremantle Mission* (Tralee, 1965)

Power, Patrick C., *History of South Tipperary* (Cork, 1989)

Sands, Bobby, *One Day in My Life* (Cork 1983)

INDEX

Y

Yeats, W. B. 11, 219, 228, 229, 243

Young Ireland 333, 334

Young Irelanders 7, 8, 12, 14, 15, 16, 27, 64, 77, 79, 80, 83, 84, 88, 89, 91, 113, 121, 138, 250, 333, 334, 336, 341